DEPORTATION INTO THE UNKNOWN

Among the generation of Poles born and brought up in Britain since the Second World War, few, perhaps, fully realize the suffering that their parents experienced during the occupation by the Russians following Hitler's invasion of Poland.

In the telling of this dramatic story the author, a doctor, conveys her feelings during the deportation of herself and her mother into the depths of the Russian steppes, and describes the misery, deprivation, and degradation with, thankfully, a brave humour which sustained proud people during these troublous times.

DEPORTATION INTO THE UNKNOWN

DANUTA TECZAROWSKA

MERLIN BOOKS LTD.
Braunton   Devon

To
MY DAUGHTER
with love

ISBN 0 86303 267-2
Printed in England by Maslands Ltd., Tiverton, Devon

CONTENTS

PREFACE

I am but one of the million and a half Polish citizens whom the Russians deported to the USSR during the 1939/45 war. Less than three weeks after Hitler's invasion of Poland, the Russians (without any declaration of war) entered Poland from the east and moving quickly into the depths of the country, occupied a large tract of Poland with the effect that the country ceased to exist as an independent state and became dismembered between Germany and Russia. At the end of the war in 1945, the area of Poland seized by the Russians unfortunately became incorporated into the USSR: the south-east part of the region which had been seized became known as West Ukrainian USSR, with Lvov as its capital, further to the north the region became Byelorussian USSR, and the land to the extreme north was annexed to Lithuania which became Lithuanian USSR.

A few months after having seized eastern Poland, the Russians initiated mass deportations of Poles into deep Russia, wanting to be rid of the population, in particular the intelligentsia who was hostile towards them. The first wave of deportations took place in 1939/40 even whilst there was yet a state of co-operation between Russia and Germany. During this time the Russians deported (a) 'prisoners of war', (b) political detainees and (c) the civilian population who was sent officially to the USSR under orders of 'compulsory resettlement'. Prisoners of war and a section of the political detainees were sent to three camps: namely, Kozielsk, Starobielsk and Ostaszkov. The rest of the political detainees were detained in prisons in the USSR or sent to penal forced labour camps in Siberia. The second wave of deportations was executed towards the end and immediately after the war when the whole of Poland was 'overrun' by the Red Army.

Over half a million Poles were evacuated from the USSR after the war from the one and a half million who had found themselves in Russia — the rest, about a million Poles were doomed to remain in the USSR in various settlements, prisons and penal forced labour camps.

In 1939 the Russians took 15,000 Polish officers as 'prisoners of war'. After the declaration of war between Russia and Germany on the 22nd June, 1941, when the Germans occupied part of Russia, they found in Katyn, near Smolensk, a mass grave containing the bodies of over 4,000

Polish officers each of whom had been murdered with a shot in the back of the head. There was no trace to be found of the remaining 10,000 Polish officers; their fate remains a mystery to this day, and up to now their graves have not been found.

By some miracle, about three hundred officers, from the three camps (Kozielsk, Starobielsk and Ostaszkov) were saved from death and after the outbreak of war between Russia and Germany and the amnesty for the various Polish internees, these officers joined the Polish Army which was being formed in Russia under the command of General Anders. My husband is one of them.

In 1942 the Polish Army under General Anders's command and the civilian members of the families, in all numbering over 114,500 people were evacuated from the USSR to the Middle East.

I come from Lvov, a city in south-east Poland, now in USSR. I was born there, finished schooling there and later studied medicine there, at the University of Jan Kazimierz. From Lvov, I was also deported to Asia. I love that city, where three nationalities lived together, Poles, Ukrainians and Jews. In my childhood, the Ukrainians called themselves Rusini and behaved towards the Poles as brothers. One celebrated Christmas twice, 'ours and yours'. (According to their calendar year, Christmas falls during Epiphany.) Jews, that wise and, to us, enigmatic race, upheld their traditions and customs and added much charm to the city. In spite of all differences, bitter fighting and memories, I cannot suppress my feelings that the Ukrainians as much as the Jews are kindred spirits.

My profession enabled me to come into contact with a large cross-section of people — Polish, Russian and, too, the natives of Asia. I often had occasion to recognize the 'Soul of Russia', not the official one but the intimate and private one, where sentimentality and personal charisma are mixed with a certain inherent cruelty. I think that by the grace of my profession, I had more opportunities to watch and observe, than the average deportee, who mixed in his own small circle.

Coming into contact with the generation of Poles, born and brought up in Britain, I have noticed that a certain proportion of them bear a resentment towards their parents, for failing to provide them with a 'normal' sunny home, in what is to them a foreign environment. A 'normal' home that is, which can be expected by the average British child. How can one, being an *emigré*, torn out by the roots from one's homeland, create a normal, sunny home? Children of *emigrés* in Britain bear the stigma of the foreign origins of their parents and occasionally experience it. Can one wonder that some of this youth rebels and will have nothing to do with anything 'Polish'? This youth does not want to be burdened with the stigma of foreign origins, it wants to assimilate into British life and be like 'everyone' here. Few of the Poles born and bred in Britain can overcome and cope with this problem.

Yet another section of Poles who have been born here, understands their parents' situation and suffers for them, which does not help to alleviate the parents' feelings. Altogether, this section of youth does not want to know what their parents lived through, it is simply too painful for them. Some young men suffer from inferiority complexes and envy their fathers for having passed the 'ordeal by fire' of the war (unfortunately, often literally true). May these people be spared such an opportunity of proving, as their fathers did, that they are 'strong'. Perhaps one of the Poles born here will read this and pause to reflect?

I give no names, solely the first letter of each name. If anyone should 'recognize' themselves, I should like the 'good' to learn that I valued them and the 'bad', of whom I met very few, to examine their consciences. I became familiar with much kindness and help from people of various nationalities, Poles as well as Kazakhs and Russians. Without their help, I should not have survived my deportation.

I have written this short précis of the history of Poland and the Poles during the war years of 1939 to 1942 to provide the reader with a better understanding to the background of my book.

THE BEGINNING OF WAR 1939

For nearly a year, I have been living with my husband and mother, in Jeleśnia, near Żywiec, which is almost on the German border, in the west of Poland. Both my husband and I are doctors and are working in general practice. The 'reclamation' of Zaolzie (the part of Silesia which had been given to Czechoslovakia after World War I) finds us here and I am a witness to the 'joyous' celebrations caused by this event. Bands are playing, crowds singing and I — I am ashamed and afraid because I can scent war in the air. I am very ashamed for Poland. She is 'raking in' a piece of Silesia, which has been thrown as bait to her by Hitler. Hitler has tossed us his pickings, we are pleased with it whilst his aim is to mislead us as to his future designs for Poland. The bands are playing but I fight back tears of shame.

Summer is almost upon us and we begin to sense the unrest. The army arrives in Jeleśnia and prepares to entrench. Threat of war is in the air but the newspapers assure us that we are 'strong, united and ready'. Therefore we should have no reason to apprehend war. With the army arrives a doctor who commences private practice under our very noses. Jeleśnia is a small village, too small to support three doctors. We hear of individual call-up papers which arrive in the surrounding villages. In the middle of August, it becomes obvious to us that war is coming and that regardless of what the politicians may say, war is inevitable.

My husband cannot leave his work. Apart from the private practice, he attends the Health Centre, schools, and out-patient clinics. So he must remain, but my mother and I resolve to return to Lvov, in eastern Poland. I send two train wagons full of furniture (from the whole house) to a cousin in Lvov, who has an empty room and can store our belongings. A few days after dispatching the furniture, my mother and I set off for Lvov, leaving my husband in Jeleśnia. Since his mobilization papers are allocated to Lvov, we expect him to join us soon.

In my cousin's empty room, we cram the furniture up to the ceiling, leaving a narrow passage clear to the window, under which we stand a small table and two chairs. My mother's bed occupies half the passageway. For myself, I put down a mattress on the floor and this effectively blocks the remainder of the clear space available.

Panic reigns in Lvov. The shops become empty, as goods which appear,

10

are soon bought up. The whole city lives in the grip of tension and fear. I walk through Lvov, which has suddenly changed from a lively city, full of bustle, into a city of fear and drab sadness. We are all waiting for some miracle to happen so that we can again breathe freely and smile. No miracle happens — the atmosphere becomes heavier.

General mobilization is announced and my husband arrives in Lvov on the 31st August. As yet nobody has been killed but war is practically here. On the morning of the 1st September we hear explosions and learn that the main railway station has been bombed — and now war is here.

I go to the mobilization point with my husband and on the way there, we are caught by an air raid. Aeroplanes appear in waves and bomb the city. We take cover in a basement which is packed with terrified people and together, we wait for the raid to end. The falling bombs whistle; it appears they must hit us; however we have been told that the 'whistlers' fall at a distance — the bombs which kill are the bombs one has no time to hear coming.

At last we reach the mobilization point, where I report in as a volunteer doctor and my husband presents his call-up papers. All is in general chaos and disorientation. Nobody knows where and to whom to report to and we are sent from desk to desk. Finally, we manage to get 'mobilized'. The next problem is to assemble our uniforms (gas mask, haversack, etc.) I am to join 'the army' as a volunteer, in civvies.

In the evening, it is as though the city were under a spell. There is a general black-out, people pass each other like ghosts in the streets: all are terrified and all are hurrying somewhere. The best café in Lvov attempts to be *comme il faut* and is selling cakes — not as good as they used to have but nevertheless, cakes! We buy some and turn our steps towards 'home', to that one-roomed furniture store.

Great is our joy when Britain declares war. We expect British aeroplanes to appear over Poland almost immediately, to defend us. How naïve we are! Instead of British planes, German ones continue to circle overhead bombing the city.

My husband and I are allocated to a field hospital which is due to move to the lines of action, any day. We feverishly pack two small suitcases and my husband's haversack and pile into military buses which move off towards the east of Poland on the 12th September. Why are we travelling east when the Germans are attacking from the west? Understand this we do not, but we believe that those at the top know what they are doing, we still believe we are 'strong, united and ready'.

We sleep in villages, housed in private quarters and eat from the camp cooking-pot, mainly peas and bacon. It all seems rather weird to me and I start to have the unpleasant feeling that nobody knows what to do and what will happen. As though in a scene from an operetta — here I am, in my dress, minus a uniform, attached to a field hospital.

Presently, my husband and I receive orders to load the wounded on to a train, so that they can be evacuated behind the lines. As there appears to be no 'behind the lines' or even lines, it is all rather baffling. However we are glad to be of some use at last. Naturally the evacuation takes place during the night in the black-out. The station at which the train is standing is small and is crowded with the wounded. They moan, they beg for help and water. In tomb-like darkness, we help the orderlies to carry the wounded on to the train. Several soldiers are in a state of shock — they have no wounds but are shaking and have no idea what they are doing. They are the ones who cause us the greatest worry and trouble. They continually meander off somewhere in a hurry. We pile them into the train through one door and they wander back on to the platform through another; there are too few of us to attend to them. At last, all the wounded are on the train and the train is ready to move off. Regrettably the train for some reason, remains stationary and then day begins to dawn. With the dawn come the German aeroplanes. The train is strafed by machine-gun fire, in spite of the carriages being clearly marked with the Red Cross. This raid was probably only a reconnaissance sortie and the strafing 'for amusement' because several hours later when our train had departed, the station is erased from the face of the earth by bombers. Meanwhile the German aircraft are 'playing games'. They dive low and try to shoot down people who are standing on the platform. Both my husband and I attempt to hide behind the trees which grow alongside the station. The aircraft fire from the nose, directly in front, so we attempt to shelter out of the direct line of fire. Nobody is killed or wounded and, after this foray, the train moves off.

With the orderlies we make our way back to the field hospital, meeting on the way, our colleague, Dr B., whose head is bandaged. It appears that during the raid, he had taken shelter under a bridge, which collapsed and lacerated his head. Though his wounds are slight, our colleague is highly agitated. This does not surprise me as I also feel shaken. Everything appears unreal and I find it hard to believe that I am participating in a war.

Our field hospital continues to move east. It is dark and we cannot see anything in the black-out, neither houses by the roadside nor villages. Suddenly, in the distance we see a small town which is aglow with light. Our convoy halts amidst general consternation and bustle. After a time we are approached by people, who bring the information that the surprisingly illuminated spot is Sokal where the Red Army has entered. As proof of this information, they show us leaflets, written in a bad style and grammar and also half in Russian, announcing that the Red Army has entered Poland to liberate her from the bourgeoisie.

We move on, skirting Sokal, travelling faster; we are simply fleeing. Behind the convoy of vehicles carrying the officers and our command, marches a column of orderlies. Two doctors are detached from the vehicle convoy, every few hours, to join this column, as ranking officers. They are to be returned, after a couple of hours to their vehicle and two other medical officers dispatched to the rear of the marching orderlies. This procedure takes place several times. Several medical officers find themselves thus 'on foot' with the medical orderlies, without means of contact with the vehicle convoy. There comes a moment however, when we realize that Captain B. returns from the rear alone with the chauffeur. Nobody is being brought back from the rear and this time there is no reply to the call "Who will volunteer?" An embarrassing silence pervades the vehicle, an irate Captain B. repeats his 'request'. Should there be no volunteers he threatens, he will have to issue an order. The situation is saved, my husband and another colleague stand up. They are dispatched to the rear of the orderlies' marching column, in Captain B.'s vehicle. Meanwhile this column is falling further and further behind the convoy of vehicles which is making full speed towards the east.

I am not to know that from this moment it will be two years before I shall see my husband again and that then it will be in Tatischevo in Russia near Saratov, where General Anders's Polish Army will be forming. The separation which is to be one of several hours only, will last two years. I am ignorant to this day as to why several medical officers should have been thus abandoned to the Bolsheviks: the majority of them are to perish later in Katyn, and Captain B. is to return to Poland and to live there comfortably. This information would be revealed to me by a friend who would come to visit me in Britain.

Now alone, with our two small suitcases, I travel on, surrounded by my depressed and apprehensive colleagues. Several qualified with me, so we are no strangers but I feel bitter because I know they are all single. Yet not one of them raised their hands to volunteer. For shame of them my husband has volunteered. My husband and the other colleague are the last medical officers to be dispatched by Captain B.'s vehicle to the rear of the marching column of medical orderlies. The doctors who now remain in the travelling vehicle are therefore already safe in one sense. I still delude myself that I am with an army which is organized, that this army will take care of me and that the medical orderlies in the rear, will not be forgotten.

Our convoy of buses, cars and ambulances overtakes many military units, which are travelling faster and faster. Ahead of us we see more and more of the army; everyone is moving in the same direction. On the 19th September we arrive in Nadvorna, a small provincial town on the Hungarian border and here we halt. We watch as our command alight from their vehicles; we see them deliberating. So we all step down from our car and await to see what we will be told. I learn that there is talk of crossing the border into Hungary, of flight from Poland. We are penniless; at least I have no money because as yet we have not received our pay. I decide to look for the pay-officer who always carries the pay-case, full of money, on him. Lt. Z. is nowhere to be found — he has disappeared along with his case. He must have already realized which way the wind was blowing.

There is discussion, deliberation and various rumours; and as I see that the chaotic situation is becoming prolonged, I decide I must go to see the Commanding Officer of the field hospital. "What are our orders?" I ask him.

To which he replies, "Madam, there are no longer any orders," and "you must do as you think is best."

My mother has been left behind in Lvov, without any money, in a room bulging with our furniture. My husband has been left in the rear with the orderlies. I choose to stay in Nadvorna to wait for him. It would be quite unreasonable of me to bolt to Hungary, alone. I expect my husband to reach Nadvorna and then we can decide what is to be done. I lift our suitcases down from the vehicle and go to search out the local doctor.

The doctor in Nadvorna turns out to be a senior colleague of mine from Lvov. How lucky I am to have chanced upon Dr B.! He is an exceptionally hospitable person and invites me into his home, as sincerely as if I were his sister. He lives here in an attractive villa, with his wife (who is in the last stages of pregnancy), his mother and his sister who is apparently staying with them only temporarily. They are all so very good to me, making me feel one of the family; utterly safe amidst kind people.

Leaving my suitcases with them, I set off to the roadside to keep watch for my husband. After a completely sleepless night, I am very tired but I stay by the road all day long. I dare not leave my 'post' even for a half-hour to have a meal with Dr B., in case I should miss my husband. During the whole day, the army marches along the road, large and small columns of tired and frightened men. I am witnessing the death of Poland. My mind refuses to accept that such is the reality, that the army is leaving the country and leaving the nation to the mercy of its enemy.

Towards the end of the day, the soldiers march past with an ever-increasing tempo; chaotically, ranks broken, without their kits, without their rifles. They are fleeing from the Bolsheviks. I realize this but I still hope that my husband will manage to escape ahead of them and will appear in Nadvorna. I see men of the police force fleeing — never in my life have I seen such despair etched upon human faces. They carry no arms; they have lightened their loads; anything to enhance their chance of escape from the enemy. Many of them are openly weeping. They are broken; they flee in order to escape with their lives. Physically exhausted, barely able to walk, in despair and stunned by the fate of Poland.

The number of fleeing soldiers decreases towards dusk; there are now gaps on the road whereas before, column after column of organized soldiers marched on. Now small groups of terrified, stupefied people pass by. Sporadically, lorries come speeding along, loaded with soldiers, aiming their rifles at the Ukrainian civilians who are standing by the roadside. It is quite obvious that the soldiers feel uneasy and threatened by the local population. I fear that perhaps our Army has already come face to face with the hatred which many Ukrainians feel towards the Poles. I am greatly saddened — I grew up amongst the Ukrainians, in Lvov; I walked here in these mountains and never questioned if this territory was 'theirs' or 'yours' — these mountains were 'ours'. The Ukrainians speak a different language, which I understand however and I used to be at ease in their company. Now even this feeling has been destroyed: my whole world has collapsed and apart from fear about the future, I feel a pain, which is almost physical. After all, my father had Ukrainian friends, he used to visit them when they were celebrating their own Christmas, which commenced when we were finishing our celebrations on Twlefth Night. I remember as a child envying the Ukrainians, they had all their festivities to anticipate just at the time we were taking down our Christmas tree. And now Polish soldiers are pointing their rifles at them. (Unfortunately, as I was to learn later, they were justified in so doing.)

Meanwhile it is getting dark and I am literally dropping on my feet. I cannot wait any longer. Help comes in the form of Dr B.'s sister, who offers to stand vigil in my place. Having given her a careful description of our unit, I return to Dr B.'s house to get some sleep.

I again return to my spot at the roadside, early next morning, only to learn that no more medical orderlies have come by. Dr B.'s sister had stood all night, straining her eyes, peering into the night and calling out my husband's name quite unnecessarily. I have now lost all hope of finding my husband — the road is deserted, soldiers appear only sometimes. Those who appear are without any equipment, their uniform jackets are unbuttoned and in disarray. Those who were able to, have by now escaped. The rest who stayed behind have been taken by the Bolsheviks. Although as yet there is no war with Russia, I am at this time not to know that Polish officers nevertheless, are taken prisoners of war, whilst the ranks are set free to 'go home'. We are left in Nadvorna in total limbo. The Polish State as such, has ceased to exist whilst the authority of the enemy has not yet made itself felt. The road is empty and silence reigns, a sinister silence; we are afraid what will happen next.

Dr B.'s house is full of refugees, the soldiers. They are busy ripping buttons and various insignia from their uniforms. Those who have civilian clothes don them. Dr B. helps as much as he can by giving out his own clothes. The ladies of the house busy themselves with cooking and feed all, with anything which is to be had. We use all the rooms for sleeping, side by side, on the floors. Only one bedroom is left for the private use of Dr B. and his family.

Dr B.'s sisters are teachers who work in nearby Ukrainian villages. We seriously begin to fear for their safety on hearing rumours that the local Ukrainian population is looting and murdering Poles in this area. One of the sisters arrives with her husband, from a village beyond Nadvorna — they have barely escaped from the mobs. Now groups of people appear on the street in front of the house. They carry sacks which are slung over their shoulders, they loiter about on the street, looking into the house windows. We are getting afraid of being attacked, the more so, as night is falling.

After deliberating what should be done in the case of such a nocturnal attack, Dr B. takes us out to the back of the house so that we can spy out the lie of the land. It is decided that it would be best to split up into small groups of two or three people. We arrange in which directions we will scatter, if we are attacked. By using such tactics, we hope some of us at least will escape with our lives. The revolver which I have carried on me, I now throw away into the bushes before returning to the house. To have made use of it, would have provoked the slaughter of us all.

We bed down, fully dressed, on the floors; ready to flee at any moment. It is almost impossible to sleep because we are constantly on the alert, listening to detect if the house is being approached. A few of the men do fall asleep deeply and this results in a tragi-comic incident. We are startled in the middle of the night by shouts and yells of "Help, murder!" All of us leap up and my heart is thumping like a sledge-hammer. Although I have been jerked out of semi-consciousness, I realize that the shouting came from the adjacent room whilst there is no yelling or noise elsewhere. Having opened the door to the room, we realize that one of the refugees has been having a nightmare. This man dreamt that he was being murdered! We can now laugh but at the same time we are annoyed at having been scared and for having been given a taste of what could have happened. He had really chosen his moment well for shouting in his sleep . . . .

When morning comes the roads in Nadvorna are deserted — there is an absence of any authority and nobody moves from their houses; all await to see what will next happen. Around ten o'clock an enormous Russian tank rolls into Nadvorna with an almighty roar. We breathe a sigh of relief! Given an impossible choice, it is better to have to deal with an organized and controlled enemy rather than to be at the mercy of greedy and wanton rabble.

Dr B.'s house has been left in peace up to now. When I was to return to Nadvorna from Lvov, two weeks later, to collect our suitcases, the B. family would still be safe. And in the interim a son was to be born to Dr B. I was never to know of the future fate of the family. I shall never forget their hospitality or the picture of Dr B.'s young and attractive wife bravely and calmly awaiting the birth of her child under such horrendous circumstances.

As soon as the Bolsheviks have taken over control, I go to the railway station to enquire about the possibility of returning to Lvov. The rail tracks had been bombed in several places but have not been destroyed completely and there is hope that the lines to Lvov will be reopened in two or three days' time. Whilst at the station I meet a colleague, Dr M., who also wants to return to Lvov. We arrange to travel back together on the first train, as soon as they commence to run.

The whole of the next day, I wait for him, but Dr M. does not appear. When I accidently come across him on the third day, I see he is shaking and half-conscious with fear. The previous day, he tells me, the Bolsheviks caught a group of uniformed men, amongst them himself, and took them into a field. There they were all lined up and the Bolsheviks took aim at them with their rifles. They kept them in suspense like this for about a minute and then ordered them to disperse. I suppose some people can thus amuse themselves. Dr M. leaves Nadvorna the next day and does not contact me. I know colleague M. well and did not expect him to let me down in this way. I had been counting on his company and help during the journey to Lvov. After the war he is to disappoint and upset me even more because I am to learn from credible witnesses that he went over to the Germans and declared himself to be Volksdeutch (that is a pure bred German). His surname was German, something which in itself was not uncommon in Poland but he had never let it be known that he felt and was a German. I leave Nadvorna on the 27th September a day later, on the second train to run to Lvov.

LVOV UNDER THE BOLSHEVIKS

I arrive in Lvov at the main railway station which has been badly damaged by the Germans; with fear choking me, I walk to 29 Listopada Street where I had left my mother. Is she alive? Luckily the street has not been bombed and I find my mother alive and well in our 'furniture store'.

I immediately begin to look for a job because at present we are living on our stores which we had bought as our hoard 'for the war'. We have no ready cash. I visit friends whose husbands had left for the war and who have also failed to return. We can do nothing but await nervously to see what will happen. My mother and I manage to pickle some cabbage and we store it in the cellar of my cousin's house — who knows, we may have to survive on anything.

A few days after I have returned to Lvov, two soldiers come to our room. They have promised my husband to let me know what has happened to him. And now they have kept their word! To my regret, I fail to ask and note their names and can never thank them for their message. Apparently my husband had remained in the rear with the medical orderlies. Their column failed to reach the Hungarian border in time and they were all caught by the Bolsheviks. The men were allowed to go free but the officers were taken prisoner. In the confusion, my husband had had several opportunities to make his escape and to join the men who were set free. He did not do so because speaking no Ukrainian, he feared to expose both them and himself, knowing that the local Ukrainian population was murdering Polish soldiers.

The two soldiers go on to tell me about the atrocities which they have witnessed on the way. It is only thanks to their fluent Ukrainian that they have arrived safely in Lvov because they pretended to be Ukrainians. They assure me my husband is well and unharmed but is a prisoner of war. They regret only that he could not be persuaded to return to Lvov with them. I am extremely happy on hearing their news as I do not yet know what danger is to threaten him and I think he is at least safe whilst he is a prisoner of war.

I try to find employment with the District Health Authority. And there, in that large three storeyed building, I am taught a lesson, the effects of which are to last me a lifetime of what it means to belong to the middle class. I used to come here as a student, seeking to be allocated to do smallpox vaccinations to earn some money. I always had to climb up to the third floor because the use of the lift was reserved solely for officials. I expect it to be otherwise now that 'equality' is here and so I go towards the lift. But nothing of the kind! The lift attendant casts his eyes over me, deems that I belong to the intelligentsia and says, "The lift is not for the use of the likes of you, it is for the working class." Once again I have to get myself to the top floor on foot! I realize in later life that the middle class is always the class to suffer. For the Left it is 'too high' and for the Right it is 'too low'. This belief is also to be proved true in Britain.

A few weeks after the Russians have entered Poland, they start to reorganize the Health Service. Polyclinics are formed which stay open for twenty-four hours of the day. The general practitioners have their surgeries here and accept calls for domiciliary visits during surgery hours. The doctor on duty goes to emergency calls and decides whether the patient should be sent to hospital, to the Polyclinic or whether his general practitioner should visit him at home and take over further treatment. Various specialists also have their surgeries in this building. The organization is well thought out.

I manage to obtain the post of duty doctor, the so called 'Chergov-iylikar'. The position entails forty-eight hours of work per week (in two twenty-four hour duties). For the first month this seems light work. Later the twenty-four hour 'shifts' prove so hard that one barely has time to recover from one rota when the next duty commences. Whilst on duty, it is not worth trying to get any sleep because although there is a couch in the duty office, the telephone rings frequently during the night. It is less exhausting to sit up, fully dressed in readiness for a call, than to pretend one is getting rest in mock sleep and then having to jump off the couch. Occasionally during a duty, there is inadequate time even to get one meal. One has to exist on sandwiches on these occasions and even then they can only be eaten a bite at a time.

There is no transport and it is necessary to walk to visit patients, and even to have to walk several kilometres, if the call comes from an outlying village. On returning from a visit, the next calls are already waiting. The duty starts at 9.00 a.m. and ends at 9.00 a.m. the following day. Thus the night part of the duty is particularly demanding as one has already had twelve hours of rushing about during the day.

I find my greatest problem is in attempting to get to sleep the following night after sleeping during the day at the end of the duty. I am caught in a vicious circle. I go about constantly exhausted and badly in need of sleep. It would be possible to reverse the sleep pattern and do only night work but I find it impossible to sleep one night and to work the next night.

On one occasion I am called out to a patient who lives in a village on the outskirts of the city, about an hour's walk away. To get to the patient means I have to walk through the town and across fields. It is in one field that by chance I come across a patrol of Russians. There are three of them, uniformed and armed and they shout to me in Russian. I show them my doctor's pass though at times such as this it is a completely useless chit of paper. I am allowed to go on my way but the encounter has greatly unnerved me. I had been completely at their mercy, alone with them in the field, in the middle of the night and far from the city. Obviously I had been lucky and they had happened to be decent men whose behaviour towards me could not be faulted. They had only checked my identity, which had been their duty. As a rule it is unwise to find oneself on the streets at night because according to Russian mentality, there can be no possible need to be abroad at night. If one is, then they assume it must be for some secret ill-intentioned purpose. During the night, the street patrols will arrest anyone who is 'loitering' and so I could well have been arrested.

On reaching my destination, I find that my patient is not seriously ill and therefore I would not be justified in asking her general practitioner to come and see her. Her husband is polite and attentive towards me. I think he is somewhat embarrassed as he knows they have called me out unnecessarily. I think he also expected to see a male doctor — a bourgeois — and when I turned up he felt uncomfortable. I pretend not to notice his unease, tell them there was no cause for the anxiety which prompted them to call me out and even console them that the patient is not threatened by anything more sinister and will soon recover.

Perhaps the husband in his embarrassment, is grateful for my tactful behaviour because he later brings me a piece of sole-leather for shoes as a reward (I have no idea how he discovered my address) and will accept no payment for it. In these times, leather for soling shoes is completely unobtainable and worth its weight in gold. I cannot help liking these Lvov rascals! (called in the local slang 'batiar'). His lilting accent is delightful and in him I have come face to face with a 'decent' rascal! We both know he has come to apologize for having called me out unnecessarily but neither of us so much as hints that the other realizes the reason for his having come.

Presently and, of course, it has to be during a night, I get called out to see a Russian 'Komandir'. He is quartered in a private house and when I enter his room, the heat hits me so that I nearly suffocate. The stove is incandescent and all doors and windows are firmly shut. The patient is in bed, soaking with perspiration. He allows himself to be examined and I discover that he is wearing three sets of warm underwear, layer upon layer, like an onion. He watches me suspiciously all the while and when I complete the examination, he pulls out a revolver from under his pillows, shows me it is loaded and threatens to shoot me if in any way I try to harm him. This dramatic situation is on a par to a third-rate film and rather than being frightened, I am amused that I find myself an actor in this unlikely scene. Later, when I get to understand the 'Russian mind', I become convinced that this was the Komandir's idea of a joke because he had expected to see a male doctor. Nevertheless the fact he had a pistol under his pillow proved he feared the Poles.

Without any warning the Russians invalidate Polish currency and we are given no opportunity to exchange our money. People are despairing but I am not. I had no money to exchange and so I have lost nothing. The couple of Zlotys I had had in my pocket I had used to buy sweets — they too are a source of calories. Unknowingly, I must already have been affected by the Bolshevik attitude because I feel I want to laugh at the panic of the 'magnates'.

The director at the Potocki Street Clinic where I work, is Dr H., a highly esteemed man. He cannot openly oppose the Russians but wants to help the Polish doctors. I do not envy him his position or the great responsibility associated with it. Apart from the doctors at the clinic we also have an informer in our midst, a Mr C., who comes from Krakov. He is a Jew and his official post is that of general factotum. Mr C. keeps a watchful eye on everything that happens at the Polyclinic, particularly on the doctors, to ensure that they are carrying out their various functions. During my night duties I often have discussions with him; this in effect means that I sit and listen to him. He so intensely wants to initiate me into his ideology. Naturally, I never contradict him. Later, when I am to be in Kazakhstan, I am informed by a cousin in Lvov, that Mr C. was the first person to appear in our room, with the first light of dawn to loot, pilfer, and carry away as many of our belongings as possible before the official powers arrived on the scene.

Time flies and Lvov, with each day, becomes a sadder city. The streets are littered with rubbish and the inhabitants are intimidated and harassed. The Russian soldiers are keen to purchase watches. 'Times' or 'Tchasiy' as they call them are unobtainable in Russia. They are willing to buy any 'time' available. Even pedestrians are stopped on the streets and asked if they have a 'time' for sale. Like children, the soldiers will hold the watch to their ears and smile broadly when they hear it ticking. Also as popular with them are opera and field-glasses. Having a pair of my father's Zeiss field-glasses and needing the cash, I try to find a customer for them. Before I have a chance to find a buyer, I meet an older Jewish colleague who will not allow me to carry out my plan. He insists on giving me a loan. He says it would be a pity to dispense with such an item and as he has some money he presses me to accept some on an indefinite loan. He is not a very close friend of mine so his action is prompted out of the goodness of his heart. He wants to help me by making sure I keep the field-glasses to sell in a darker hour of need. Happily, I am able to repay the loan, just before I am deported to Siberia. Did he survive the war? Did he have adequate money to escape from the Germans?

Money is now very short and it is even worse with food. Peasants from the outlying villages of Lvov bring potatoes into the city. We store some in my cousin's cellars. The shops still sell dried peas, beans and sometimes cereals. Fat of any kind can only be bought on the black market. We melt down some pork fat so at least we will have a few jars of lard for the 'dark hour'. It becomes increasingly more difficult to get bread. Even after queueing outside a shop for several hours, one often has to go away empty-handed. My husband's brother knows a baker, who would gladly sell him some bread, only he is worried he will be accused of favouritism. Favouritism is strongly frowned upon in the USSR and is punished accordingly.

I now hit upon a brilliant idea! I stuff a pillow under my coat, over my stomach, and guided by the elbow, with deference by my brother-in-law, make my way to the bakery. There is a long queue outside the shop, which we ignore and walk round to the private entrance at the rear of the building. Once inside I shed the pillow and again stuff the coat, this time with two loaves of bread. Supporting my heavy 'burden' with both my hands in my pockets, I leave the bakery with composure. I can hardly restrain myself from laughter and fear I will betray myself. Perhaps my escapade was not quite 'the thing' but life has already taught me that often to 'do the thing' handsomely can result in perishing handsomely.

The beginning of December, 1939, brings me the first letter from my husband, who is being detained as prisoner of war in Russia. Yes, a prisoner of war without there being officially a state of war between Poland and Russia! The address given in his letter is only the number of a wartime post box. I am relieved that he is healthy and relatively safe. Naturally my husband's letters are censored so he is unable to give me any details. He can only ask to be sent some warm underclothes and a pair of ski-boots. He tells me that he will be allowed to write to me once a month. Straight away I parcel up the boots, making a separate parcel of each boot. This is a precaution, if I made one parcel of both boots, I could be tempting somebody to steal it. Even so, the boots fail to reach my husband. Obviously somebody found even one boot could be put to some use!

My husband's sister-in-law speaks fluent Russian, so I make all haste to go with her to see the War Procurator. I mean to ask him to intervene on behalf of my husband. Since he is a doctor and not a professional officer, they have no right to be detaining him as a prisoner of war. Of course, as could be expected, the War Procurator is of the opinion that as my husband was in uniform and with the army, he can do nothing to help me. At least I have done all I could.

Christmas is spent sadly in the company of my husband's brother and his wife, who live near by. Conversation is stilted — we do not know what to talk about. We are lying low, waiting to see what will happen, and it seems pointless to be making any plans for the future. I sometimes see old school friends. One friend is reluctant to go into town with me because I only have a beret and no hat to put on — the poor soul does not realize that the times when 'one wore a hat' to go out are no longer with us. Another friend will not move from her 'nest'. She and her small daughter keep to their flat, where the windows are still taped up with strips of paper. This had been done 'in case of war' so that the splinters of possible broken glass would not injure the baby. She is trying to convince herself that there is no need for any anxiety. She exists on the money sent to her by her husband who is in Hungary. A third friend is able to view the present situation objectively in the same level-headed manner as she has always had in life. All three of these friends are to survive the war.

The Russians order a population census to be taken. We are all apprehensive about this since the questionnaire is obligatory and very detailed: name, place of birth, origins of parents, name of spouse, whereabouts of spouse, etc. I very much fear that I will be displaced from Lvov because a year before the outbreak of war we had moved to the west of Poland to Jeleśnia and we are still registered there as permanent residents. Therefore I could be classed as a refugee in Lvov from the west, even though I had been born in Lvov and have lived here all my life. I am also afraid to write down that my husband is a prisoner of war in the USSR. Eventually I write down the truth because if I am to get into hot water, I prefer to get into it by telling the truth and not by lying. Unfortunately my permanent residence in Lvov was interrupted when we had moved to Jeleśnia and I could now be moved back to my 'official place' of residence in Jeleśnia which is now occupied by the Germans. The Russians who have stepped into Poland from the east, to 'liberate' us, are anxious to clear the area of undesirable persons of the intelligentsia. So I am nervous. It does not cross my mind that apart from resettling people, the Russians may have other methods of eliminating us.

We were next ordered by the Russians to vote to elect representatives to the West Ukrainian Parliament. It is obligatory to go to vote and the caretaker of the tenement attends to make sure we all do this. In the evenings certain officials also come round to check if we have fulfilled our civil duty. It is practically impossible therefore to evade participating in the elections and I am obliged to go. I vote for some Ukrainian woman; at least I can vote for a woman! In any case the elections are a mockery because the outcome is prearranged and decided beforehand. Even so, it irks me to have to put my cross against a name.

The Russians are attempting to educate and organize us with full force! A meeting of the Health Authority employees is convened and as I work at the Polyclinic, I am obliged to attend. The huge room is packed with people — mostly strangers with only a few familiar faces. The meeting is opened by speeches in praise of the new Russian regime, condemnation of the past — we must 'greet the new regime with joy, work and plan with enthusiasm'. There are many speakers but all the speeches are stereotyped. The University of Jan Kazimierz representative takes his turn in speaking. Professor G., professor of Paediatrics, steps on to the podium. He was one of my examiners whilst at Medical School and I shudder with apprehension as I wonder what he can possibly find to say. Please do not let me become disillusioned with him, please let him prove himself to be the sort of person I took him to be! And indeed, Professor G. does not let me down! He struggles, he meanders round various topics and gives an outline of the history of the Grody Czerwienskie. Let me explain that this part of eastern Poland, during the Middle Ages, was claimed as their land by the Cossacks, Ukrainians and Poles. There was constant unrest and squabbling over this question. After World War I, the Grody Czerwienskie were officially deemed to belong to Poland, and had belonged to Poland up till now. The Ukrainians had never come to terms with this arrangement, and now under the Russian regime were claiming the territory to be theirs as the west Ukraine.

So Professor G. was careful not to incite trouble and talked in general terms about this area and Lvov as its capital, managing to avoid using the name west Ukraine. To use that name would obviously have stuck in his throat. He had to be very careful not to appear openly hostile towards the Ukrainians and Russians but nevertheless he had said enough to endanger himself. A brave man.

DEPORTATION AND THE JOURNEY TO KAZAKHSTAN

It is on the 10th April, 1940, when a Jewish woman doctor, who also works at the Polyclinic, warns me of the possibility of deportation. One day, she comes into work in a very agitated state. She had been called out during the night to visit a patient and this person has been deported. That night was the first night of the deportations. Her patient had given birth to a child a few days before and when the Russians had come in the night, under the pretext of 'resettling' her, she had demanded to be seen by her doctor. In spite of the doctor trying to reason with the Russians that a woman, a few days after labour and a new-born infant, are unfit to be moved and to travel, she and the baby are deported. It was deemed that labour is not an illness. I cannot believe that I may be threatened with deportation — after all I had a job here.

The woman doctor, whose name I cannot remember, urges me to make my preparations, with all speed, for possible deportation. To make matters worse, I learn that her patient, had also written in the population census, that her husband was a prisoner of war in the USSR.

We had heard rumours that the Border Guards were being deported, but this did not unduly worry us since the Russians could be said to have just cause for this action. The Border Guards know all the paths and crossings over the borders of Poland and could assist in the smuggling of arms and people across the border. It never crosses our minds that the Russians will deport civilians. I fool myself that as I belong to the 'working intelligentsia' as a doctor, I cannot possibly belong to the category of people who are being deported.

The woman doctor continues urging me to pack. She tells me that it is insignificant who I am and what I do, it is only relevant that I am the wife of an officer who is a prisoner of war in the USSR. From the details I have given in the census, the Russians will categorize me as 'army family'. The Russians possess lists of ordinary and reserve officers' families and are deporting them. I still will not accept that this can happen. However my colleague is so shaken and so insistent that I should pack, without any more delay, that I am forced to consider deportation as a serious possibility.

Arriving home, I commence preparations for deportation, thinking I shall have several days' time to get organized and ready. My mother remains

25

calm and helps me to sort out our belongings. Having packed various valuable trinkets, I take them to an old school friend for safe keeping. I also pack all the silver cutlery into a suitcase which is now so heavy I can barely lift it. I will take it tomorrow to a friend. 'Tomorrow' is never to arrive as tomorrow I shall already be locked up in a cattle wagon in the main railway station.

I pile all our documents, my husband's, mother's and mine into a brief-case. I destroy my grandparents' birth certificates by burning them. I think they could be called 'bourgeois' and I fear that the certificates could harm me. My mother and I then cut up two family portraits and burn the pieces in the stove. We do not want the portraits to fall into strange hands. I wash a few 'smalls' and hang them up in the kitchen to dry, before going to bed.

The fact that I had all my documents with me, was not going to make things any easier or pleasanter for me in the future. Most people I am to come into contact with during my wanderings did not have the time or presence of mind to pack their documents. Frequently, therefore, people were to think it very suspect that I had mine. Some were to think I was in favour with the Russians because of this. In other words that I was on the Russian payroll. Others were to suspect that I faked the documents. The possession of my documents was to cause me maximum distress much later in the autumn of 1942 when Dr G., the commander of the Polish Hospital in Teheran, was to query the validity of my medical degree, giving as a reason for his doubts the very fact that I had it with me! Dr G. had become used to verifying claims of people to being doctors. He wanted me to present two credible doctors who would testify that I was qualified. I showed my outrage at being suspected of falsification and so Dr G. gave way, but was quite obviously annoyed with me. I had disrupted his routine procedure and had wounded his self-importance. To this day I feel the urge to laugh when I recall the situation. Indeed the psychology of human beings is most interesting: for a person to 'dare' to be different is frowned upon. It seems there is an accepted 'set' order and an individual may not disrupt the format of a specific situation. I was only to understand this manner of human reasoning after many years. In Teheran I was to feel very hurt that Dr G. suspected me of cheating. I naïvely thought he would be pleased and would praise the fact that he had met a person who had kept her head when being deported and had had the presence of mind to pack her degree certificate. Years later, this observation of human psychology was to be borne out by a French film, in which the population of a whole village attends the funeral of a family who have died by eating poisonous fungi. The people weep on seeing the line of large and small coffins but they are annoyed by the one small boy who survived because he was away from home and so did not eat the fungi. His survival has upset the entirety of the tragedy.

The cousin, in whose home we live, is also afraid of being deported and makes me promise that if she is deported, I should have her beloved dog put down. I naturally promise to do as she asks, should the need occur. The cousin and dog are to remain — we are to be deported.

Soon after our return to Lvov from Jeleśnia, my mother had sewn all her jewellery into her suspender belt. Not only does she wear it during the day but also sleeps without removing it. This suspender belt is later to save her life.

We go to bed around eleven o'clock but we find it impossible to sleep well. At about one o'clock I am aware of a lorry stopping outside the building and almost immediately comes a hammering at the gates. We are now fully awake, our hearts begin to beat faster and we are so very certain they have come to deport us that we leap out of bed before the concierge has had time to open the gates. Within the next couple of seconds we hear them banging on our door and shouting in Russian. It flashes through my mind — we live on the ground floor, the kitchen door opens into the yard which adjoins the gardens of the houses opposite — I could escape even now, the building is not surrounded. But I cannot abandon my mother, I cannot possibly leave her to be deported alone. I am helpless in this situation and must allow myself to be caught like a trapped animal.

Three thugs come into our room, one obviously the senior in uniform, one soldier with a rifle and one in civilian clothes. This one speaks in broken Polish and tells me he is taking us to join my husband. They elbow us to make way for them because they want to search the room. My mattress lies next to my mother's bed and there is no way into the room so I have to stand in the doorway. We are made to dress in front of them. They watch us intently to see if we are trying to conceal anything. What providence that my mother has been sleeping wearing her precious suspender belt and that they do not notice it as she is dressing. It only takes us one or two minutes to dress and now having moved my mattress, they start to search the room. The contents of various drawers are thrown out: even the lard, which we have stored in jars in readiness for the winter, is pierced with a bayonet — they are searching for weapons. They look into every nook and cranny and at the same time tell us to hurry with our packing, even though there is no room to move. In the dresser they find some First World War ordnance survey maps of the mountain regions of Gorgany and Czarnohora. My father had been given the maps by an army friend and greatly appreciated them since he used to do some serious walking in the mountains when out trout fishing. Every path and track was marked on the maps, each smallest stream and every possible crossing, into Hungary and Czechoslovakia.

I am now paralysed with fear as I see their eyes gleam at their find! How keenly they pounce on the maps. They are bound to think I am a spy! Aggressively and sternly they ask me: "From where and for what reason do you have these maps?" How do I explain to them that from early childhood, I have been used to spending my holidays in these mountains? They will not understand the walking in the mountains, sleeping in Koliby (shepherds' huts) by an open fire, in the company of the Huculs (the local highland people) is my only holiday pastime. Throughout the whole of my life all my holidays have been spent in these mountains. In the USSR it is not customary to go walking in the mountains with a knapsack on one's back: because people are incapable of making such an 'unnecessary' physical effort for sheer pleasure. In any case, border areas of the USSR are forbidden territory to the Russian people. I suddenly realize that, in their eyes, the maps prove that I must be a spy. My present situation is far worse than I expected it to be and they could imprison me for spying. I attempt to hide my fears and innocently launch into a long tale of my mountain holidays, explaining that for walking, the maps are an indispensable part of my equipment, if one is not to get lost. I cannot tell if they believe me or if they cannot be bothered to arrest me but they apparently decide it will suffice to carry out the prime objective of their task, which is to deport us. The maps are brushed aside and they continue to search the room. I am relieved that it now looks as though I shall 'only' be deported and not arrested and imprisoned as a spy.

They rush us all the while and we are given ten minutes to pack in this cramped and crowded room, into which the five of us are squeezed with not even enough space to turn around. There is no time to stop and think what we will need so we just throw some personal clothes into two suitcases. We fail to pack any cooking or eating implements but later in Kazakhstan I find a useless clothes-brush in my suitcase! We have a large trunk in the room which we use as a general store and pantry. Sugar and soap is packed away in the bottom and this trunk now proves very useful. We throw in some sheets and bedding and I add a suit of my husband's though I disbelieve that we are in fact being taken to join him. I simply do not think to take a single pan, or a cup or a knife, fork or spoon. Under the circumstances of this horrendous moment I cannot foresee that wherever we will be taken, we shall have to eat off something and with something. The first items I grabbed when we were told to pack were our documents and finally I snatch the still damp tea-towels, which I had washed before going to bed and which have been hanging up to dry in the kitchen. The kitchen, where the door exits to the garden and freedom . . . .

The Russians help us carry our baggage and help us up into the waiting lorry. The lorry is already full of people — all poor wretches like us. We are the last to be put on to the lorry which moves off immediately. We are all silent and people sit on their suitcases, baskets or bundles in complete stupefaction. For the last time, we look out at Lvov. The city is asleep, the streets are empty, dark and silent, the silence only being broken by the sound of our lorry. In the morning there will be no trace of us and those who have remained, will speak only in whispers about this night's happenings. As always in Russia, arrests and deportations always take place at night in secrecy.

We eventually arrive at Lvov's main railway station. The train is waiting for us on a siding, surrounded by armed soldiers. The lorries drive us up to the cattle wagons, which have even had their small windows boarded up. The sliding doors are pushed aside and we are ordered to get in. The wagon is filled with people already so it is with difficulty that we push and heave our luggage aboard. We stack all the suitcases and bundles into a large pile in the middle of the wagon. We are expected to sleep on two benches which run the width of the wagon, at either end. There certainly will be inadequate room for us all to use the benches so we shall have to bed down in two tiers. Twenty people on the floor under the benches and another twenty on the benches. We have estimated that there will only be space for the forty people at a time, to sleep lying down, whereas there must be approximately fifty persons here, men, women and children of all ages. The young folk offer to sleep or rather 'rest' in a sitting up position on the luggage, during the night, and to stretch out on the benches during the day, when the elderly can then sit up.

We find a hole in the floor by the door of the wagon. This is our 'convenience'. Level with the benches, the four small windows have been boarded up. We can only see out by peering through small chinks in the boards. Day begins to dawn and we can see that the train is guarded on one side only, by soldiers who stand on the platform. On the unguarded side of the train there are fields. We can see some movement through the chinks in the windows. We carefully prise away some of the thinnest pieces of boarding, to see small groups of people on the platform. Our friends and relations have come to aid us by trying to pass small parcels through the windows. These humane actions are thwarted by the soldiers who usher the people away with their rifles. We soon realize that the guards turn the relations away, if they attempt to hand us the parcels whilst they can see what is going on. Once the guards have passed by, they ignore the parcels being handed over. We signal to our friends that they should wait until the guards have walked on beyond the wagon before coming over to give us their parcels.

I see my husband's brother and wife have come to look for us but cannot get near to the wagon. I manage to fight my way to the window and shout loudly to attract their attention. I ask them to bring us eating utensils, also cups and bottles for water. Somehow, few of us have thought to bring any containers for holding water. There are two pails in the wagon but we are told these will be used for holding our soup rations. So we do not even have any utensils for fetching water! Later in the afternoon, my brother-in-law and his wife return and manage this time, to pass spoons, mugs and two bottles, to us. I do not realize that this is the last time I shall see them for thirty-seven years.

During this, our first day in the wagon, they give us a little bread to eat and the guards escort a few men away to bring us water. We have to resort to improvisation now because we have no large containers for water. We collect together anything which can be used: bottles, flasks, milk cans, etc., and tie them together so that the men can carry as many of these containers as possible. The amount of water brought back is little to be shared out between us all. We have to ration it out. For all our requirements, we get approximately one litre of water per person, in every twenty-four hours. In the next three weeks of our journey, we are all badly to feel the shortage of water. The hole in the wagon floor, which is to serve us as a convenience, becomes a nightmare. No one has the courage to use it; not only because of the lack of privacy, but also, in such a confined space we are forced to stand shoulder to shoulder. Blankets, curtains and other oddments of material, are searched out from amongst the luggage, and with the aid of string, we rig up a makeshift screen round the hole. The men have emptied their pockets, to find not only the string but also penknives and nails!

There is so little room in the wagon, that one passenger finds her feet 'spending the night' in the toilet, when she lies down to sleep. We have to be extremely careful not to fall over them when using the 'loo'.

We are left in complete darkness in the wagon. Luckily, some people find several candles amongst their belongings. The candles are used very sparingly because perhaps in the future there may be a greater necessity for them. Perhaps it is as well we are in darkness because even in this tragic situation there can be moments of comedy. The old and obese gentlemen cannot manage our 'convenience'. The cubicle round the hole is so small and they are so big that they are unable to close the curtains once they are inside! It is physically impossible for them to fit in completely. Like ostriches however, they appear to be happy if their heads are hidden by the screen; not caring that the rest of their 'anatomy' is on public display! Not infrequently I laugh quietly, until tears stream down my face.

During the first night, whilst the train is still stationary at the railway station, several people make their escape from the adjoining wagon. We hear a commotion and shots but they have escaped by breaking away the boards from the windows. I envy them — I would have done similarly had it not been that my mother is with me.

The train remains yet one more day in the station. They check the lists of people in each wagon, repeatedly. They check and compare the lists with other papers. We can hear footsteps on the wagon roof. Somebody is walking along, stopping, tapping and then going on. We are puzzled and hazard a guess that they are installing bugging devices. We try to talk in whispers. Every few hours they tap the wheels of the train, causing much disturbance.

Eventually, as night falls, the train begins to move: we do not know where we are being taken to or if we will ever see Lvov or Poland again. As the train leaves Lvov behind, I am overwhelmed by despair and cannot hold back my tears. I am aware of a base and abominable feeling of resentment towards my mother. It is her being with me that has resulted in my being caught and deported, like a helpless animal in a cage. My mother, thank God, is unaware of the reason for my tears (at least I do not think she has guessed the reason). I weep tears of resentment and anger against my mother's presence.

We are now travelling in locked wagons, eastwards. Somebody keeps walking along the roof of the wagon — for what reason or purpose? I doubt that they have installed listening devices because for what reason? In having deported us they have rendered us harmless.

The train stops frequently, most often before it reaches the stations, which we pass at such speed that we are unable to read the place-names. At other times, we stop in the middle of fields, sometimes for a few minutes, sometimes for an hour or more. Each time the train is at a stand-still, once again the wheels are tested, the undercarriage checked, and we hear them calling to each other and walking on the roof.

During one of these halts, Russian soldiers who have jumped down from the train, walk along the wagons offering to sell us tins of crab-meat, ham, fruit and also sweets. I was to learn later that the train included a special wagon of provisions for us but we are only fed on bread (about 300 grammes per person per day). Several times we are given a few sweets each and once a few cubes of sugar. The food which has been supplied for us, is sold to us by the crew of the train on and off during our journey.

We buy some tins of ham — which has gone off. I later feed it to dogs in Kazakhstan. The tins of crab-meat are cheaper and go further, so they are beter value for our money. The crab-meat is top quality 'Kamczatka', sweet and delicious. Eventually after a while I find the crabs become so nauseating that I cannot look at the meat. For years later, I am to feel ill at the sight of a tin of crab-meat! The tins from the ham we will find very useful later as pans for cooking.

Once every twenty-four hours we are given soup; watery but warm. The soup would be waiting for us at a prearranged station but as the train is often delayed, we get the soup at odd times of day or night. Two men are allowed out of the wagon to collect the soup in the two pails provided. The soup is shared out between the fifty of us.

There are mothers and infants in some other wagons. Fortunately we are not faced with the problem of babies in our wagon. From the shock of their traumatic ordeal, the nursing mothers have become dry and have nothing to feed to the sucklings. Chewing up bread, they attempt to give it to their babies. They are given a cupful of milk for the babies once a day. There is a shortage of water and no facility for washing nappies. Thank God that I am spared the sight of these women and infants. No infants die during our journey but also no child under the age of three is to live for longer than a year after our deportation.

People in our wagon are changing into animals, and changing very rapidly. I watch as a man steals his wife's meagre bread ration from her and eats it surreptitiously; I watch a schoolteacher blowing his nose through his fingers, though he has a handkerchief; I watch men jostling and fighting to be chosen to fetch water. And fear grips me.

Being cooped up together, as though in a mixed prison, people begin to break up slowly into natural groups. One couple who are part of our group, is an engineer, Mr C. and his wife, from Gdansk. Mrs C. is a vegetarian (and apparently became so, after some family catastrophe) who is placid, composed, patient and good-tempered. Mr C. however is, I think, extremely self-centred. His life is ruled by the principle that one must push oneself forward, with disregard to the circumstances — this becomes apparent during our journey. Poor Mr C. is not to survive the war. I am later to see him, dying of avitaminosis, in hospital in Teheran in 1942.

Schoolteacher Mr B. and his wife are both charming and brave. They are thrilled to have brought with them a Persian rug, which now serves them as a portable bed. They are quite right to be pleased because the rug proves to be thick, warm, and indestructible! Later they will be using it to sleep on upon bare earth, without feeling the cold or damp. Mr B. acts as our priest; at his instigation we all join in communal prayers and singing in the evenings, making our journey more tolerable.

Schoolteacher Mr P., resembles a typical 'gentleman farmer'. He is tall, stout and paunchy, red of face and with a bristling moustache. He is pompous and self-important. His wife is very pleasant and gay and addresses everybody as 'ducks'. They have a son, who is a politically active student at Lvov Polytechnic. He had not been sleeping at home but in a different friend's house each night because he feared being arrested. When the Russians came to their house to arrest him and found he was not there, they deported his parents instead. Later, in Kazakhstan, Mr and Mrs P. receive letters from their son! They learned that after their deportation, their son stayed under cover for a while in various houses. Presently, as though nothing out of the ordinary had happened, he returned to their vacant flat and attended lectures, as normal. They were also to receive food parcels from him. The Russians were only interested in deporting the intellectuals *en masse* and did not waste time or efforts in pursuing the individual. That explains why their son was left in peace in Lvov.

Another schoolteacher Mr L., is a person who is kind and gentle. Throughout the journey, in a scout-like fashion, he plans how to survive the 'exile'. He contemplates making bird nets, animal traps and how to find and collect fungi and berries. Unfortunately, in the territory to which we are being deported, there will only be sparrows and wolves and there will be an absence of fungi and berries.

There is also travelling with us an intelligent and widely-read student. I am often to recall him because even at this moment he predicts that Communism will spread all over the world. He thinks the flood will come from China and the Chinese will eventually rule the earth. His postulation is logical but the outcome seems to us to be improbable and fantastic. However perhaps the future will show his 'prophecy' to be correct? I only hope he proves to be a false prophet!

Also with us are the wife of a Public Notary from Lvov and her daughter. In looks and demeanour, the wife resembles a quiet mouse. The daughter, who is very short-sighted, big and blonde is a little 'queer'. Neither mother nor daughter talk to anyone but all the while rummage about in their belongings.

The lack of exercise begins to tell on us all soon. All day we can only sit or lie down and therefore the opportunity of being allowed to step down from the wagon to fetch water, is much desired by all. But it is always the same few men who manage to do so. Twice a day the lucky beggars get off the train, breathe the fresh air and can stretch their legs. Till one day, several of the young women protest against this arrangement; demanding that a fair rota system be organized. To comply with the demand, it is decided to give each person their turn in going out for the water. When my turn comes, I festoon myself with all the bottles, cans, etc. and position myself by the doors in readiness for their opening. At the very moment when the doors are slid open, I am pushed aside by a man who has a wild expression on his face and the same group of men as always exit for the water. With each day there is a little more bestiality and power of the fist.

We often sing to help while away time during our journey — we sing hymns and popular and patriotic Polish songs. The Russians are startled by our gleeful voices. They cannot fathom, not only how we can sing under these circumstances but also often sing with smiles on our faces. We get enormous satisfaction from being able to hide our fear and despair from the enemy. Through a chink in the boards, I one day see two of my friends, daughters of the Chief Medical Officer of Health in Lvov, going to fetch the water. They are in excellent good form, laughing and joking together and the Russians are bewildered.

We pass through a small station, travelling too fast to be able to decipher the name. Just beyond this station, the train grinds to a halt. It is then shunted several times on to different tracks and once again the wheels are tapped and checked, etc. Something significant is happening. After a few hours we start moving forward again and we notice that the rail track is very wide. We are in Russia. The construction of the wagons must have been such, that it was possible to adjust the wheels to fit the wider Russian tracks. Poland is now left behind us. Now we are completely disorientated because the station names are written in Russian Cyrillic alphabet. None of us can read the writing. We cannot even copy down the names, to be deciphered later, because the train rarely stops at the stations.

Judging by the sun's position we are travelling all the time eastwards. We pass beautiful rivers, mountains and forests. We must be in the Urals!

On the mountain slopes can be seen large and attractive sanatoria and we are even able to discern the white-clad medical staff. It is very beautiful here. The streams sparkle in the sun, the forests are fragrant with the scent of pines — all is sheer paradise. The train stops at one of the small stations in this 'paradise' and a horde of ragged and dirty children crowds round the train. They start to beg for bread and by gesturing show us that they can 'exchange' soap for it. Not everybody has brought any soap with them, so seizing this opportunity, some people throw the children their meagre bread rations. The honest children give them soap in exchange. My travelling companions eye me suspiciously because I do not exchange my bread. As it happens we have plenty of soap with us which was packed in the bottom of the trunk where we were storing provisions for 'the winter' in Lvov. This is the first paradoxical situation I see in Russia: they are without bread but they have plenty of soap — how odd!

We are hit by a sandstorm just beyond the Urals: the strong wind forces sand in through every slit in the wagon. It becomes yellowish-grey inside the wagon and it is very stuffy. The older people start coughing and all of us feel we are going to suffocate inside the cage-like wagon as breathing becomes difficult. The train has to stop due to poor visibility and we can see nothing through the windows except a yellow murkiness. It has helped that we have halted because now the sand comes through the cracks with less force and we get some relief by pressing damp cloths over our noses and mouths. In fact the sandstorm is not a particularly important occurrence. What is of greater significance is the feeling of being caged like helpless animals who are imminently to suffocate. The storm takes about two hours to pass and we move off again.

They frequently come to check us. Our names are called from a list and like schoolchildren at a roll-call we have to answer 'here'. Theoretically the transport is quite well provisioned with food. Were it not for the fact that some of the food was being 'sold' to us and the rest being stolen by the crew, we would have been adequately fed, bearing in mind the circumstances and the purpose of the deportation.

In practice we receive 300 grammes of bread and the watery soup, every day for three weeks. Apparently it was not 'foreseen' that we would require any water because they did not provide us with containers for it. Of washing, just the hands only, there is no question. Gradually we become encrusted with grime. One of the worst things is the amount of water we are able to fetch in our bottles, etc., is insufficient to quench the thirst of some individuals, and they suffer.

We are travelling rather slowly — lengthy stops, at times lasting several hours, in the middle of nowhere, fill us with fear. As we see vast, uncultivated stretches of land which are dotted with dwarf birches, we realize we are in the Siberian tundra. Increasingly we fear where they will put us off the train, let it be not too far to the north!

As the train snakes along, by watching the position of the sun, we rejoice when it heads south and worry as it heads north. One thing is certain: our overall direction is to the east. Presently, the tundra and its dwarf birches vanishes and before us opens the vast steppe. We see people of Mongolian features on the stations we pass, wearing strange clothes. They are dressed in quilted jackets and large fur caps. The ear-flaps of the caps stick out at the sides like wings. They look friendly and pleasant and smile at us. I find their Mongolian faces most attractive: thin noses and lips and large black slanting eyes like dark saucers in flat, olive faces. There is no snow here at the moment but if we are to judge by their clothes and caps with ear-protectors, it must be extremely cold here in the winter. Without any limits, the steppe stretches endlessly beyond the horizon: there is only a carpet of dry, yellow grass, not even a sign of any bush in this total flatness.

The train, now most perceptively, turns to the south and joy breaks out in our wagon. There are more Mongolian people standing at the stations, whole groups of these friendly-looking people. I cannot say why but they inspire me with confidence and I am attracted to them rather than being afraid of them. My instinct will prove not to be misleading.

Our joy caused by the train heading south, is quickly dispelled because after another hour the train comes to a halt at the station of Dziangistobe. It is the first of May, 1940 and our journey has ended, aptly on the workers' day of holiday.

KAZAKHSTAN — IN THE AK-BUZAL KOLKHOZ

The station at Dziangistobe is but a tiny hut in the steppe but there must be some habitation near by because we can hear sounds of music and singing in celebration of May Day. As the soldiers slide back the wagon doors, a line of lorries comes towards our train. We are ordered by the soldiers to get off with our belongings. There is one lorry to each wagon-full of people. We have no way of knowing that each kolkhoz has been allocated to take in a certain number of deportees. We get into the lorries, each of which has been sent from a different kolkhoz and our fate will be in the hands of chance or luck. During the first winter, three-quarters of Poles in some kolkhozes will die of starvation.

We imagine that all of us from the whole train will travel on together. However, the lorries packed to bursting with people and belongings drive off in different directions. Our lorry drives into the steppe along a rural road. Not a shrub nor a tree anywhere, only the flat, dry steppe. No huts or signs of civilization anywhere in sight.

We travel deeper into the steppe, nobody speaks, for indeed — what is there to say? We are afraid. The lorry comes to a standstill after about two hours of travelling — in the middle of nowhere, in the steppe. They order us to get down. We have arrived at our allocated destination. Our Russian escort gives us each five roubles, climbs back into the lorry and we are left alone in the steppe. In answer to our shouted enquiries, he laughingly points to a hut which we had not noticed because it is so low to the ground.

We now understand that the hut is 'home' where we are all to live. At this moment we can no longer keep up the pretence of being brave, despair can be seen on all faces. We look around us and on closer inspection we spot some more huts, close by but they are so low that they barely rise above the level of the ground. People emerge from the huts and start converging towards us. We have no idea where we can be. We speak no Russian and only a few of them speak Russian and that, badly. We communicate by sign language which they seem to understand and pointing to the settlement say 'Ak-Buzal', gesturing more widely they say 'Kazakhstan'. So at least we know now where we are. I learn later that Ak-Buzal means White Calf.

The Kazakhs are a dignified people: the men in their quilted jackets or ' fufajki ' and fur caps with ear-flaps, the women in white headdresses which

36

flow down their backs, like veils, and long skirts. They have brought us bowls of milk which they give to the children (I do not yet realize the full meaning of this hospitable gesture). I notice that some of the old Kazakh men have tears in their eyes and are weeping at our plight. There is a marked absence of any young men. I am aware of the pitiful sight we present: women of all ages, children, old men and a few youths. All dirty, frightened and clutching our handfuls of belongings.

It is already late afternoon and encouraged by the Kazakhs, who help us carry our bundles and cases, we move off towards our allocated shed. It is apparent that this barrack has only recently been erected, without any base, directly on to the soil of the steppe because the 'floor' is still green! The fresh green grass had had no time to turn yellow. The roof and walls are made from old rusty tin. We make up our beds, from what little we have, on the floor and lie down. I cannot remember if anybody bothered to eat anything. Somebody lights a candle and we hurry to get organized before it burns out. We are incapable of planning for tomorrow, being emotionally exhausted, deportees in a wilderness, at God's mercy. I feel as though I have been 'hit over the head'.

The Kazakhs appear again in the morning. Amidst much gesticulating they make us understand that we can 'buy' milk and eggs from them in exchange for goods. My mother and I proceed to 'buy' some eggs which we mix raw with some sugar. The sugar has travelled with us, packed in the bottom of our trunk where we had stored it for the winter in Lvov. We are relieved that at least for the time being, we have something to subsist on.

One problem is the shortage of food, the other problem is our filthy condition. We must wash but we have neither bucket nor basin. There is no worry about the supply of water because each hut has its own well. The helpful Kazakhs lend us a couple of buckets and motion us to walk away into the steppe to have a thorough scrub. The wells are deep, the sides ice-encrusted (and to remain so, all the year round) and the water is clear and sweet.

My mother and I therefore trek out into the steppe with our buckets of water and an empty 'Kamczatka' crab-meat tin, which we can use to sluice ourselves down with. As the sun is already hot and the sky a cloudless blue, we strip completely and pour the icy water over our bodies. Itching to wash away the dirt as quickly as possible, we do not feel the cold. We soap and rinse but the grime refuses to be washed off, especially where it is ingrained on our necks and up from the hands to the elbows. We resort to scrubbing ourselves with handfuls of dry grass and this helps to remove some of the filth. It takes us several days of washing and scrubbing to remove all traces of dirt.

The steppe smells of wild thyme and wormwood and is not so completely flat as we initially thought. We would barely walk away from our shed to have some privacy for washing, when the huts of the settlement would disappear from view. We have to take great care to find our way back to Ak-Buzal and not to wander by mistake further out into the steppe!

Returning to the shed after our unsatisfactory ablutions we find commerce with the Kazakhs is in full swing. The Poles are exchanging their things for food, the food being eggs and milk. The items which 'sell' like hot cakes are fine white towels, sheets, basins and pans. We exchange a sheet for a bucket with a Kazakh woman. The women are very greedy for our sheets because they cannot obtain the long white material necessary for their traditional head veils.

Expectantly we await the arrival of somebody to tell us how to cope — we cannot get it into our heads that we are alone to manage as best we can, the more so since we are two-thirds women with dependent children or old parents. We wait and delude ourselves that we will be taken care of. Instead, at dawn the next morning we are woken by shouts and a hammering on the door. A Kazakh enters and says something in broken Russian. Eventually we understand that he is the Priedsiedatiel or headman of Ak-Buzal and has come to drive us out to work. The Kazakh shouts but massacres the language to such an extent that we can barely catch the odd word. And even if we could understand completely we are disinclined to go to work not knowing what it may entail — so we are either too old, or too young or cannot leave the children alone. I have no problems, because the Kazakh on learning that I am a doctor, leaves me in peace and somehow becomes reconciled that I am only prepared to work in my profession and will not labour manually. Neither does he attempt to drive my mother or the other elderly women out to work. The sole outcome of the rumpus is a lot of shouting. I think the Kazakh has only been trying to execute his duty because all his shouts and threats have lacked conviction.

On the third day in Ak-Buzal it becomes apparent that nobody is going to come to our aid and nobody will guide us how to manage here. Judging by the Kazakhs and their dwellings, it is obvious that there is great poverty amongst them — there is no question of the Kolkhoz being able to feed us because they have nothing to eat themselves. The 'elders', that is the old gentlemen in our group, hold a council to discuss our next steps. It is decided that we will endeavour to discover the name and location of the nearest place where there is likely to be some authority and to go there to demand help. Our elders are disgusted: "What do they think they are doing, to abandon us like this?" "This is impossible," etc. Unfortunately our old gentlemen still think along old lines. The Council of Elders (as I call them) decides to hire the services of a Kazakh and his cart in order to go to Gieorgievka where we know there is a Post Office, a Health Clinic and also the 'authorities'. I am pleased that I shall have the opportunity to call on the Regional Health Authority in order to ask for employment, but I soon discover tht the old gentlemen do not wish to take any females with them. They prefer to go alone to handle 'our affairs' because 'things are impossible'.

They hire a Kazakh with his cart, the cart being pulled by a camel! What a novelty — we did not think camels could be bred in this climate. Off the elders go. They return with crestfallen expressions. They have been told that we have not been just resettled but deported to Kazakhstan for a term of ten years. We are here as 'zsylni' (deportees) to be punished. I presume our crime is that the majority of us here belong to the intelligentsia class. We have grossly misjudged our situation. The old gentlemen were told that if we are to survive, it must be by our own efforts, by working, because, "He who works not, eats not." We are expected to work, 'nada rabotat' (in Russian), in the Ak-Buzal kolkhoz. We would then receive a percentage of the crops due to us, in autumn, in accordance with the number of days worked. It is now only May — we are expected to live and work on thin air for four months.

We are woken each morning by the shouting 'Priedsiedatiel' as he endeavours to drive us out to work. Since day by day he shouts more and more it becomes impossible for some of the youths and girls to continue finding excuses. I witness their first day's departure to work. What happens is this: we are woken at dawn as usual by the 'Priedsiedatiel' and our 'work-force' leaves the shed for the picking-up point. There they sit down to await the cart which is supposed to come for them to take them to the fields. Two hours later they are still sitting there, waiting. Eventually the bullock-drawn wagon appears and they trundle off to work at a ponderous snail's pace.

They tell us later that the journey to work took an hour and a half and the work was light, entailing weeding and earthing up. They were permitted to work at leisure, choosing their own pace. It was unimportant how much work was achieved, it was only vital to appear to be occupied. They were allowed long breaks and were given one small meal. On returning to Ak-Buzal at about ten o'clock in the evening, our 'labourers' are in excellent spirits, sunburnt and relaxed after their romantic two hour drive through the cool, moonlit steppe night. In this instance, the ponderous pace of the bullocks only added charm to the general atmosphere.

Inside our shed the 'workers' get down to the business of feeding on the food which their womenfolk have bartered from the Kazakhs and have prepared for them. If this is the picture of a working day in a Kazakh kolkhoz, it is hardly surprising that people are poverty-ridden because as the harvest is so scant they have little to eat.

We shall have to settle down here somehow, we cannot continue as we are, living in this barrack, sleeping and squatting on the ground, in worse conditions than boy scouts on an expedition. On reflection, it might be preferable to separate into smaller groups and to rent rooms from the Kazakhs. I think we have no alternative because it is unlikely that anybody will survive the winter if we remain in this shed. So far as I am concerned, I shall hope to extricate myself from Ak-Buzal before the winter comes by finding a position as a doctor.

With this aim in mind, I resolve to walk into Gieorgievka because I have no money to hire a Kazakh with his cart. Gieorgievka is approximately fifteen kilometres away and to return the same day will mean I shall have to cover thirty kilometres. However, I am a capable hiker and from my experience in the mountains I know I can easily walk forty kilometres a day.

My newly acquired knowledge of a few Russian words is of little help since the Kazakhs speak no Russian and therefore I have to ask directions to Gieorgievka by using sign-language. I manage to make myself understood and the Kazakhs give me instructions with the help of single words and gestures. I diligently jot down the directions because the last thing I want to do is get lost on the steppe. The wide road through Ak-Buzal peters out into a narrow path just outside the hamlet and eventually remains only as a narrow earth trodden track which then also disappears.

My instructions are to follow the track and then continue in the same direction across the steppe until I see the 'kurhan'. I think a kurhan must be the burial mound of some historically significant figure. I am to pass the mound on the right then I must turn right, etc., etc.

I make a very early start whilst it is still cool and a light thyme and wormwood scented breeze is blowing gently. I am completely alone, around me the endless steppe and above me the cupola of the sky: I feel light-hearted and totally detached from reality. The walk would be delightful were it not for the circumstances which had prompted me to embark on it. At the start of my expedition, I had doubted the wisdom of my decision in setting off, alone, across the steppe but when I pass the various landmarks given me by the Kazakhs, I pluck up my courage and reach my destination in good spirits. It is ten o'clock in the morning and I am well pleased with my achievement. The Kazakhs, so it proved, had given me correct and precise instructions.

Gieorgievka is a typical, small Russian village which straggles for several kilometres along the road called Stenka Razin. Razin was a colourful Cossack rebel who was active in the seventeenth century in Astrakhan. The cottages here are taller, whitewashed and surrounded by small vegetable plots — it is evident that there is some semblance of order and relative affluence here. Affluence, by Kazakh standards that is. I espy trees for the first time since we have been in Kazakhstan, tall poplars lining the roadside and rustling in the breeze. It could almost be a Polish village. My heart lurches sickeningly.

The village consists of the main street and several other 'roads'. These roads are inhabited by ghettos of ethnically differing Russian peoples. One such settlement forms the district of the 'zsylni' who were the deportees sent to Kazakhstan during the Tsarist times. These days their children are free citizens who were born here, have established their own families and consider Kazakhstan to be their homeland. Separately is another quarter, that of the voluntary settlers who were lured to this area in the Tsarist times, by the rich fertile soil. And now their children and grandchildren also feel their roots to be here in Kazakhstan.

An old Russian woman tells me this region used to be a land flowing with milk and honey. The wheat would grow practically without any need for cultivation, wherever the grain happened to fall on the soil and the immeasurable steppe would graze innumerable cattle. The black velvet colour of this rich earth imprints itself on my mind. Gieorgievka is surrounded by cultivated fields a few of which are already turning green, others still as black as night. The main crops here are potatoes and wheat. It is evident that the Russians work the soil and obtain good harvests. Gieorgievka is a wealthy village!

When I reach the Department of Health I find that the Director is away. I am seen by an elderly and distinguished Russian, one Ivan Siemionovitch, a past deportee. During the Tsarist times, Ivan Siemionovitch was a white-collar worker in Moscow. He was arrested by the Bolsheviks and after serving several years in prison, was exiled to Gieorgievka. His son was allowed to remain in Moscow and is studying at the University, whilst his wife died during the time Ivan Siemionovitch was in prison. Ivan Siemionovitch is sad and cowed and appears to understand and to sympathize with the position in which I am placed. He would like to help me. Since there is a shortage of doctors here, he thinks I should be hopeful of being employed. However, I must wait until the Director returns. He tells me to come again in a fortnight's time and in the meantime he promises he will talk to the Director and do all he can to help me. His attitude gives me confidence and I trust he will do as he promises. I am to return in two weeks' time.

At the Post Office I mail one letter to my husband in prison camp, giving him my new address and another letter to his brother who is in Lvov. On the way to the Post Office I notice several large posters which depict a Polish noble trampling over the head of a Polish peasant. I am unable to read the Russian writing but the posters speak for themselves. One cannot help admiring the ingenuity of the Communist organization which has sent the posters to this outback preceding our arrival, in order to prejudice the local inhabitants against us! I am also highly amused because the noble on the posters happens to be the absolute likeness of Mr P.! The same posture, the same paunch, the same features, the same moustache and identical colouring. I see now why our Mr P. returned from the crusade of the elders to Gieorgievka, with a very abashed and sheepish expression: it cannot have been very pleasant to see one's own caricature under such circumstances. Fate had paid him back for refusing to take females with him!

Having posted my letters, I squat by the side of the Post Office to rest awhile and to eat a piece of dry bread which I had kept from the train journey for such an eventuality as this. At five o'clock in the afternoon I start back for Ak-Buzal. I walk fast to return before nightfall but darkness descends before I reach our kolkhoz and I have only the barking of the dogs in the distance to guide me. At last I reach the huts but cannot find our shed. I have no stick or any other implement to ward off the dogs so I must attempt to skirt round them, keeping my distance. Still no luck with finding our shed, I must ask somebody the way. As I enter into the yard of a hut, six or seven large dogs attack me and knock me to the ground. In answer to my cries for help, the Kazakhs come running out of the hut and call them off. They are very worried that I may have been injured by the animals, but I am unharmed — the dogs have not actually bitten me. Everything happened with such speed that I have had no time to be frightened. The Kazakhs breed dogs for their fur and use it in the making of caps and gloves. So as not to damage the hides they hang the dogs to die!

By-passing the huts and barking dogs I eventually reach our shed. I can see the light (of the one candle) and feel safe to be 'home'. Home, though with a rusty tin roof and grass for carpets, is where my mother is, where I can lie down and sleep. How lovely it is to be back home from Gieorgievka!

We are all convinced it is essential to quit this barrack of ours and somehow to make alternative provisions. We arrange with a Kazakh woman to rent a single room in her hut in exchange for some of our things. Three 'families' of us move into the rented room which is unfurnished. We spread out our suitcases and at night will sleep side by side on the floor. Apart from my mother and myself, the other two 'families' are Mr and Mrs B., with whom I became friendly during our train journey and the wife of a Public Notary with her 'odd' daughter, Miss Sophy. Our landlady is very sullen or perhaps only mournful? She tells us, by using sign-language, that her husband is away from home. It may be that he is languishing in prison.

Commotion and loud talking wake us during the night and we are conscious of loud male voices raised in obvious anger. Our Kazakh landlady can be heard answering quietly and calmly. There is a great deal of loud and fast conversation — being unable to understand a single word we are terrified. We all expect the worst — perhaps they want to murder us? By local standards, our suitcases contain treasures and our disappearance would interest nobody. We can but pray. We are completely helpless and must wait to see what will happen. The altercation lasts about an hour after which the men leave. We never find out what it was all about.

Bread cannot be obtained but we can get hold of brown flour from which we make noodles; how to cook them presents us with a problem since we have no fuel to get the stove going and we cannot expect the landlady to give us her 'kiziak'. Kiziak is dry cow-dung which they collect on the steppe. In readiness for the winter, the Kazakhs make a special concoction from fresh cow-dung which, when alight, gives off the same amount of heat as wood. During the summer, which is here at the moment, they cook over fires using dry cow-pats only. We shall have to go out into the steppe to fetch ourselves some fuel for cooking, so we set off, all three families, armed with sacks and pillowcases.

We find that in some places our 'harvest' is bountiful, elsewhere one has to search far to find a cow-pat. Some pats have obviously been on the ground for a long time and the grass has grown through them, these have to be kicked and kicked hard and adroitly to free them. With practice I become very adept and tear the green pats away with one hard kick. We make our way back to our hut, shouldering our 'elegant' burdens and compare each other's takings. Mr and Mrs B., my mother and I have had to walk about the steppe a great deal to collect the kiziak but Miss Sophy is triumphant because she has gathered plenty of kiziak without effort, near to home. She proudly empties her sack of human excreta and not cow-dung. We do not have the heart to disenchant her! She can be excused to some extent because she is very short-sighted. We give vent to our mirth behind her back!

Miss Sophy is fated to be unlucky. She goes into the steppe again to collect the kiziak (not to the ditch by the hut this time) and meets a cow. The cow is placidly grazing but on seeing a human figure approaching, starts to walk towards Miss Sophy who gets scared. The faster Miss Sophy walks away from the animal, the faster the cow follows, until Miss Sophy breaks into a run, with the cow behind her all the way. Out of breath and terrified, Miss Sophy arrives home blurting out that she had escaped from a bull! Miss Sophy's mother is very thrifty. She has only one pan for cooking and all and whatever food they can obtain is thrown into it. The pan never gets cleaned because we have to save every scrap. Both of them sit over their suitcases and are always scrabbling around amongst the contents, particularly during the night. They keep rearranging their belongings and talking in whispers. In our cramped quarters their behaviour is embarrassing and annoying. My mother and I find it impossible to make close friends with them as we have with Mr and Mrs B. In fact, I feel sorry for the two of them.

We continue to exist by exchanging our things for food. Apart from sheets and towels, good barter items are pyjamas and tea, especially the tea — if one has any. Tea is so valuable that it is measured out pinch by pinch. In exchange for our things we can get eggs, milk, potatoes and sometimes brown flour, but all in small amounts or even in instalments, for example, a glass of milk every day for several days. One day I manage to get a morsel of pork fat which proves to be a useful deterrent for my landlady's mother. This old lady has acquired the habit of helping herself to our potatoes whilst they are in the pan cooking. Knowing that she is a Muslim, I 'contaminate' the potatoes by throwing in a piece of the pork fat thus making them taboo for her. She soon drops her habit but I feel rather guilty for exploiting her religious beliefs and for cutting off her extra supplement of food. However, there is little enough for the two of us alone and I cannot allow her to share our meals. She also pesters us for tea and it is very difficult to refuse her when she can see that we are drinking it. I have come to realize, after our first few days here, that the Kazakhs drink tea in the Kazakh fashion — compulsively. They will give the last crumb of bread away for their 'chai'.

The stoves which the Kazakhs use for cooking are very cleverly constructed. The sides are made of clay and the cooking top is a sheet of tin. The stove performs therefore a dual purpose, cooking and the heating of the room. In winter the stoves keep the rooms very warm but in the summer it is too hot to use them indoors. The Kazakhs then resort to building, quickly and competently, outdoor stoves in front of their huts. For some inexplicable reason they are not content to leave them in the one place: one day the stove will appear in the porch of the hut, the next day it will be demolished only to be rebuilt outside, then knocked down after a few days to be put up once again on a different site still, a few metres away.

As coal and wood do not exist here, they use the kiziak for fuel, but to kindle the fires, dry calf-manure is burnt because it catches alight very speedily and gives off a pale blue flame not dissimilar to that of methylated spirits. If the Kazakhs want the stoves to heat up very quickly they will use what is called 'karahanik'. These are tinder dry, small shrubs which are blown by the wind over the steppe during autumn. As the shrubs tumble over the ground, some of the side branches get broken off and one has to chase the resulting small, white, lacy balls. The shrubs do not grow in this region, they must be blown here by the autumn winds, from afar. I watch a Kazakh woman kindling a fire with the karahanik. She squats on the ground and has to work quickly to feed the fire with more karahanik as it flares alight immediately and very noisily, burning with its blue flame and giving out much heat. In fifteen minutes the stove is too hot to touch.

It is most uncomfortable for the three families to live in the one room. At night one cannot walk past because we sleep side by side on the floor and during the daytime we have to sit on our packed suitcases because there is no space to unpack.

There is no guarantee if and when I shall get a job in Gieorgievka, so I have to prepare for eventually having to spend the winter, here in Ak-Buzal. We decide we must separate and my mother and I rent a room from an old majestic Kazakh. Our landlord is very dignified and will not touch the kiziak with bare hands, donning leather goves, probably made from dog skins, for the task, and gesticulating to us that kiziak is most unclean. I get the impression that he is sympathetic towards us and would like to help.

On our very first night in his house, he asks us to dinner and we find ourselves receiving VIP treatment. A very low, round table stands in the middle of the room: and on the table, all the very best which the Kazakhs can offer. Flat unleavened bread, which has been cooked on a griddle, hard boiled eggs, some cottage cheese in a bowl and sour cream. Earlier, I had seen a Kazakh woman skimming the cream off the sour milk, using the palm of her hand as a scoop and then scraping the cream off her hand on the side of the bowl! There is no seating and we take our places round the table, squatting on the floor. My mother is very uncomfortable so they bring her a cushion to sit on. As my mother suffers from rheumatism and cannot bend her knees anyway, the cushion does little to help.

There is an abundance of food and conversation — using sign-language and throwing in the odd 'Russianized' Polish word. All would be fine were it not for the cockroaches! As soon as it gets dark, our hostess places a small paraffin lamp on the table and whether they are attracted to the light or blinded by it, I decline to guess, but the cockroaches start to drop down from the ceiling on to the table. Yellow, revolting creatures, swarming about. Our hostess must think this a natural phenomenon and languidly knocks them off the table on to the floor with her hand. We most certainly do not belong here.

After the feast we return to our room, which is completely bare of any furniture except for two iron bedsteads with their palliasses. We extricate sheets and eiderdowns from our trunk and get into bed, happy to be sleeping in proper beds for the first time since our deportation. Our happiness does not last for long. As soon as we douse our little paraffin lamp we become aware of an odd rustling and humming. Relighting the lamp we can see that all the walls and the ceiling are absolutely crawling with cockroaches and bedbugs. There are bedbugs in the beds with us and from time to time a cockroach will drop on to us from the ceiling and start to scurry around frantically in the bedding. Sleep is now out of the question. I ask Mother to stitch me up inside a sheet to try to stop the vermin from crawling over me but I still cannot sleep because I am now too hot and stuffy. We get dressed and spend the night sitting up by the light of the lamp.

We shall have to find different lodgings, and fast, because we cannot spend another night in this place. But what do we say to the landlord? How can we risk offending him after the hospitality lavished on us? He is unlikely to understand our fear and revulsion of these vermin. There is no other way out and he accepts our notice to leave with due decorum, does not question our decision to leave, and returns our deposit of rent before we even ask for it. How very embarrassed and guilty I feel!

We now move into Ajsha's house. Her husband is away from home and the hut is relatively spacious, so she is more than willing to rent us a room. Inside the dwelling, narrow winding passages radiate in all directions from a large vestibule and lead to the living quarters. There are no windows in the corridors which are therefore very dark and the doors to the rooms are shut by complicated wooden locks, which baffle me until I am shown how to operate them. The corridor system is very ingenious because in winter the cold cannot reach the rooms and in the summer the heat cannot penetrate into them. And up to now we have seen no vermin in this house.

The two iron bedsteads which we are given have straw-filled sacks in lieu of mattresses. We move in. The trunk we deposit in the middle of the room, in its place of honour, and here it will perform its function of table, pantry, shelf, etc. I think I am seeing things when I look at the trunk the next morning: from every nook and cranny in the weave of the trunk, protrude two small waving antennae — it is the cockroaches again, which have moved into the trunk and have established residence in it!

I drag the trunk outside where I begin to beat it with a stick to remove the invaders. It is impossible to dislodge them all, especially the smaller ones which have hidden deeply within the wicker weave and even shaking and throwing the trunk down proves quite futile. I have to resort to drastic measures: I proceed to drag the trunk down to the irrigation channel where I submerge it in the deepest spot I can find and sit on it to keep it down. I spend the next hour sitting in the water until all the cockroaches are drowned. The trunk is as clean as a whistle! I laugh at myself because I must have looked extremely funny!

We still continue to exist by exchanging our goods for food, mostly 'selling' in instalments because the Kazakhs do not have enough for themselves and live on a day-to-day basis. This is in direct consequence of methods of the local husbandry: each family is allowed to own only one cow, which is put out to pasture with the communal kolkhoz cows. For the right to graze their cow on the steppe and for the services of the kolkhoz cowherd, each family must give away, to the kolkhoz, a certain amount of their milk — so their cup does not overflow.

Putting the cows out to pasture is an organized affair: they are milked in the morning and then led out into the steppe for the whole day, returning before sunset, when they are milked again before the night. It is a picturesque scene: in the morning the kolkhoz cowherd leads the communal cows on to the road where they are joined by the private family cows, each emerging from its own hut. The process is repeated in reverse, in the evenings, when they all return to the village after their day on the steppe. By instinct, each private animal separates from the herd and turns into its own byre.

Apart from the milk from their own cows, each Kazakh family will have a few potatoes and some flour. They are unable to keep many hens because there is little to feed them on and therefore eggs are scarce. I must add, that in this climate, the cows are dry during the six months of winter and the hens lay no eggs.

It is now June and blisteringly hot during the day. The nights are cool, short and light, light enough to be able to read out of doors at midnight. It is too hot to cook inside and the Kazakhs build stoves outside, in front of their huts. They instruct me how it should be done: to start with I must find myself a length of pipe, for the chimney, in the rubbish tip, also a piece of tin for the griddle and several unfired bricks, called 'samans'. Secondly, I must find some horse-manure and must mix it to a pulp, by hand, with some water. This will be used to cement the samans together. I am told that cow-dung will not do for this purpose because it would disintegrate with the heat generated and the stove would collapse. My experience of holidays in the mountains stands me in good stead and I erect a stove which draws well, faces in the correct direction into the wind, and does not smoke, so we can now cook our potatoes and noodles using relatively little kiziak. Eggs are eaten uncooked because we want to preserve the vitamins. I attempt to cook 'spinach' from pigweed — an edible weed — but it proves to be quite revolting. As we have little tea, we use it very sparingly. We use a pinch at a time, then dry the leaves and brew them afresh repeatedly, until we finally boil the leaves. We feel the hunger but we survive — how shall we manage later? Being unemployed I would not be entitled to buy bread, even if I had the money and even if there were a shop here. Here we are without a shop, the Kazakhs are without bread, eating only flat cakes baked from the flour they have earned by working. They are physically unsuited for agricultural labour and so accumulate few 'trudodni' (they are paid by the number of trudodni worked — a trudodni is eight hours work for the kolkhoz). Thus they receive but little flour. They are undernourished. Besides, in Ak-Buzal there are no young men; only the old men, women and children are left. Most of the young men are away working somewhere to earn money and some are in prisons. How are the villagers to survive? I pray to God I get a post in Gieorgievka.

We discover that Ajsha's family have been rifling through our suitcases. They were only curious to see what we have and nothing has disappeared. So, I arrange to show them our belongings. I empty our suitcases, exhibit everything and explain the purpose of each item. They show how delighted they are by clicking their tongues and nodding their heads. During the course of this occasion, I strike up friendship with a young girl of about fourteen who is, I think, Ajsha's sister. We go together to the irrigation channels to get washed, both of us using my soap which she loves. Although she washes her hair each day in the cold water she is still infested with lice and hopes the soap will rid her of them. I try to explain that it will be ineffective and that it would be possible to eradicate the lice using home remedies such as vaseline and vinegar. I cannot tell if she understands, or if it is possible to get the necessary ingredients here. Besides, she would need a fine-toothed comb and I only have the one. Whenever the Kazakhs have a spare moment, they resort to delousing each other. To put one's head on a friend's lap and to feel their fingers probing and searching in the hair constitutes a pleasant and useful pastime. Just like the apes.

My young friend accompanies me into the steppe on forays for kiziak. As she walks she sings Kazakh songs which I should love to be able to write down. One melody, in particular sticks in my mind because it seems to have been taken straight out of *Aida* — or perhaps it was the other way round?

I can only reproduce the melody rather poorly because I never master the rendering of the final note, finding it impossible to imitate the Kazakh pitch of voice.

The same young friend shows me how to make their winter fuel, the kiziak. I may be forced to spend the winter in Ak-Buzal so I prefer to be prepared. My mother and I collect the cow-pats on the steppe and as much as we can from the road. However, twice a day when the cows walk down the road past the various huts, the Kazakh women dash out to collect whatever has been 'dropped' in front of their house. I have to be cautious therefore not to be accused of 'pilfering' somebody's cow-dung. We pile the dry steppe kiziak and the still steaming dung from the road, into a heap, with the addition of a few handfuls of dry grass. Each day we pour several buckets of water on to the heap. When the mound is large enough and has been left for several weeks it then has to be processed into kiziak. Amongst the wealthier Kazakhs, a horse is tied to a stake and by walking round and round in a circle over the mound, mixes it all to a uniform paste, water being added continually.

In the poorer households, and most of the Kazakhs in Ak-Buzal are poor, they have no horses and the mixing is done by people who tread the dung. Before starting on my heap, I pour several buckets of water over it, then I hitch up my skirt and step bare-footed into the cool, moist mass which reaches up to my knees. Much to my surprise it is quite pleasant! The sun is scorching from up above, my feet and legs are beautifully cool and I start treading enthusiastically and systematically so as not to miss any lumps and to mix everything into a homogenous 'dough'. The Kazakh girls supervise me and are pleased to see me learning how to make kiziak. It is just as well that I have these teachers because in my inexperience I cannot, for example, tell at what stage the manure is adequately mixed and what one must next do. They show me that the mixture has now to be spread with a shovel, into a huge flat 30 cm thick pancake and left to dry in the sun for several days until it partially dries. It is then ready to be cut up with a spade, into half-metre sized blocks and again left to dry further. When the blocks are dry enough not to disintegrate when lifted, they are turned over. Eventually when they appear completely dry, they are stacked upright on their sides. Now this is where the Kazakhs show off their artistic talents: they arrange the blocks, using a few each time, into little pyramids of different designs and shapes. Each Kazakh settlement stacks the kiziak in different traditional patterns never deviating from its own particular design. After a few weeks, the blocks are taken home and stacked tightly packed together against the wall of the hut, making sure the wall chosen, is one which will not be buried in snow-drifts.

I have acquired the skill of making winter fuel but only I know how many times I had to bend and stoop when collecting the kiziak on the steppe, how many buckets of water I had to draw and carry from the well and how exhausting it was to cut the blocks.

The blocks of kiziak are as heavy as wood and when burning, give off much heat. It would be difficult to estimate how many calories I used up during this hard work and how many I gained in the form of heat in the winter.

July is approaching and it becomes increasingly hot. The almost tangible heat pours down from the cloudless sky — no trees and no shade. Kazakh fashion, I make myself a veil from a towel, being anxious not get sunstroke when out on the steppe. The veil will at least protect my head and neck each day, when I have to go into the steppe to collect our fuel for cooking. I understand now why they wear veils here.

During the whole of summer 1940 there is only one storm and the rain falls but for a very short while. It is magnificent to see the storm on the steppe — dark navy blue clouds on the horizon on one side and the sun shining from the opposite direction making the huts glow orange against the backdrop of the practically black clouds. Rumble after rumble of thunderbolts can be heard rolling across the steppe. Lightning forks down to earth in the middle of the horizon, illuminating the whole land with its weird ultraviolet light. I begin to weep, remembering the storms and lightning in the mountains in Poland. This storm is even more majestic and awe-inspiring. An old Kazakh woman comes up to me and is curious to know why I weep. I too gesticulate, and using the sign language answer that I am remembering home. She understands. Meanwhile the storm rages over the steppe. I have the impression that I am standing in the bottom of a huge cauldron, an unearthly cauldron, which is reverberating all around me. Nature asserts its might and beauty, making me feel as small and insignificant as a speck of dust. I shall never forget this feeling of being transported into a world of different dimensions.

Chores associated with the essentials of survival keep me fully occupied. To get something to eat, to cook it and to stay relatively clean are tasks which take all day — I can only rest at night. It is during the cool and light nights that the whole settlement comes to life. Fires are lit in the stoves in front of the houses by the old women so by the time the young women return from work in the kolkhoz, the evening meal can be cooked. There is laughter and noise round each stove and as the huts are near together, there soon develops the atmosphere of a social gathering, lasting well into the night. The sky is star-spangled and the night is light and nobody feels like turning in, especially as inside the huts it is dark and stuffy. We Poles are also cooking, socializing, discussing and taking the opportunity to read letters and sometimes even newspapers.

We have a Mrs T. here, who has been deported with her two sons, boys of about eight and ten years. As yet she is coping extremely well because she has managed to bring copious amounts of tea with her. She exchanges this chai for flour, eggs and milk and is able to live fairly comfortably because the

Kazakhs cannot resist tea. The Kazakh woman, with whom Mrs T. is lodged, wheedles pinch after pinch of tea from her, in a neighbourly fashion, without repaying her in kind. Mrs T. writes to Poland and receives a large parcel of tea which 'feeds' her for a long time. When the tea is all gone, Mrs T. and her sons begin to go hungry. Later when I meet her in Gieorgievka, in the winter of 1940/41, she tells me a moving story. When she had run out of tea, she and even the children had nothing to eat. Her old landlady in Ak-Buzal, who had drunk nearly all her tea, then surprised her by giving her a present of two sacks of flour.

I make friends with Mrs W., who used to work as a cook in a restaurant in Poland. Mrs W. can always 'buy' something from the Kazakhs, whereas I am less successful. When I ask her how she does it, her answer provides a lesson in human psychology, because although she is uneducated she is very intelligent. She says the Kazakhs are too proud a race to stoop to business transactions being a free, nomadic race and have to be given the illusion that one has come to pay them a social call and not to buy eggs or milk. A visit should be conducted in the following manner: after an exchange of greetings one should squat down beside the Kazakh, who will usually be found sitting on his doorstep — and one should remain seated in silence until such a time when the Kazakh himself will begin to 'converse'. Sometimes the silence will last a long time; one must be very patient and when the Kazakh says something, usually in broken Russian, it is essential to maintain the conversation by throwing in the odd word here and there. Only, after at least a half-hour of the visit, can one ask if he has any eggs, without mentioning the word 'for sale'. Now we all know that one must say "czemurtka bar ma?" (have you any eggs?) when we want to get hold of eggs. Applying the above tactics, making casual remarks about the weather, cows, etc., I fare better with my purchases from the Kazakhs. I should have known what's what in the local etiquette — Mrs W. has shown me up.

Once, a Kazakh who is sitting on his doorstep, beckons me to follow him. He leads me out into the steppe beyond Ak-Buzal where he attempts to explain something to me. I am puzzled but eventually I realize he is saying, "Here is the end of man." It is then I notice that the whole field is scattered with small kurhaniks, (burial mounds) which have no symbols or writing on them. The Kazakh has brought me to their cemetery. I am honoured and value the trust and friendship thus extended to me in being shown the resting-place of his ancestors. "Here is the end of man" — a dignified expression.

I get news from my brother-in-law that they have a letter for me in Lvov, from my husband in Russian prison camp. I am to learn later that my husband was then in Starobielsk. My brother-in-law had just received a letter from me from Kazakhstan and had immediately written to my husband in prison camp, giving him my address in Kazakhstan. My letter which I had posted in Gieorgievka, about ten days after my arrival in

Kazakhstan, had not yet reached my husband.

Letters from the prison take about a month to arrive. So the letter which my husband had written in March, 1940, reached Lvov in April 1940 after I had been deported. My husband is later to tell me that the prisoners of war were not permitted to write letters during April and May, 1940. In April, 1940 my husband was in Starobielsk and in May he was moved to prison camp in Pavlischev Bor near Smolensk. From there he wrote to me in Kazakhstan in June, 1940 as he had in the meantime received my letter with my new address, and also a letter from his brother in Lvov. His brother had also informed him of my whereabouts. The first letter which I received from my husband addressed to me directly in Kazakhstan, was written in June, 1940 from the prison camp in Pavlischev Bor. Naturally my husband was only allowed to give a war post box number, so at the time I did not know where he was.

I receive this letter a month later, when I am already in Gieorgievka, in July, 1940. The prisoners of war were forbidden to write their monthly letters during the time when the prison camps in Starobielsk, Kozielsk and Ostaszkov were being liquidated — literally. The 'liquidation' took place between the second half of March to the second half of May, 1940. They were liquidated in stages — officially the transports of men were destined for Poland and 'domoj' (Russian for home) for reunion with their families. Impatiently, my husband awaited his turn for the return to Lvov and he was in one of the last transports to leave Starobielsk — and survived. On the wooden walls of the wagons of the train, carrying my husband from Starobielsk to Pavlischev Bor, previous officer prisoners of war in Russia had scratched names of places through which the train had passed. My husband's train now passed through the same places. One of the messages written on the wall of the train was 'We are in Gniezdowo and lorries are waiting for us.' All traces of the officers who had left that message had been lost. The train carrying my husband also arrived in Gniezdowo and the officers were off-loaded from the train into the lorries. The local people must have seen the previous transports of 'Polish War Criminals' because the Russian children, apparently suitably primed, taunted the officers with abuses and threw stones at them as they were marched from the train to the lorries. The lorries carried my husband's transport of officers to the prison camp at Pavlischev Bor and not to Katyn, as was the fate of previous transports of officers. This handful of officers was thus saved. Nobody knows why they did not meet the fate of the others. Maybe somebody 'at the top' became nervous and suddenly had the orders changed? In April, 1943, the Germans were to announce that they had discovered a communal grave in Katyn, containing the bodies of over four thousand Polish officers who had been shot through the back of the head. The camp at Pavlischev Bor was a reasonably comfortable and well-equipped place of detention for the prisoners — they even had bed sheets! It is only a few kilometres away from

Katyn. My husband is later transferred to a prison camp in Griazoviec but nevertheless, from June, 1940 to the time of his release, he writes to me regularly each month.

I was to be the only officer's wife in Gieorgievka who did not lose contact with her husband in Russian detention. The other wives in a similar situation, were to become suspicious because I was in regular receipt of letters. We had all received letters before our deportation to Kazakhstan. It will even be whispered that my husband has 'gone over to the other side' and that is why he is allowed to write. My husband is to survive imprisonment, theirs are not. But at present, in Kazakhstan, we are not yet to know this and nobody has even heard of Katyn. The poor women write regularly from Kazakhstan to their husbands in the prison camps but suspecting that their letters are not being allowed to reach their husbands also write to relations in Poland, begging them to forward their own addresses in Kazakhstan. All the efforts to make contact with their officer prisoner husbands fail. No more is heard from the imprisoned officers after April, 1940, that being also the time when we, their families, were deported to Asia. So far as I am concerned the Katyn affair is clear — I have no doubts whatsoever that the Russians killed the Polish officers.

As there are no young men left in Ak-Buzal, the people remaining, that is the women, children and old men, cannot cope. The women are of slight build, slim, have tiny feet and hands with slender fingers. These nomads, who have been forced to settle by the Russians, are unsuited to work on the land, either physically or mentally. They are ignorant of cultivation methods and lack the physical strength required for agricultural work. All these factors result in poverty and misery amongst them. They are only able to exist and survive thanks to the one cow each family is allowed to own. If the family is a large one, it has practically nothing on which to subsist. Additionally, TB is rife amongst them.

The Russian settlements, however, present a complete contrast — their inhabitants have arable fields, live in larger superior huts and are well nourished. There are several Russian kolkhozes in the Ak-Buzal environs. Mrs W. and I, set off across the steppe, to see one of these settlements, called Vozniesienka. My heart bleeds for the way the Kazakhs are forced to live when I see the Russian kolkhoz, with its fields of cabbages, cucumbers and marrows. Its people are well fed, healthy and strong; its huts have small gardens where they even cultivate flowers, and poplar trees line the roadside. In the distance I can see fields of wheat, shining golden in the sunlight. To think the Kazakhs have to comb the steppe for the sparse wild onions! I come to pity the Kazakhs all the more — they are being slowly and methodically destroyed.

There is great excitement in Ak-Buzal: we are to have a wedding — a genuine, legal church wedding! The young pair met and fell in love on the train during our journey and are desperate to get married. As we have no priest amongst us and there is certainly no church, the families concerned are faced with a problem. What is to be done with them? A schoolteacher, Mr B., who was in our wagon, comes to the rescue. Even during our journey Mr B., was concerned with our spiritual morale and would organize hymn singing and communal prayers in the wagon. He now takes charge of the wedding problem. He must have known a thing or two because he writes to the Bishop of Lvov in Poland, explaining the situation which has arisen and receives permission to act as priest in this exceptional instance. A document with the Bishop's signature and official stamp authorizes him to perform the ceremony. I did not know that the Church was prepared for such contingencies!

The 'church' wedding therefore takes place in a hut, a group of Poles acting as witnesses. The young pair repeat the words of the sacrament, a marriage certificate is written out by Mr B. and the document of authorization enclosed. They are legally married! The newly-weds rent a splendid room for their first home — it has four walls and the sky for a ceiling. Many of the Kazakh huts have these roofless extensions because in the summer they like to sleep in the open but also like to have some assurance of privacy. The young pair spend their wedding night (and will spend many more) under a star-spangled sky, shut away from the world by the walls and a locked door. In the future unfortunately, I am to lose contact with them.

In early June, as previously arranged with Ivan Siemionovitch, I return to the Department of Health in Gieorgievka. Now, being familiar with the route, I can walk confidently. When I arrive, Ivan Siemionovitch tells me he has mentioned me to the Director of Health and I may permit myself to be optimistic in obtaining a job. He regrets however, that the Director is away today but will be available tomorrow to see me — I shall have to stay the night.

I know there are some Poles in Gieorgievka, still encamped in a shed somewhere in the village: they were fortunate enough to be allocated to Gieorgievka in the first instance. I manage to find them and they welcome me, giving me shelter and food for the night. The next day at long last, I meet the Director. He is a young, pleasant, and energetic man, favourably disposed towards doctors and, of course, is a member of the Communist Party. Although he is a lay-man, he is very enthusiastic to promote medical services in the area, having plenty of initiative. He makes a good impression on me and I feel an affinity towards him. Later, I will not change my opinion of him, even though he gets thrown into gaol for some corrupt practices. Here, being slapped into gaol, is a common occurrence and people are not ashamed to be imprisoned: their attitude towards a sentence can be likeneed to the admonishment of a child who is slapped for a misdemeanour: after serving one's time, one is then fully accepted back into society again.

The Director says that as they are short of doctors, he will employ me but it will have to go through the official channels and I am to contact him again in a month's time. In spite of the delay I feel he is being straight with me and I am on the right path towards getting a job. After concluding what is to me the most important matter, we spend the rest of the time in social conversation. Or rather, he talks and I mumble, attempting to make the mumbling sound Russian. The Director smokes and offers me some 'karitchki', which is the finely chopped root of the tobacco plant. Upon seeing that I do not know what to do with it, he rolls up a small piece of newspaper, pours the tobacco granules into it, bends over the end of the 'cigarette' and hands it to me. I had finished all my cigarettes and have not had a smoke for two days, so I accept it with great joy. We light up simultaneously, I inhale the smoke and — my breath stops. Impossible either to inhale or exhale the smoke. Tears fill my eyes and I am convinced I will choke. The smoke from the newspaper and the tobacco 'grits' is no joke! The Director roars with laughter! This is my initiation into the secret of smoking the 'Russian way'. I am later to learn how to smoke without a hitch and even to hold the small tube between the ends of a piece of split grass, so that the cigarette can be smoked to the very end without wasting one granule of the root-tobacco. Not only tobacco but also the karitchki is difficult to get — and it is no less difficult to obtain the newspaper, which is only sold to smokers (kuriaschim). The newspapers are old and out of date by at least a week or more but I find them invaluable because using them I can teach myself to read the Cyrillic alphabet.

Knowing that basically, we are not supposed to leave the locality to which we have been deported, I ask the Director what will happen about getting permission to move to Gieorgievka from Ak-Buzal. The Director laughs and tells me to ask the permission of nobody, just to come to Gieorgievka as soon as I get the job. He also advises me to find some accommodation now, so that I should have a place to move into. And regarding transport from Ak-Buzal to Gieorgievka, it would be best to hitch a ride from a lorry passing through the village. What a very kind, helpful and pleasant man — in one phrase 'a grand lad'!

The Poles with whom I have spent the night, say there is a vacant hut somewhere here and give me the owner's address. I find him and he readily agrees to rent the hut, giving me the key to the padlock on the door. Satisfied that my business is progressing well, I turn towards Ak-Buzal but it is already late in the afternoon, after five o'clock, and I am uneasy that I shall not reach 'home' before dark. To make matters worse, I barely reach the steppe outside Gieorgievka when I spot a Kazakh walking behind me. I feel uncomfortable but there is little I can do about it. It will seem odd to walk all the way to Ak-Buzal, keeping either in front or behind him, far better strike up a companionable conversation because in any event, I shall be forced to be in his company during the three to four hours. I am certainly not going to meet another living soul on the steppe, so if he has any bad intentions towards me perhaps by talking with him I can steer his thoughts towards other matters. The Kazakh proves to be completely harmless and whilst talking in broken Russian, he discloses he is a lorry driver from Ak-Buzal. He has had to leave his broken down vehicle in Gieorgievka and is walking back home. Each steppe kolkhoz owns a lorry but they have no idea how to maintain or service it and the lorries are forever breaking down — mechanization does not seem to work here. My companion is a solemn and pleasant man, so I cease to fear that he will rape or kill me or both. I arrive home safely and in amiable company. I am ignorant that at this time in the USSR, rape is punishable by death. I am never to hear of any rape during the whole of my time in deportation.

The next morning brings me 'tragedy' — whilst I was staying the night with the Poles in Gieorgievka, the lice must have infested me! I weep for the second time — the first time being during the storm on the steppe which evoked a longing for my homeland — and for what will be the last time during my stay in Kazakhstan. I weep now with humiliation and revulsion. I have reached the very bottom of degradation and shall never be able to rise up again. My mother now comforts and cheers me, trying to inspire me with some hope for the future. She always knows when to say the right words at the right time to lift my spirits — and I had wept that I was being deported because of her, that she was a millstone round my neck . . . .

Once again, I find myself waiting, waiting for the job in Gieorgievka but in the meantime life goes on in a manner which for us has now become a normal routine: food and kiziak — these two problems occupy all our time. The only interruption in the routine is if one amongst us falls ill, when I try to help, if I am so able, thereby getting some variety and satisfaction.

My friendship with Mrs W. begins when she goes down with an attack of gallstones. She asks me to call on her, without expecting a cure in these circumstances but hoping I shall at least, be able to give her some relief from the intense pain. But I am able to help her far beyond her expectations! When I had been packing our documents in Lvov, I had also put together a small first-aid kit, which included a syringe and injections for any possible sudden mishaps. I had grabbed my small dispensary when we were deported. So now I have with me the appropriate drugs and am able to restore Mrs W. back to health in a short time. The attack does not repeat itself because Mrs W. is on a 'Kazakhstan diet' and such a diet is hardly likely to predispose to this complaint! Mrs W. presses me to accept payment for the visit and the injections. It has never crossed my mind to take advantage of my profession under our present circumstances for personal gain, and in spite of her insistence, I refuse any payment. By so doing I gain a friend upon whom I can rely and who will do me many a good turn. Mrs W. is to 'escape' from Ak-Buzal to Gieorgievka not long after me, and we will spend many pleasant, spiritually and bodily (because she will always treat me to some bread) uplifting hours together. I will see her for the last time in Teheran in 1943 where she will be ill, though not seriously, with smallpox.

The other medical case in Ak-Buzal is a Kazakh woman, whom unfortunately, I cannot help. Her husband has been in prison for several years, the woman is young and attractive — and pregnant. She is terrified that her husband will kill her when he returns and finds her with a child. The poor creature turns to me for the help which I cannot give her. A few months later when I am in Gieorgievka I will learn that she has given birth to twins.

Slowly, my mother and I start to plan our 'escape' to Gieorgievka. We keep a look-out for the lorries which infrequently pass through Ak-Buzal and enquire amongst the Kazakhs when and how often could we catch a lorry which would take us to Gieorgievka. It becomes apparent that on certain days it is always possible to get transport, so we should have no problems in getting to our future destination. I also arrange for some of our friends to be at the ready to help us load our baggage on the 'great day'.

Now, July, 1940 is upon us and I must go to Gieorgievka for the third time. The Director's face is swathed with smiles and well pleased with himself, he announces that I have got a job! My duties will be to take charge of an Out-Patients Maternity Clinic and of children of up to five years of age. The post is to be taken over immediately.

Directly the next day, my mother and I pack our things, friends are asked to come and wait, whilst I step out into the road to hail a lorry. Two pass, but they are travelling in the opposite direction. The third one which I stop, is going to Gieorgievka and the genial and friendly Russian driver will give us a lift, with pleasure. He drives up to Ajsha's house where the friends are waiting to help us load our luggage on to the lorry. It does not take five minutes to find myself, with my mother and our belongings in the lorry, which moves off instantly. Hearing the commotion round Ajsha's hut, the Priedsiedatiel comes running over, shouting and even running after the lorry. But the driver was not born yesterday and I have been briefed by the Director, to go without asking permission, so I have no intention of allowing myself to be intimidated, we take no notice and do not stop. The lorry accelerates and within minutes, Ak-Buzal disappears from view. Nobody will ever investigate why I had left my place of exile without asking for permission.

I have spent three months amongst the Kazakhs and have come to like the race — I commiserate, and will continue to commiserate with them. Certain of their habits which shock me, are only the outcome of their way of life on the steppe. They blow their noses through their fingers but do it so expertly that they never soil their hands and the phlegm comes to land away in the distance. They never do this indoors and find our habit of using handkerchiefs most repulsive, not understanding how we can not only carry such filthy rags on us, but also handle them and even wash them.

Toilets are non-existent, one visits the trenches beyond the huts but the trenches are not malodorous: in the summer the sun beats down incessantly and in a very short while the excrements are dried rock-hard. Miss Sophy illustrated this point when she collected the 'rocks' for fuel. In the winter everything is frozen instantly and then covered with snow. By the time the snow melts in the spring, there will be left no trace of the dirt. Besides the trenches which serve as latrines, there are the water irrigation channels, which criss-cross the entire settlement. In the summer, the water flowing along the channels keeps them very clean. When nature calls, the Kazakhs go into the steppe, carrying a small kettle of water for washing their hands. Men do not stand but kneel, so that they are less obvious against the flat steppe. They are nearly all of them lice-infested, the hair being a prime target — but what is the companionable occupation of nit-picking for? They manage to keep the lice under reasonable control and are not excessively overrun with them.

The Kazahk houses are low, half built into the earth, the windows very small and barely above ground level, and the vestibules and twisting corridors which lead to the living-rooms, result in a design of hut which is as well adapted to the local climate as possible — cool in the hot summer and warm in the freezing winter. The huts are built of large blocks of dried, unfired clay, called samans and on the outside, the walls are smeared with a thick layer of cow-dung. Inside, the floors, that is the dirt floors, are also spread with cow-dung and present a smooth dust-free, glazed surface. The Kazakhs live as cleanly and hygienically as conditions will permit.

Forty years later, astronauts will land in this region and there will be sputnik launching pads here. What will have happened to the Kazakhs? Will they have been resettled? How will the new technology and culture have affected them? But the steppe will for ever remain the steppe, the region is too immense to be urbanized and populated. During my first weeks on the steppe, as much as I longed for the sight of trees, I am later to long for the sight and scent of the boundless, open spaces of the steppe. When standing on the steppe, one has the impression one is standing in the middle of a sea of dry grass, spanned by the dome of the blue sky. I have no feel for poetry but often, as I gather the kiziak, I recite aloud the Polish Poet Mickiewicz's *Steppes of Akerman* which faithfully mirrors the atmosphere and feel of the steppes. The steppe is freedom and space, simultaneously; it is identification with nature, where man feels he is a fragment of its might and at the same time, only a very small speck of dust. As well as collecting kiziak, I and the Kazakh children gather the wild onions and wild asparagus which grow here. Is it feasible to think that the steppe is the homeland of the asparagus? The steppe is a staff of life: it grazes the cattle, provides fuel and building materials. How I pity the Kazakhs, that they are poor and hungry, when if they had the means, they could be happy and well-fed. My friends and I have never had any harm done to us by the Kazakhs and have never been caused any distress by them.

KAZAKHSTAN — GIEORGIEVKA

The lorry drives us into Gieorgievka taking us to 'our' hut and the driver helps with the luggage. Our home has two roomy chambers: a kitchen and a living-room. There is a well in the yard. Nothing else comprises our home. We spread our palliasses on the floor, unpack a little, and go to sleep.

The next morning, I go to the Clinic which is situated in a fairly small, low building of six rooms, where I shall be working. The elegant villa near by is the dispensary and the home of the pharmacist and his wife.

The personnel of the Clinic have already been warned that I, a 'Polack-deportee', am coming. I almost panic at the thought of having to cope with the language or rather the two languages, Kazakh and Russian, both spoken and written. Also, maternity and paediatrics are not my favourite branches of medicine. Frankly, I am nervous of infants — what does one do with these tiny mites, who can only howl, cannot tell me what is ailing them and when the mothers' history of the case cannot always be relied upon? In any case, I may not be able to understand the mothers. I have little knowledge of midwifery, except for the experience gained during my studies. I take comfort from the fact that the Clinic has been functioning totally without a doctor for several years and yet the patients are somehow dealt with, so perhaps I shall be able to cope as adequately as the nurses have coped.

In 'my' office I find the senior nurse Zenaida Alexandrovna, who has been assuming the duties of the doctor here, sitting at the table. She relinquishes the chair to me. Through no fault of mine, it seems I have acquired an enemy even before I have started. I can tell she is humiliated by her 'degradation' and will almost certainly not attempt to make life any easier for me, on the contrary, will probably try to catch me out on any small mistake in an attempt to get rid of me. Regrettably, however, I am dependent upon her. I speak very little and can barely write Russian; Zenaida is Russian; she knows the patients and I do not. It will be even worse when I have to deal with the Kazakhs because she speaks their language fluently and I only know how to ask for eggs!

Zenaida Alexandrovna is past forty, slim, slight and cantankerous, bordering on the malicious. She is an exile too and lives with her 'husband' who is not in fact her husband — they talk about it here in scandalized whispers and very soon I am told of her 'transgressions'. Zenaida never mentions her lawful husband. Her daughter is still in Moscow.

From the beginning I have problems with my broken Russian when I talk to the mothers. Zenaida smirks ironically. Speech with the Kazakhs places me in an even worse position because they are fooled by my few words of Kazakh, which I have learnt in Ak-Buzal and answer in torrents of, to me, incomprehensible speech. I am forced to ask Zenaida to translate, making her gloat and humiliating myself even more. In my first hour at the Clinic, I have to let the cat out of the bag that I cannot really write in the Cyrillic alphabet when the mother of an ill boy asks for sick leave from work in order to look after her son. And I have not a clue either how to formulate or even write out such a chit. Yet again I am forced to seek Zenaida's help and have to ask her to write it out for me and then I can sign it. Zenaida smiles all the more maliciously. I make out a copy of the certificate of sick leave for myself and mean to memorize it so that I shall know what to do in the future. The amount of Russian I have tried to learn from Kazakhs, who in any case speak it very badly, is totally insufficient. I now learn the printed Cyrillic from newspapers, picking out words which bear a resemblance to Polish ones, puzzling over others and guessing the rest. I shall have to learn the longhand from Zenaida. The future will show that I am able to maintain the proper and correct relationship with Zenaida to the very end — but with what an effort in self-control and constant vigilance on my part!

I am also faced with problems in treatment of the patients because here they use those drugs internally, which we in Poland applied only externally, to the skin. I find myself prescribing drugs which, apart from the pharmacist, they have never heard of here. Initially, I confer with Zenaida to ascertain which drugs she would use for a given case and write the prescription out under her dictation. Later on, I become convinced that certain drugs which we would never have prescribed in Poland do indeed help, so willingly and voluntarily I now apply them. In the meantime, I reassure myself that as a doctor I must have more knowledge than the nurse and am therefore less likely to harm the children than Zenaida A. would.

Apart from Zenaida, there are two young nurses in my Out-Patient Clinic — both sixteen-year-olds! They are Ukrainian and having completed their 'training' have been detailed here to Kazakhstan for two years' practical experience. At the end of which they hope to be transferred back nearer to home. One of the girls has parents and relatives in the Ukraine, the other is an orphan who has been brought up in a 'dietdom' (orphanage). Their attitude towards me is ambivalent; as a doctor they respect me but as a deportee and 'an enemy of the people' they hold me in contempt. However they carry out my orders, ask about various things and are keen to learn as much as possible. I am forever having to explain: why, what and how. I have to be very careful in all I do and say because it is quite evident that they keep me under constant observation and would not miss an opportunity to report me were I to give them reason. And I have just overheard one Russian woman saying to another, in the waiting-room, that there was a new doctor here, a Pole, who would probably kill off all their children!

Several weeks after my appointment, the wife of the head doctor is employed as the so called 'pomwratch' (a doctor's assistant). A pomwratch is more highly trained than a nurse but less so than a 'felcher'. In Russia, a felcher is a person who is almost as highly trained as a doctor and is therefore virtually a 'junior doctor'. Thank God the pomwratch is pleasant, without prejudices, level-headed, young and attractive and I shall have no need to fear her. In the future I am to be convinced that she is a fine person, confirming my original opinion of her.

Her husband, the head doctor Kuzienkov, is also young, handsome and intelligent but has been sent here for penance — he drinks. We hold long discussions on medical matters and although frequently I cannot convince him — or he me — we nevertheless get on very well. He will not believe me that in Poland, Dr Weigel discovered vaccine against typhus; he refuses to believe it even when I show him the ampules of vaccine from Lvov. Dr Kuzienkov believes that Russia stands foremost in all fields — nobody can ever discover anything which the Russians have not already discovered. He also firmly believes in the Party, claiming that the Party can never be wrong. Naturally both he and his wife are Party members, so in discussions with him, I never raise my doubts concerning Party doctrine. I merely keep quiet and nod my head. Any discussion about the infallability of the Communist Party would not only be dangerous for me but would also be completely pointless: they have faith in the Party and against faith there is no argument.

As soon as war had broken out, I had gone to Dr Weigel's Institute in Lvov and had obtained some typhus vaccine for my husband, my mother and myself. I had had time to vaccinate my mother and myself before we were deported but my husband who was taken prisoner of war in September, did not manage to complete the course of injections. I had written to Lvov asking to be sent the rest of the injections and when they had arrived had sent them on to my husband. My mother and I must be completely immune to typhus because in spite of being louse-infested and being in contact with people suffering from typhus, we do not contract the disease. Because there was a time lapse in his course of injections, my husband caught typhus but not severely.

We are six women in the 'Out-Patient Clinic for Mother and Child' as my place of work is officially titled. I — the doctor, the wife of the head doctor — the pomwratch, Zenaida A. — the chief nurse, the two sixteen-year-olds — junior nurses and the orderly. The orderly is a middle-aged, pleasant, intelligent and good-looking Russian woman: she has been exiled to Kazakhstan whilst her husband has been arrested because — they had both been working on the construction of a rail track near the Chinese border. This employment resulted in them becoming very well off financially and also becoming 'polluted' by the 'decadence'. She cannot find adequate praise for the Chinese or for their goodness and wealth. When the work on the rail track was completed, the labourers who had been 'polluted' by contact with the Chinese culture and wealth were eliminated. In this instance the elimination was lenient because they were merely arrested or exiled. They could not be allowed to return to their native regions in case they 'contaminated' the locals with their newly acquired decadence.

At the Clinic everybody observes me. I come from another world and many things about me amaze them. They cannot understand how I had been able to buy my gold watch and wedding ring legally because in Russia, gold can only be bought in state owned shops and then only in the larger cities. They look at my gold items with gleaming eyes and I feel my possessing them labels me as bourgeoisie. I decide to remove my wedding ring and watch from public view and now wear them pinned to the inside of my blouse. I shall make sure nobody ever sees my gold again.

The head doctor and his wife live in a rent-free house which comes with the job, together with free fuel and a cow. The cow grazes with kolkhoz cows but they have to milk it themselves morning and night. The two sixteen-year-old nurses live with them and have been entrusted into their care. In return, they have to obey and listen to them as they would their own parents. It may seem cruel to post young girls far away from home to Siberia into the depths of Asia but it must be admitted that they are assured of good care and supervision.

In the same building where I work, Dr Kuzienkov has his surgery hours in the Out-Patients Department for Adults and felcher Anna Sacharova sees patients throughout the whole day. Anna Sacharova had been exiled to Kazakhstan for ten years but although the sentence has ended, she has decided to remain in Gieorgievka since she is too old to start a new life elsewhere. She is now 'free' and people's attitudes towards her have changed, making her life all that much easier so she is reluctant to move to a new and strange place to start afresh. She is free to settle where she will with the exception of Moscow which is her place of origin and where she has relations and friends. She has grown roots here, is well liked and esteemed as a felcher and so now had no alternative but to remain in Gieorgievka to the end of her days. Her husband had been arrested and there had been no further traces of him. Sacharova does not know where her husband can be or if he is still alive. She is over fifty, short and plump, with a broad, very pleasant face. We often talk of many things. She is very kindly disposed towards me and frequently helps me with problems at work. Anna Sacharova is a great Russian nationalist. During one occasion she tells me, with an apologetic smile hovering round her mouth, that she wishes Warsaw could once again be 'ours'. She had been to Warsaw during Tsarist times and had come to love the beautiful gay city. She turns her statement into a joke since she is talking to a Pole, and we both laugh.

I make new friends amongst the Poles in Gieorgievka. I meet Mrs S., her daughter Irena and son Eddy, with whom later, I am to become great friends. Mrs S. is German, married to a Pole and had lived in Poland for nearly a score of years. But she still speaks Polish with a German accent and makes grammatical mistakes, which if anything, gives her speech a certain charm. She is extremely pleasant, straightforward, artistic and smart — which is not easy to achieve in Gieorgievka. Her attitude to life and people is similar to mine so we discuss many things with enthusiasm. Her daughter Irena has a beautiful voice and had dreamt of a singing career when the war broke out, interrupting her singing lessons. Her son, a handsome and energetic boy is charming or rather possesses his mother's grace in a masculine form. Mrs S.'s husband had been arrested and they have no news whatsoever of him — his disappearance is total and complete from the moment of his arrest. The whole family are my friends, we help each other out and mutually try to keep up our morale to survive Siberia. Mrs S. gives me the one and only photograph she has of her husband — her most prized possession. I will keep the photograph for many years but I lose contact with the family in 1943 when I see them for the last time in Teheran.

My other new friends are Mrs O., the wife of a judge, her two daughters and her almost adult son. The family's story is identical: her husband arrested, the rest of them deported. Mrs O. is sensitive, cultured and diffident whilst her daughters make up the balance in being full of life and zest. The son is very close to his mother and tries to help her as much as possible. The daughters, Jasia and Olenka have a flair for business: very soon after arriving in Kazakhstan they had sent multiple letters to relations and friends in Poland, pleading to be sent parcels 'because we are starving to death' — laughing at themselves for using the expression. Parcels from Poland started arriving and are still arriving. Thank God they never did starve to death because amongst other provisions they were sent tea and coloured silks for embroidering blouses — and one could make a living from the last two items.

Mrs O.'s son has an adventure and his sisters and I have occasion to have a good laugh. He had become friends with the local Russian schoolteacher and had gone with him to some surrounding villages to see if they could buy any flour. They had to spend the night with a Kazakh who had only the one bed, so as is customary and usual in such circumstances, they had slept together. During the night, the schoolteacher had begun to behave rather 'strangely'. The naïve boy had not a clue what the man desired. Quite openly, he related the incident to his mother seeking an explanation of the Russian's behaviour. His mother's embarrassment is such that she cannot bring herself to enlighten the boy. She compromises by forbidding him to see the teacher again. As a contrast his sisters and I have a good laugh at the expense of an innocent boy. Far in the future I shall meet the sisters again in Britain.

I am also great friends with Mrs T. and her seventy-year-old mother. Mrs T. is well-read, educated and energetic. When talking with her, one can forget if only for a few hours, our present situation which at times seems so hopeless. Her company transports me into different realms — into the sphere of the intellectual which is far removed from the world of bread and kiziak. After a couple of hours of pseudo-philosophy we usually both feel better. Mrs T. had 'married beneath her' which her mother cannot forgive her to this day. 'Granny', as I come to call her, though she has no grandchildren, refuses to mention the matter. Again their story is the same: Mrs T.'s husband arrested and they, deported. One can talk seriously but also joke and laugh heartily with Mrs T., which is an advantage in our circumstances. The one thing about Mrs T. which stuns me is her honesty — uncompromising exaggerated honesty. I think I am an honest person but I would have far to go to equal her. Two years later in Teheran Mrs T. gives an example of her honesty. She is qualified in the craft of making artificial flowers and is employed in this capacity by the Department of Social Welfare of the Polish Government in exile, in Teheran. She offers to make me some flowers for a dress, assuring me she will use her own, private, tools. I am a little surprised for, would it really matter for example, were the Department's scissors to be used for cutting my material? She arrives, bringing all the necessary equipment, including a small spirit-lamp for melting the wax. The lamp is full of methylated spirits but I have to add some of my own because she cannot bring herself to use the Department's methylated spirits for private purposes.

We visit each other frequently and when we do meet we both smoke a good deal having bought as much tobacco as possible from the one and only shop in Gieorgievka. Since at present I have a job I can afford to buy the karitchki or tobacco providing there is any at the shop, but the shop has just run out of stock and my own supply is almost finished. I have enough tobacco to roll only a few cigarettes more when I decide to go and see Mrs T. I stay for a couple of hours and we smoke away nearly all my tobacco. I know that Mrs T. has been without a smoke for two days and is gasping. When there is left enough tobacco for only two more cigarettes, Mrs T. urges me to keep it for myself. However, there is no point in begrudging her a last cigarette because in any case I shall run out of tobacco and it makes little difference if this happens sooner rather than a few hours later. We smoke a lot because we are hungry and the nicotine helps to alleviate the pangs. In spite of having a job I go hungry — my salary is inadequate to buy food for two people, besides, there is no flour, cereals or fat to buy. On my way back home I begin to ask if I have erred in sacrificing myself thus, by which action I shall have to manage without a smoke. How shall I manage to work tomorrow? I am left with the nagging hunger and no nicotine. That evening a Kazakhstan 'miracle' happens. A few minutes after returning home, somebody knocks on the door and a Kazakh woman enters. She has run out of urgently needed cash and has come to sell me a packet of cigarettes — even twenty cigarettes! I am shaken by a wave of shivering — it might almost be thought that 'somebody' is watching over me and has instantaneously rewarded me for my self-sacrifice and lack of egoism. Never before had anybody wanted to sell me cigarettes and oddly enough, never again will they want to.

My friend Mrs W. and her daughter have escaped from Ak-Buzal and have arrived in Gieorgievka. I am so pleased because I am fond of her and it is most comforting to be surrounded by friends. They manage to set themselves up very well indeed, finding work in the Central Veterinary Clinic. They live there, occupying a large, bright and clean room which is provided with two beds and even a radio! Apart from the free room and fuel, they also get a wage and hence the right to buy bread. Their duties are to clean and keep the whole building warm. They have to be up very early to empty the ashes from five stoves which then have to be relit, so that by eight in the morning the building will be warm. The work is heavy especially having to carry the kiziak but they are both healthy and strong, so they can cope. Mrs W. has had no further attacks of the gall-bladder because her diet consists of mainly bread.

As well as having a warm room and a radio, they quite unexpectedly have access to unlimited amounts of soap: admittedly this soap is grey, semi-liquid and is kept in barrels in the store-room, for the use of the veterinary surgeon, nevertheless it is some soap at least and soap is not to be found in this area of Kazakhstan. I have never seen any, either in the shop or the pharmacy. As befits the civilized Russian nation, the pharmacy has great stocks of toothbrushes and perfume but no soap! Mrs W. gives me a bucket of soap! I boil this grey mess until it thickens and when it has cooled, am able to cut it up into cubes. The soap cubes lather well and now I have something to launder with. My supply of soap which I had brought from Lvov is running low and soon I should have had nothing with which to wash even myself.

A visit to Mrs W. always becomes a party, when we will have some tea or coffee substitute and a piece of bread. They both work and so are entitled to buy bread and can purchase over a kilo and a half daily, not to mention the fact that Mrs W. gets on well with people and can always be relied upon to procure some other food. They also give me various snippets of gossip from Ak-Buzal, amongst which is the information from Mrs W.'s daughter Mila, that lesbianism flourishes in the settlement. Can one condemn or blame the Kazakh women? There are no men left in the village and the women are young.

A market is held every ten days in Gieorgievka. The working week now has nine days and the tenth day is the day of rest, or rather the day one has to perform all those household chores for which there was no time during the week. As it is now summer there are some vegetables for sale in the market, mainly carrots, marrows and infrequently water-melons. On one occasion I taste a fruit which is a cross between a melon and a water-melon. It is delicious: with the texture of a water-melon and the taste and smell of a melon. I wonder if and when the world will be introduced to this new fruit? The Russian whom I met at the market and who had explained to me how this new breed had arisen, tells me that in Russia they are experimenting with new methods of growing potatoes. Each potato is cut into several pieces, making sure each piece contains an eye and the pieces are then planted on three levels in the soil. Apparently a three-fold yield is obtained in this manner from one potato in three times as little space. Eggs and milk sometimes appear in the market but always in very small amounts which are snapped up immediately. The sight which gives me most pleasure is all the people at the market: the Kazakhs who have been drawn from the surrounding hamlets are all parading in pyjamas! They had bartered these from the Poles in exchange for flour and think the pyjamas are lightweight summer suits! The Russian women, on the other hand, are dressed up in Polish nightdresses. We see the world and his wife parading before us in night attire! It is quite like a masquerade and we cannot restrain our laughter which comes easily and eagerly because being so down we have forgotten how to laugh and we make the most of the smallest opportunity to forget reality for a moment. We have no heart to tell the Kazakhs that they are wearing night-clothes — they would not understand in any case, that special clothes for sleeping exist and if they were made to comprehend they would feel ridiculed — best say nothing. The Russian women too would feel ridiculed and would become even more hostile towards us than they already are. The people at the market never do discover why the Poles are in such excellent spirits — we leave them unenlightened and proud of their costumes.

Zenaida A. from the Clinic also buys a nightdress from me to send to her daughter in Moscow to wear as an evening gown. I have no intention of misleading her: she asks me if I have anything to sell her for her daughter, I fetch the nightdress but before I have time to explain that it is a nightdress, Zenaida A. joyfully pounces on the 'evening dress'. So the nightdress goes to Moscow — to a ball. Should I have put her straight and ruined her pleasure? Indeed not.

The market is a social occasion, the Kazakhs, Russians and Poles are here, each and everyone dressed in their best finery. There are many people but few goods. But everybody is ambling around, nobody has stopped at home and even if one has no money one comes to the market for the company. There is a meat stall at the market but I have yet to see any meat there, only once having seen some bones, hanging up for sale. Only once and that was in Ak-Buzal, did I manage to buy a piece of scraggy meat from a Kazakh who had illegally and on the quiet killed a cow. That was the one and only time I was to have any meat during the whole of my deportation.

Also, only once did I manage to buy any milk on the market and that was in the winter, when the milk, from a newly calved cow, was handed to me in the form of a solid yellow lump. I took the solidly frozen milk home in my hand.

Now, during the summer, I meet many friends here. Even Ivan Siemionovitch has arrived and is walking about dressed elegantly in well polished high boots, wide black trousers tucked into the boot tops and a beautiful silk 'rubaschka' with an embroidered collar. The outfit is all that remains to him from his past life. Although Ivan Siemionovitch has come to the market he keeps to himself. He lives alone and spends all his free time looking after his small garden. He proudly shows me round his 'estate' where he cultivates marrows, cucumbers and tomatoes. Really, Ivan S. is a very good kind man. He is most disturbed when he learns that my mother and I sleep on the floor and insists it is extremely dangerous to do so for: in the summer one can be bitten by poisonous spiders and in the winter sleeping on the dirt floor is to court certain illness. He arranges to get me two old hospital iron bed-steads which are in the store-room. He sends me there and I am sold two beds at a relatively low price on his recommendation. My nurses at the Clinic are annoyed that the Polack is furnishing her hut and seems to have no intention of kicking the bucket. They laugh that although I have bought the beds I shall not manage to bring them home because nobody will 'demean' themselves to carry them for me. They are mistaken. I transport the beds by myself, one by one, carting them along the distance of almost two kilometres and resting every few paces. They stop laughing. The Polack is stronger than they imagined.

It transpires that thanks to Ivan S., I have indeed narrowly missed danger: there are some fairly large, round holes in the dirt floor of our hut and I had not realized that the poisonous black widow spiders, whose bite can lead to death, are nesting in some of them. Ivan S. had become quite worried when I mentioned these 'peculiar' holes in the floor. This is why nobody sleeps on the floor in Kazakhstan. After I leave Gieorgievka my conscience will prick me to a degree for never writing to Ivan S. to thank him. But I am afraid to expose him to possible accusation of being in contact with an anti-Communist Pole. I hope he will understand and will not think me ungrateful.

A Mrs B. is here with us in Gieorgievka, the mother of a school friend of mine. She has just received a letter and a photograph from her daughter in Warsaw, the photograph showing her daughter in a ball gown. Can it be possible that ball gowns still exist? Mrs B. is extremely energetic and since she feels drawn to agriculture, she applies for work in the kolkhoz in Gieorgievka and is very happily employed there. She enjoys working in the fields because it reminds her of home — she used to be the owner of wealthy estates. There comes a day when Mrs B. disappears — nobody knows what can have happened to her and people are afraid to talk about her disappearance. There are rumours that she has escaped. Suddenly, after about three weeks she reappears and as though nothing had happened returns to work at the kolkhoz. She is unwilling to say much, except to a few people and I discover that she had managed to escape back to Lvov by pretending to be Russian (she speaks Russian fluently) but once there she found herself caught as though in a trap. There was no question of being able to reach Warsaw because she was without any personal documents or money and was in danger of being arrested if she attempted to go further. The only thing she could do was to return to Kazakhstan! For several days she goes into work until one night the KGB come for her, take her away — and there is no more news of her. Fear weighs us down — each and everyone of us could 'disappear' — any night. We talk little about her case and then in whispers because there is always the possibility that we might be accused of having collaborated with Mrs B. in her attempted escape.

There is a deported Russian orthodox priest wandering round Gieorgievka. His given task is to clean out the public toilets in the village. Nobody is prepared to give him any other work, so he exists in this way because without work one perishes from hunger. The public toilets here are just latrines without any sanitary installations. The priest stinks. He is without friends, completely isolated, ragged but still wearing the full length robe. Filthy and smelly, he evokes in the Russians a terror and revulsion but in me, admiration for his very dignified posture and bearing. This old man with the long beard is and remains a priest, faithful to God! Nobody will speak to him, nobody will go near him for fear of incurring anger of the authorities. The priest is damned, even more than a leper because nobody will even give him a bowl of water to drink.

It becomes much cooler now in August and winter is fast approaching — the steppe is losing its colour and in the mornings the fields are white with frost. The first snow falls in early September. There has been virtually no autumn and within three weeks, summer has turned into winter. We are petrified to think how we are to survive the winter in our hut, which, having the two rooms is too large for us to be able to heat adequately, since the kiziak is very expensive. We shall not be able to manage. It is also unwise because we are living in the hut, completely alone. We must seek other quarters. I turn to Ivan S. for help, who cannot agree with me more that we must not spend the winter in our present accommodation and promises to look for something more suitable for us.

He finds us an 'apartment' with the kolkhoz cobbler who lives in a hut which is practically in the centre of Gieorgievka and where there is a room to rent. We like the room which is entered directly from the vestibule and has two small windows on the frontage wall. The stove is built across the room in such a way as to nearly divide it into two separate areas, a bedroom and a kitchen. The space between the two windows we shall be able to use as a common-room for sitting and eating. The accommodation is exactly the right size for us — we shall fit in but shall not require too much kiziak to heat the room. Better still, the landlord gives us a small table and two chairs which we stand under the windows. In the 'bedroom' we stand the two beds between the stove which reaches up to the ceiling, and the wall. On the other side of the stove will be our 'kitchen', with its hearth and griddle for cooking. There is space also to store the kiziak which must be allowed to dry after having been brought indoors, before it will burn. There is even room for a basin so that we shall be able to wash in warm water, by the warm stove. Beside the door we stand a bucket — our WC.

Our landlord is a Russian who was born here and, poor fellow, born a cripple, without the use of either leg. He can move about only by dragging himself along the floor. However, he seems quite content with life and is a cheerful man. As he can only work in a sitting position because of his disability, he is employed by the kolkhoz as a cobbler. He manages very well, patching, altering the 'valonki' (thick, felt winter boots) and earning a little more on the quiet. He is happy, liked and needed by everybody. His wife, a stalwart and buxom Russian woman has presented him with three children. The marriage appears to be a very happy one and I suspect that his personality plays a major role in it being so.

Our cobbler takes his responsibilities as master of the house seriously and helps us by giving some advice. Primarily I discover from him, that I must have a pair of valonki because without them I shall not be able to leave the house in the winter. I argue that I do have a pair of excellent white, felt boots from Zakopane, in Poland. When I show him the elegant, knee high boots, the cobbler laughs — and with good reason. Zakopane boots are just about as suitable for Siberia as a stockinged foot would be, in comparison to the valonki. My landlord has a pair of old, torn valonki which he mends and sells to me. He does not swindle me and they serve me well. The valonki can usually be bought only in the large cities or towns, for example Moscow, Kijov or Leningrad. There are none to be had in Kazakhstan not even in Semipalatinsk. The men working in the kolkhoz have to order them through the kolkhoz, contributing towards payment, a suitable amount of sheep's wool. Some of the Russian women have valonki from Moscow: brown, grey and white, light and smart — the very height of elegance. Here we wear only black ones which are clumsy and heavy but warm. The valonki are invaluable in this climate and being knee-high, protect the legs against the cold and wind. They can easily be brushed free of snow. They are rather rigid and stiff so one has to learn how to walk in them but they are easy on the feet and soft and quiet to wear. Before putting on the valonki, the feet are first wrapped round with strips of cloth called 'onuce' — soldier-fashion, as in old army days. Socks, even the thickest ones do not protect against the frost as efficiently as these strips of cloth. Anyway, there are no socks or stockings here and my feet never get cold, even in the most severe of frosts.

My mother sews me a pair of trousers from a trench coat lining which is camel-hair and which by chance we must have thrown into our trunk in Lvov. My mother's blue fox boa had also happened to be in the trunk. From it, my mother now makes me a cap, an excellent copy of the Kazakh design, with fur round the face and ear-flaps which can be fastened under the chin. I wear all the warmest clothes I have; a dress, two cardigans, trousers, coat, cap and valonki. Only — I have forgotten that I have no gloves! Rising to the emergency, my mother fashions a pair of gloves using rags and cotton wool taken from the Clinic. I must say, that bundled up like this, in all the things I possess, I do not feel cold. Only my eyes and nose are exposed to the frost.

When we had been taken from Lvov, we had been told they were taking us 'to join your husband'. Just in case this was true, though I did not believe them, I had thrown one of his suits into our trunk. Now, this suit 'buys' us fuel for the entire winter. The Russians are more than keen to buy men's suits but as the only 'in' colour is navy-blue and my husband's suit is dark grey, I am forced to accept a lower price for it, payment, naturally being in cash. I then find a Kazakh who needs the ready money and who sells me his own private store of home-made kiziak. I do hope he has left himself enough not to freeze during the winter. The Kazakhs, not the best kolkhoz workers, usually had only a small tally of worked days to their credit and therefore received a correspondingly smaller issue of fuel. Thus they need to supplement this kolkhoz fuel with kiziak made at home. The Russians on the other hand, never need to make any extra kiziak at home because as they work well in the kolkhoz, they receive the fuel due to them which is adequate for their needs — it is always very warm in the Russian huts.

The Kazakh delivers me the cart-load of kiziak and I pay him the agreed amount in rolled up rouble notes which he pockets without even checking and departs. I stack the kiziak blocks compactly and directly against the outside wall of our room, as best I can. The landlord makes an observation that I should have chosen a different wall — the wind tends to blow from this side in the winter and the kiziak will get buried in a snow-drift. Being so exhausted with carrying and stacking the heavy blocks, I do not feel up to moving it again and make light of his advice. Later, I bitterly regret my inertia! The snow does cover over my heap completely and to pull out a few blocks, I have to dig the snow away with a spade. As the kiziak is used up, I eventually have to dig further and further making tunnels in the snow through which I have to crawl on my stomach to reach my daily requirements of fuel.

I panic that evening when I count how much money I have left. I have given the Kazakh three times too much! I had forgotten that in this country, apart from one and five rouble notes they also have a three rouble note! Whoever heard of having notes in denominations of three? Anyway I had forgotten, and instead of the one rouble notes, I had given the Kazakh three rouble notes. I have lost a fortune! The man did not bother to count the money, did not even look to check what I gave him, just took the wad into his hand and put it into his pocket. How can I convince him that I made an error? I do not know if it is even worth going to claim it back from him. He would prove as stupid to return the money as I was to give it three-fold to him in the first place. But I cannot let my pride stand in my way — however much I am ashamed to admit my stupid mistake. Plus the fact that I cannot afford to lose such a large sum of money without putting up a fight to retrieve it. It is unfortunately already late at night and I shall have to wait until tomorrow. I sleep badly that night and as early as possible next morning I go to see the Kazakh. As I begin to explain what has happened, my heart starts to thump all the more quickly. Will he be honest or not? The Kazakh listens in silence and the silence seems interminable, until at last, pointing up to the sky with his finger he says: "Allah is still there," and returns my money! I should like to hug him but can only express my thanks. I depart, with joy radiating from my face. I think that had he seen my joy, he would not have regretted his honesty. How can one but help like the Kazakhs?

People advise me to weatherproof the windows of the hut against the winter cold. Acting upon the advice, my mother and I fill up all the cracks with cotton wool, with the help of a knife, and then paste strips of paper over the top. The cotton wool I take from the Clinic, the paste I make from flour and water. Utilizing the fact that the windows are double ones, I make a sort of pad from straw and also place that between the two panes at the base. I breathe a sigh of relief when we have completed all the preparations for the coming winter: I am certain that this winter at least, we shall not perish from the frosts. It has not been pleasant to hear the Russians predicting that we shall fail to survive the winter and shall freeze to death. Zenaida A. is particularly fond of 'pitying' us in such a manner.

There remains only the problem of food stores for the winter. We must lay in a few provisions for a possible dark hour, and which in our situation will have to be chiefly flour. We never know what may happen and it is better to be prepared for the worst contingency. My salary is barely sufficient to feed us both, so we sell and exchange the rest of those belongings which we can manage without, for flour. It is to be wondered at that we still have anything to barter but the Russians can make use of most items: handkerchiefs, belts, needles and thread. I hide my gold — the wedding ring and watch — for a time when we may indeed be starving to death.

The one and only shop in Gieorgievka, naturally state-owned, is open for one hour from midday when the Kazakh shopkeeper sells to the workers the bread due to them. I am entitled to buy 800 gr. of bread per day, as the working head of the family. My mother is entitled to 200 gr. a day, as my dependant. So we have a kilo of bread each day between the two of us which would be quite sufficient provided we had other things to eat: eggs, or milk.

We do not own a cow or chickens and during the winter nobody will sell us a drop of milk or a single egg. They have little enough for their own needs. All there is to buy apart from bread is: salt, substitute coffee, and sometimes a handful of sauerkraut — none of which has any nutritional value.

But the bread here is delicious! Made from wheat flour and baked through well, even though the loaves are enormous. By weight, my ration of bread works out as one eighth of one huge loaf. The bread is made in the kolkhoz and they certainly know how to bake well. The flour is dark but pure wheaten — sometimes white bread is baked, the so-called 'roll' which is very tasty but has the one fault in that one is hungry again two hours after having eaten it — it shoots through!

All of us at the Clinic prefer the dark bread, the white roll is too light and fluffy and although by weight one appears to get a larger piece, having eaten it, one is convinced that there must have been less than of the dark bread. The Communist Party members go to the shop in the evening and enter by the back door. Their rations of bread, assuming it is strictly their rations, are ready waiting to be picked up as are also various other goods which we never see in the shop.

I never see any sugar during all the time I live in Gieorgievka. I am to become so disaccustomed to sweet things that later in Teheran I cannot drink tea with sugar — it tastes insipid and dreadful. On one occasion the shop gets some tinned fruit and in the blink of an eye a queue instantly builds up because 'there is something in the shop'. I join the queue too, and am able to buy a tin of quince which I put away to have on my birthday. We get a bigger and even more improbable surprise when the shop gets some chocolates from Moscow, beautifully packed in boxes which bear a picture of a Kazakh. They have been sent here to celebrate the anniversary of the 'liberation' of Kazakhstan. Gieorgievka goes berserk — people dash hither and thither, shouting to each other to run to the shop because some chocolates have arrived. I follow people's example and also rush to the shop although I cannot believe my ears. I am able to buy a pound of chocolates! Unhappily, only about fifty boxes have come to Gieorgievka. I am one of the lucky ones and then thanks only to a friend who ran to fetch me before a large queue had formed. The chocolates are delicious (perhaps because I am hungry) and the box is beautiful. I decide to keep it as a souvenir but it is to get lost during my later displacement. How well Mother Russia looks after her 'liberated' countries — she sends them chocolates on their 'birthdays'!

I start to feel at home at the Clinic and try my hardest not to fall out with anybody. Those two chits of girls, the junior nurses, are ill-disposed towards me but are impressed by the fact that I am a doctor and to thwart their efforts to catch me out, I keep explaining what and why I do and prescribe. I have already learnt sufficient Russian to be able to communicate well and though I make grammatical mistakes and my accent is atrocious, I can manage. My patients — the children — if I sometimes do not help at least I do not harm. I have great sympathy for my small patients and often cannot help wearing my heart on my sleeve when I am prescribing them drugs. I do not use any drastic or new drugs but rather stick to old, well tried methods. How dreadful that I am having to learn Paediatrics on them!

The Kazakh infants are beautiful. Small, round, ivory-skinned and with huge black eyes in those flat faces. They have no eyebrows and their little noses barely protrude, like little buttons. They have a wee fold of skin in the inner corner of their eyes, the so called 'third' eyelid which gives them a mischievous look. They also have a peculiar racially characteristic feature: a small purple blemish on the small of the back which is present at birth and which disappears after a few months. They have the real authentic 'mongol stain' which can occur in our race in pathological mongols. They are well-proportioned and 'appetising' in contrast to the Russian babies who are overfed and pinkish-white with expressionless faces.

I notice that all the small Kazakh boys have shorn heads except where one or two tufts of hair have been left in various places according to their mother's fancy. I am very intrigued and start to question the mothers why they leave the odd tuft on their sons' heads. My enquiries only embarrass the mothers and I receive no replies. They smile and remain silent. A Russian woman explains the custom to me: the male children are left with the tufts because they can quickly be grabbed and held by them to stop the devil from stealing them away. The children howl so much when being examined that I am deafened. I am in despair — I cannot even hear what the mother is saying, so how am I expected to listen and to hear what is going on in the lungs of the child? It is impossible to give them the usual medical examination and I have to be guided only by what I can see and by using a thermometer. It takes me quite a long time to learn how to examine infants. By the time I am due to leave Gieorgievka, the infants do not howl any the less (and I have three of them at a time in my office) but I have become accustomed to working above the noise. I can ask the mothers for details and am able to hear the replies, I can listen to the infants' chests in the 'normal' way and can hear what I am supposed to hear. The secret of my progress lies in the fact that I have abandoned my stethoscope (of which the children are very scared) and listen to the lungs by lifting up the child and by placing my ear to its chest. I have to pick up the lung sounds in that moment when the child is filling its lungs with air for the next howl. I develop a factory-like system: one child is being weighed and recorded by the junior nurse, a mother with the second child on her lap is giving Zenaida A. the details of its illness, which usually takes ages, and the third child I am examining. The mothers, as always, very frequently give unnecessary and irrelevant details of the malady, omitting those which are most important and relevant. It is essential to have a system because frequently I have to examine up to thirty children between eight o'clock in the morning and one o'clock in the afternoon.

My first function on returning home from work is to search for lice which I often catch at the Clinic. Luckily I have a fine tooth comb with me so I can comb my hair out thoroughly. My method of examining the infants leaves me wide open to becoming louse infested. I also strip down to bare skin and search in all my clothes each day.

The working week in 1940 still consists of nine days, the tenth being the 'Sunday'. One would not think that such an extended week would make such a difference but however, nobody can really take it in their stride. On the seventh day everybody still copes, on the eighth day everybody is very tired and by the ninth day it is quite impossible to work. We are fit for nothing except to dream of getting away from work, escaping from the treadmill and getting some rest even if it is only mental and not physical. Nobody can concentrate or work conscienciously and efficiently. It seems that at the maximum, the human being is capable of working only six days consecutively.

On 'Sunday', the tenth day, not only do we have to catch up with the chores at home but also it is expected of us to 'eagerly, happily and voluntarily' participate in community work — which in our case means re-covering the hospital walls with clay because winter is approaching. Walls which are not treated each year become damp and will crumble. Everybody in the Clinic beginning with the Chief Doctor and ending with the orderly loses one 'Sunday' smearing the walls with the clay-dung mixture.

There is a return to the normal length of the working week in the winter of 1940/41 — seemingly the work efficiency diminished so much that it was not worth expecting people to work the nine days without a break. In Russia everybody works an eight hour day. In designating the number of hours of work for doctors, the demanding nature of the profession is taken into consideration and doctors work only seven hours per day. From the total, six hours are allocated for actual work, the seventh hour is supposed to be spent supplementing one's knowledge, reading medical journals, etc. We hold 'surgery' for five hours a day at the Clinic whilst domiciliary visits are supposed to be made during the sixth hour. These visits are rarely required because the population is so well disciplined that the doctor is called out only when absolutely necessary. In my Clinic for Mother and Child I practically never have to make a domiciliary visit because children up to the age of five are supposed to be brought to the Clinic. The over-discipline in these people worries me because they bring me seriously ill, feverish children who should not be exposed to the freezing air or moved from bed. I shall have to forbid this practice and shall have to assure them that I shall call on the child myself either the next day or in a few days' time. People are afraid that they may be accused of exploiting a state employee, such as I am, if they ask me to make a domiciliary visit and I deem it unnecessary. So thanks to the authorities and orders they drag their miserable, ill children out of their warm beds and muffling them up like parcels bring them to me at the Clinic. Thus my working day is limited to the five hours a day, from eight in the morning to one o'clock in the afternoon. Therefore, I do not feel it is unfair that I might have to remain at the Clinic until two in the afternoon when in the summer we are swamped with work.

Several medical journals regularly come to the Clinic but they are on a low level. They are helpful to me in that they touch upon problems and illnesses which I have not come across in Poland. Thanks to the journals, I am exceptionally well read in, for example, the illness which humans can get from drinking milk from a sick cow — and that is why neither I nor any of my friends ever become infected since I know what preventive measures to take.

It is forbidden to idle or talk about matters not associated with work during office hours at the Clinic. It is only in winter, when due to blizzards and snow people cannot get to the Clinic that we get any 'free' time and we are then supposed to read professional books and articles or to instruct the nurses. I am very careful to stick to these regulations because I want to give them no opportunity of reporting me to the authorities.

During one day in winter, in October, there blows from the south a very strong wind called a buran which is powerful enough to knock people over: children do not go to school and people remain indoors if at all possible. The blowing buran carries myriads of ice crystals which quickly glaze the road to a glass-like surface and which impinge on the face like a hundred sharp needles. Estimating that it will take me twice as much time to walk to the Clinic, I set off from home much earlier than usual. I have to walk into the wind which tries to push me backwards all the way to the Clinic and arrive there at one minute to eight o'clock, breathless and glowing. I find the nurses standing in front of the wall clock watching the time in order to catch me out if I should happen to be late. I have not given them that satisfaction and the disappointment shows in their faces. One is dismissed from work if one is late three times.

They have found a very wise solution to the question of paying for drugs here. With the exception of the very old and the very poor (who have to show an exemption certificate) everybody has to pay 10% of the actual price of the drug; also the dispensary is state-owned so the medicaments are cheap anyway. The system prevents people from asking to be prescribed an expensive drug when an identical but cheaper one will do just as well. It also prevents patients from hoarding drugs since nobody wants to waste even a few kopeks and therefore there is no insistence for drugs if the doctor considers them unnecessary in a given case. The charges for drugs are so low that they will never ruin anybody.

I had commenced work at the Clinic in the summer and now again, as always each year in the summer, we get an epidemic of dysentery. The open latrines and clouds of flies promote the spread of the infection so it is hardly surprising that dysentery is endemic here. As yet we have no drugs to provide suitable treatment and the children die like flies. Naturally I get the infection too, and am able to examine only about two patients when with monotonous regularity I have to dash to the closet. Diarrhoea with blood, stomach pains and a slight temperature are no reason here for taking time off from work. So at home in the evenings I take an opium powder and try to rest. I then discover that there are a few ampules of anti-dysentery serum in the dispensary and within a few days of injecting myself I am cured. The remaining ampules I use for my patients.

One day, an elderly Polish gentleman (I later learn he is a retired general) brings his eight-year-old granddaughter to the Clinic. The little girl is sweet, intelligent and physically well developed. The grandfather has brought her to see me because he is perturbed about the enlarged glands in her neck. I realize, with horror after examining her, that the condition is fatal and the child in these circumstances (and times) cannot be saved. I have to tell the grandfather — lacking the courage to talk to the mother — the awful truth. I turn to the Chief Doctor, Kuzienkov for help but in spite of his efforts and the attention which he is able to give her, little Zosia dies a few months later. She is buried on the steppe. I become friendly with her mother, who can only bear the tragedy because she also has a little son.

The measles epidemic starts in the autumn. I do not know if the infection is particularly virulent or if the children, especially the Kazakh ones, have no resistance but it might as well be the plague and it reminds me of the fate of the American Indians, when complete tribes died from this disease brought in by the whites. I had never seen such serious and complicated cases in Poland and had only read about them in books. Before the measles has a chance to end, we get an epidemic of scarlet fever which happens to be an exceptionally mild infection. The authorities having been notified of the very high mortality rate due to the measles epidemic and anxious to prevent a repetition of the mass deaths, act quickly: we receive large quantities of anti-scarlet fever serum from Moscow and I am ordered to use it in every case of the illness. The serum is old-fashioned and dilute and large quantities have to be injected into the small buttocks. I hate having to give these injections, all the more so because I know that I am causing pain whilst I consider it totally unnecessary since the children look fit and only run a slight temperature with the rash. But orders are orders.

One day at eight o'clock in the morning, a small boy who has scarlet fever is brought to the Clinic by his mother. The instructions to bring children to the doctor help to spread the infection. The little boy is strong, well-fed and does not look at all ill, in spite of having a slight temperature and a rash. I am alone in the whole building with only one of the junior nurses because the adult clinic does not open until nine o'clock in the morning. I am faced with having to give a serum injection to a four-year-old boy with the help of only the sixteen-year-old nurse. I ask the child's mother if he has ever in the past had any injections and she assures me he has had none whatsoever. I turn the child over on to its stomach and tell the nurse to hold it so that it cannot jerk during the injection, which could cause the needle to break and remain buried in the muscles. Very slowly I begin to inject the serum because I know it is less painful this way. I inject approximately one twentieth of the dose and the child has remained suspiciously calm and does not cry or move. I ask the nurse to tell me how the child looks and she assures me that it is fine. I therefore continue to inject but very slowly, drop by drop until a sudden premonition makes me pull the needle out very quickly and I tell the nurse to turn the child's head to the side. The child is unconscious and the rash stands out black on its face. Within the next few seconds the boy starts to convulse! I have put the child into an anaphyllactic shock — from which usually there is no recovery. In a flash I am aware of the fact that I have killed a strong, healthy child with an injection I had been ordered to give, in my opinion, unnecessarily. I have injected only about a tenth of the dose. I call the mother from the waiting-room but she does not realize the gravity of the situation even though the boy is unconscious and blue-black. I send the nurse to the nearby dispensary with instructions to fetch the necessary injections for such a case. I grab a syringe and give the child an injection for the heart since it is the only kind I have to hand. Within two minutes the nurse returns with the necessary drugs; she had caused a fair commotion in the dispensary and the pharmacist, sizing up the situation had quickly given her the drugs. The nurse returns out of breath because she has run there and back and cannot believe that I have already had time to give the child one injection. To tell the truth, I cannot remember either assembling the syringe or filling it with solution, I can only recall actually injecting the boy, whilst I was alone with him and his mother, when the nurse was in the dispensary. I now inject the child with the drugs from the dispensary and he revives! Thank God the dispensary is well stocked and thank God that the pharmacist and the nurse have passed the test of how to react in an emergency — as I have. But when the child begins to breathe and move and when the rash has once again returned to its bright red colour, I start to shake. The mother takes the child home without having realized what a miracle it is that her son has survived. I visit them in the afternoon because I am worried about his condition. However I find he is very lively and the mother gives me a bread roll in gratitude for my care, whereas all day, my legs will barely carry me and my stomach is quivering. It is a wonder that my hair has not turned white!

When Dr Kuzienkov and felcher Sacharova arrive at the Clinic at nine o'clock I tell them the whole story. Sacharova says I am lucky because had the child died, I should have spent the rest of my days in prison, accused of murdering a child. I make my own enquiries to discover how it was possible for the child to go into anaphyllactic shock. I discover that the child had previously received some injection whilst at his nursery of which the mother was ignorant. That was when he must have been given some serum, whilst I, relying on the mother's information did not think it was necessary to take any precautions. From this time onwards I never ask if the patient has had any previous injections but always apply a method of injecting which is time consuming but precludes the risk of anaphyllactic shock. Sacharova laughs at me, says, "It will never happen to me," and continues to give serum injections without taking any precautions. I had been most unfortunate and had brought about a classical, text-book anaphyllactic shock. It might well have finished me 'classically'!

Unpleasant incidents seem to happen to me all the time at the Clinic. On this occasion I am faced with a social-professional problem which places me in a dilemma. Sacharova calls me to see her patient, a Pole, who is suffering from a venereal disease and whom she is uncertain how to treat. Sacharova is a very good felcher without the false pride of thinking she knows it all. In her office I come face to face with a young man whom I know well socially. I also know that he is in love with a female friend of mine. He was under treatment in Lvov, the deportation interrupted the course and now he has had a relapse and is again infectious. We are both very embarrassed but I try to behave in a strictly professional manner. I inform him that he is infectious, that he must not drink from a cup which other people use, nor must he smoke communal cigarettes — my lips say these words but my mind is willing him to understand that I really mean he must not kiss her because I am worried that they have already reached that stage in their relationship. He is a decent and intelligent man so I am sure he is well aware of what may threaten my friend. I try to convince myself because I am unsure of what I should do: should I tell her and frighten her or should I keep my professional confidentiality? I maintain professional secrecy — I give him his injections personally to complete the course of treatment. I do not know how he explains to my friend that he must modify his behaviour towards her. I always feel uncomfortable when I meet him socially: smoking one cigarette between many and drinking from one mug is, through necessity, a common practice amongst us. I attempt not to look his way. Anyway, my friend does not come to seek my help professionally and seems happy in his company to the end of our stay in Gieorgievka.

Was I correct in retaining professional secrecy? I cannot tell. Perhaps it was cowardice on my part not to warn her of the pending danger? There are many Tin Gods, not everything always accepted as correct proves to be so with time and has to be modified. Should I not have followed the dictates of 'humane' ethics rather than 'medical' ethics? I am a young, keen doctor — perhaps after the experience of a lifetime I may adopt a different approach? I continue to feel guilty.

I love to talk with the Clinic orderly. She is shrewd and always ready to help — it is she who steals the cotton wool and bandages for me from the Clinic. I have her to thank for my weatherproofed windows and my warm feet wrapped in the onuce. She does it all so disinterestedly and naturally because — as she says — one cannot survive here without resorting to theft. She also tells me some interesting facts about anti-Semitism in Russia. I had thought there was no anti-Semitism in the USSR — it does not exist officially but it is considered a gross insult to call somebody "Jewrej" (Jew)! People are still prejudiced against Jews but must not talk openly against them. I come across this attitude also in other Russians. I suppose the mere admission of holding anti-Semitic views is proof of sorts of friendship and trust because officially it is a crime to think along such lines and one risks imprisonment.

Close by the Clinic, the pharmacist and his wife live in the villa in which the dispensary is also situated. In the pharmacist we have a dried-up figure of a thin, elderly, bearded man. In the wife we have the antithesis: she must surely weigh a hundred kilo and is so tall and fat that she looks like a monster. Her face is bloated to such an extent that it is impossible to perceive the features and the blubber-enfolded eyes are small and cunning. Together they look like a couple in a farce. She is a shrewd woman but not a bad woman. She keeps her husband under her thumb and . . . . she runs the dispensary, though unlike her husband she has no qualifications. I have only ever seen the pharmacist a couple of times and then only when he was peering out into the dispensary from behind the door of their private quarters. Timid and bewildered he is a nonentity and when he has no choice but to speak, does so in almost a whisper, economizing on words, and disappears as soon as possible. The person who stands behind the counter is the wife, who has familiarized herself with the running of the dispensary and it is she who assumes the role of the pharmacist whom nobody ever questions. No one dares to question her because she is in a position of some authority: she knows all the 'important' people, always has sugar and cubed at that, tea which she brews in a samovar and all the provisions which are never to be had or found in the shop. She is so to speak the mistress of her domain. When the dispensary gets anything, such as for example, saccharin, she will sell it to people but to only those whom she likes and who acknowledge her power.

As soon as I had arrived in Gieorgievka I had gone to the dispensary to buy some soap — but it was always unavailable — on the other hand there was always a profusion of toothbrushes. I had bought myself a large supply, unnecessarily as it happened because to the end of my stay in Gieorgievka there was never to be a shortage of them. But there is never any toothpaste or toothpowder. I resort to buying writing chalk which I crush and use to clean my teeth with the lamentable effect of eroding the enamel on the teeth. It might have been better had I a mortar and pestle to reduce the chalk to a finer powder.

As well as always having toothbrushes, the dispensary has a plenitude of excellent perfumes! Even in Tsarist times Russian perfumes were renowned and highly valued and used by all the wealthy people even by men and particularly by the officers in the Tsar's army. Following this tradition, Kazakhstan also gets its allocation of the 'indispensable' commodity. Only instead of being used as scent we use the perfume in the Clinic in lieu of surgical spirit which is normally used for sterilizing instruments but which does not exist here. Perhaps the reason for this anomaly is that the surgical spirit would probably be drunk in place of vodka. Particularly lovely is the sweet pea perfume which we use for boiling the syringes and the strong smell permeates through the whole Clinic. From this time onwards I cannot even bear the smell or the flowers of the sweet pea.

The pharmacist's wife is a lady: she lives in a villa and employs a servant — a Pole. Her household is large and includes a cow, some hens and a pig. We do not know from where she gets the tea and sugar. The Pole has a hard job because she has to see to the pharmacist's entire property, has to clean the whole house and light all the stoves but she does not grumble because she gets paid for her work, eats with the family, keeps warm and is well-treated — she spends her evenings sitting with her employers by the stove, sipping hot tea from the samovar and nibbling sugar cubes. They drink tea here in the Russian fashion; the tea is poured, a little at a time, into a saucer and is sucked through a sugar cube which is held in the mouth. It would be impossible to drink the tea straight from the mug because it comes absolutely boiling hot from the samovar.

After a few months of this bourgeoisie life and still during my presence in Gieorgievka, the crash comes! The pharmacist is arrested for corrupt practices. No one is surprised because it was impossible for them to have lived so well without having committed theft of one sort or another. The man is not condemned or censured but quite the opposite, people sympathize and feel sorry that he is in trouble and has had the misfortune to be caught for the thefts. Such an attitude is common and nobody is ashamed of having a prison sentence — after doing one's stint, 'honour' will be returned.

The pharmacist, in prison in Semipalatynsk, is sent parcels by his wife who manages to remain serene and collected — they know it is only a question of time and he will be released after the two year sentence. I never do find out if he returns to Gieorgievka because in the meantime, I leave myself. Since the dispensary has been left without a pharmacist, a replacement is sent from Moscow. It is a young woman, and she takes over the dispensary, the villa and the whole household, as is her due in her official capacity. It is now that the pharmacist's wife impresses me because without losing face or her dignity she finds it possible to become the housekeeper to the new pharmacist. She keeps house for her, cooks and waits on her, and gets on well with the newcomer. She knew how to step down off her pedestal cheerfully.

The influenza epidemic starts in late autumn and I too go down with the infection. I run such a high temperature that I cannot go to work. I let them know at the Clinic and by no stretch of the imagination do I think they will see fit to check that I am indeed ill. The same day in the afternoon however, who should appear but my 'friend' Zenaida A. Without uttering a word she hands me a thermometer, which shows my temperature of 39°C. She departs irked that she has not succeeded in catching me shirking from work.

Barely have I recovered when my mother falls ill with the influenza. I am not unduly perturbed because I know the extraordinary strength of my mother's constitution in spite of her weak heart. However, her illness greatly upsets our landlord who comes or rather crawls to our room to see 'Granny'. Perhaps he is motivated by pure curiosity, perhaps he is expecting some event of significance, for example, a funeral to break the winter ennui, enough that he comes and sympathizes with my mother. He stays a long while, standing supporting himself by holding on to the bed, nodding his head whilst scrutinizing my mother and saying that he is very sorry but he can see that 'Granny's' turn has come, her turn to depart. My mother has a good sense of humour so we both burst out laughing when he leaves. What a way to console a patient!

I meet an old school friend, M. M. in Gieorgievka who is here with her parents and younger sister. The reason for their deportation is tragi-comic. Mr M., an impoverished descendant of landed gentry was a civil servant in the county offices in Lvov. When the Russians had ordered the population census in Lvov, Mr M. had written as his occupation, 'uriadnik', Russian-izing the Polish word and thinking that it would mean civil servant in Russian. However, the use of this word resulted in them all being deported because in Russian 'uriadnik' means a tax-collector! And as such, a hated personage during the Tsarist times, a blood-sucker who was abhorred by the masses since the peasants would have their cattle confiscated and would face ruin for non-payment of their taxes. Unless of course the peasant had some money with which to bribe the tax-collector which in any case only delayed the eventful repayment. And thus old, lost Mr M. finds himself in Kazakhstan with his family.

Mr M.'s wife is sensitive, cultured and totally unsuited to battling for survival in these circumstances. She is a hopeless cook. If they manage to obtain even a little flour she is unable to make noodles and if she does cook something the culinary effort makes the whole family fall ill. Like all of us they have no fat to cook with and therefore Mrs M. decides to fry her batter-cakes in castor oil which she gets from the dispensary. The whole family eats the batter-cakes and later bitterly regrets it.

My friend, M. M., is very talented artistically. Even at school I remember, she used to paint and draw well, so she now exploits her talents and applies for work in the kolkhoz sewing work-room where they quickly learn her worth. She is set to embroidering a blouse and when they see that she begins by drawing her own design for the embroidery they never ask her to do the mundane work but gladly employ her as a designer of embroidery patterns. She goes round the Kazakh huts collecting the traditional Kazakh embroidery motifs which she then incorporates into her designs for embroidering on the blouses with the coloured threads. She is much appreciated and valued. She also draws Russian designs, regional Ukrainian designs, etc. Marusia has found an outlet for her artistic talents and has thus gained the right to buy bread, whilst the sewing work-room is delighted with their acquisition of an artist. M. M. sews herself a hat using newspaper, which apart from protecting her from the sun, looks charming, all the more so since she has managed to get some paints and has embellished it with a colourful design. There is no doubt that her brimmed hat is better against the sun than the kerchief which I wear on my head. The hat looks very attractive and original as she wears it when walking round the market in Gieorgievka.

M. M.'s sister, a very young teenager, is still almost a child but applies for work in the kolkhoz. Being the daughter of an ex-landowner, work on the land appeals to her. She is strong and healthy and is therefore welcomed with open arms to the work in the kolkhoz: very quickly she becomes much liked by all and is accepted as one of them. She goes far away from Gieorgievka into the steppe for three weeks' haymaking with a large group of workers. On her return she is sun-tanned, happy, has grown some more, and has blossomed before our very eyes into a buxom wench. Life in Kazakhstan on the steppe appeals so much to her that she later marries a Russian kolkhoz worker and as I learn after, voluntarily remains in Kazakhstan. My friend and her mother later on get to Persia.

Mr M. dies in Gieorgievka. I attend the funeral and am not in the least ashamed to admit that I feel no sorrow. Mr M. was over seventy and was very unhappy in exile — lost and helpless. Death rescued him from much suffering. He is the first Pole to die in Gieorgievka and his funeral becomes an occasion for a religious-political demonstration. Everybody in the Polish community is much moved by his death — the women go off into the steppe to gather grasses and some small flowers for the wreaths and sprays and the young men arrange to get a few planks of wood to make a cross. The grave is dug by the Poles themselves. Everything so far runs smoothly but problems present themselves when we face the task of getting the coffin to the cemetery: the bullocks are away somewhere working on the steppe and there are virtually no horses, so it seems the funeral will have to be postponed since the cemetery is some distance away from Gieorgievka and there is no question of being able to carry the coffin. In the end after intercession by Mr M.'s younger daughter, the kolkhoz worker, the kolkhoz lends us a cart and a couple of bullocks.

The Poles dress in whatever best clothes they possess, regardless of the colour. We worry in case we will not be allowed to carry the cross publicly but the general opinion that there must be a cross prevails over the fear that there may be trouble. Carrying the cross, a small boy heads the funeral cortège and behind him comes the wreath-covered coffin on the hay cart drawn by the bullocks who are led by the halter by a young fair man (the son of my friend Mrs S.) dressed becomingly in a short-sleeved blue sports shirt: he wears the one and only untorn shirt which he has. Behind the coffin walks the dead man's family and behind them the throng of Poles. We pass along the main street and from the roadside huts we see women emerging — mainly the older ones in fact, who kneel by the road and cross themselves three times. We sing hymns, shyly at first and then emboldened by the locals' reaction more loudly and daringly. At last we attain the cemetery, the body is committed to the earth and it is time for the orations. General S., an old man of over seventy stands over the open grave and commences a stereotyped talk in praise of the deceased's virtues and saying all which is usually said on such occasions. Standing by the side in a group of young people I am becoming bored and slightly irritated until suddenly my ears prick up as I hear, "This man has departed in the very prime of life," being said by the general, which I suppose is not to be wondered at since he is a contemporary of the deceased, but being so much younger myself I find the description rather hilarious. Glancing at my companions I see that they too are all amused and we have to turn away hurriedly to hide our mirth. Not only was Mr M. lucky to escape further deportation wanderings but he also had a beautiful funeral.

I get to know Mrs P. the wife of a border patrolman who had been arrested by the Russians immediately upon their entering Poland, as in fact they had arrested all the border patrolmen of the KOP (Corps of Border Guards): he knew the border crossing points only too well. Mrs P. was lucky because the Russian soldier who had come for her was a good man and seeing her three young children spent the whole night with them helping her to pack. He had urged her to take as many things as possible because everything could prove useful to her in the future. So she has brought an enormous amount with her, including some curtains and a radio which is a huge contraption. Her home was stripped of most things and only bare furniture remained. She was also fortunate to have been brought straight to Gieorgievka from the train and so did not have to roam through the poor, God-forsaken Kazakh kolkhozes. For local circumstances she has a 'fortune' in her belongings on which she and her children can live for several years. She is energetic, merry and everybody likes her. She exists by bartering her possessions and as the mother of three young children is not obliged to go out to work.

At the end of September 1940, a young woman doctor comes to Gieorgievka to fill the present vacancy for the post of Regional Medical Officer. The doctor comes from Moscow, where she was born and educated and is naturally a Party member. Newly qualified, young, good-looking, elegant and educated — she can even speak French! She realizes the responsibilities associated with her position but does not put on airs, does not pretend to know everything and openly admits to being inexperienced in administrative work, asking us all to help her cope with her task. Tactful and intelligent, she is at the same time full of enthusiasm and energy for her work. Later, it comes home to me that she is also a good doctor. I work with her for several months and never notice anything which would force me to change my opinion of her. She is also very friendly and I really get to like her. I feel sorry for her that she has been unable to remain in Moscow to follow the academic career which she surely would deserve — she is wasted in Kazakhstan. In this manner the Bolsheviks 'improve' their young people: they are given posts, which it would seem, challenge their capabilities and the youngsters rise and grow to meet the size of the task. Our lady doctor, the 'Rajzdrava' as we call her was able to cope with her assignment in Kazakhstan. The Party had not been mistaken in her untapped potentials.

The Rajzdrava gets down to work immediately: under her care she has the small 'cottage' hospital in Gieorgievka. She holds surgery in the Clinic and is responsible for the whole of the administration and the general state of health in the whole area. She also attempts to improve our sixteen-year-old nurses and organizes seminars during which we discuss patients' cases. She also keeps us physically fit by ushering us out to 'whitewash' (with the clay and dung mixture) the Clinic as we had previously 'whitewashed' the hospital. And whilst it is already getting cold with the approach of winter! She joins in the work — not sparing us or herself on a Sunday.

Her husband has been detached elsewhere and as it is not long since they were married, she misses him badly without making any attempt to hide her feelings. With her job she is allocated a house and fuel (the kolkhoz kiziak) and also a cow! Provisions are left for her to collect from the shop, by the back door, on her way home in the evening. Three salaries are paid her: that of the Regional Medical Officer, another as head doctor at the hospital and yet another as duty doctor at the Clinic. Although she has been sent to Kazakhstan, she is well catered for. She is a confirmed Communist but holds the conviction that Mother Russia must always take first place above all else. If we take into consideration that each doctor in Russia receives a reasonable pay increase every five years for the number of years served, then it must be admitted that the USSR takes care of her doctors, who are financially well-off for these circumstances. Regarding the relationship between doctors and the population, I experience myself that a doctor in the USSR is a respected figure of some authority.

Time flies, the first snow falls in September and by October we are deep into winter. The cows, hens and dogs are taken into the byres. I have never seen a cat in Kazakhstan — probably because cat-fur is unsuitable, being too fine, for making gloves and caps and nobody can afford the luxury of feeding useless animals.

In spite of the winter weatherproofing, our room is very cold, especially in the mornings when the stove is practically cold. Prior to raking out the ashes, and putting on some more kiziak to burn, it is extremely cold and feels all the more so since we get up from bed already perished: our beds are draughty — the hay in the palliasses has become matted and provides no insulation from the cold penetrating up from the floor beneath. They tell me at the Clinic that everybody here uses cotton wool to spread between the palliasses and the sheets. I have a new problem — where can I get the cotton wool? The dispensary will not sell it and the locals get the raw, uncleaned stuff through 'friends and connections' from Alma-Ata. One must attend to this during the summer however because now in the winter nobody will travel. We are saved by the Clinic orderly — she steals some cotton wool for me. We are now warm in our beds.

Before setting off from home to arrive at the Clinic by 8 o'clock in the morning, I have to empty the bucket after the night out beyond the hut, I have to take out the ashes and scatter them on the road and I have to fetch water from the well. These chores are not particularly tiresome on a still, cold day but when the buran blows I may be covered with ashes and drenched with water — the wind can half empty the bucket of water which I carry.

The doctors at the Clinic may, if they wish, refer patients to specialists in Semipalatynsk. This does not happen very often because travelling expenses have to be met by the patients themselves making them reluctant to ask to be referred and if anything they try to avoid it. Under the pretext of going to see a specialist one of the Poles travels to Semipalatynsk and escapes. Fortunately the man was not one of my patients but Dr Kuzienkov's who is above suspicion of helping in the escape. I feel unsafe however and my premonition proves correct when Dr Kuzienkov calls me in to see him and informs me that from now on I am forbidden to refer patients to Semipalatynsk. A few moments later he comes to see me and hands me a sheaf of letters of referral bearing his signature! I had not thought that a doctor and a Russian one at that could be capable of extending such a gesture of friendship towards me — he could be exposing himself to danger. Even so, I still feel unsure — I am certain that the attitude towards the Poles is changing 'from the top'.

One Polish woman works at the Clinic as the orderly's assistant — I know her very well and trust her. But her conduct during one of our seminars greatly astonishes me: uninvited, she delivers an aggressive pro-Communist speech. During these general staff meetings we would normally discuss routine matters and problems associated only with work and personally I limit myself strictly to medical problems only. There is no need whatsoever for my friend to take the floor. I cannot believe my ears — what a Communist she has become — for what reason? I am ashamed for her and begin to fear her. Perchance she may betray what I say to my friends? I always speak my mind amongst Polish friends. For years to come I puzzle over what may have prompted her to give such a show. Does she want to toady up to somebody or is she an undeclared Communist? In either case her behaviour is despicable. I never discuss the incident either with her or with other people but from this moment on I do not feel relaxed in her presence — the performance does not show her character in a good light. I am to see her for the last time in Teheran in 1943.

The lingering intuition that in some way I am threatened proves correct. On the 30th November, 1940, just on my birthday, I am given one week's notice from work. I am left with my mother to face the winter without an income and without the right to buy bread. At the Clinic news of my dismissal is greeted with general sympathy except for Zenaida A., who tells me, "You will most certainly perish now." It will be in Teheran in 1942 that I shall learn of the death of Zenaida A. in the winter of 1941/42, who closed the ventilation door of her stove and died of the poisonous fumes. Though it may be unpleasant to admit to base feelings, I must say that this news does not upset me. I am glad that 'somebody up there' punished her for her cruelty to me, for her smirk, when she told me that I would kick the bucket. My birthday passes sadly — we eat the tinned quinces, which I had previously bought, as planned but we cannot enjoy them and the birthday 'feast' is a dismal failure. Fear seizes me when I stop to consider how I shall continue to exist and whether I shall at all survive the deportation.

I now have to fight for life and must miss no opportunity of saving myself. Therefore the following day I make my way to see the official who is in charge of dealing and arbitrating with people's problems at work, etc. The young man, wearing the Russian Army uniform, is pleasant. He hears me out and agrees that I have been dismissed without any reason, promises to look into the matter and asks me to call again in three days' time. When I return, he pronounces that he can do nothing in my case. What he says sounds genuine and significant — we both know that an order has been issued from the top to have all the deported Poles dismissed from their jobs. It is obvious that the authorities have changed their attitude and the Polish intelligentsia no longer deserves any support. Even though I was working professionally I have become the people's enemy. I can, of course, become one of the people and work physically in the kolkhoz — that is permitted.

As always, my mother lifts my spirits, consoling me that as yet we have food and what is most important, we have enough kiziak to keep us warm during the winter so there is no point in worrying in advance because this is wartime and everything can change at any moment. This typically Polish and really rather reckless attitude of 'we shall manage somehow' consoles me because I feel I am too young to be doomed to die yet, and it is just as likely that I shall survive somehow. The other person who contributes very much to improving my mood is the Gieorgievka schoolteacher — a Kazakh woman. I know her only from her visits to the Clinic when she used to bring her son of a few months for medical checks. During these occasions we used to talk about various topics because she is an intelligent woman who is interested in all things. I never touch upon politics or religion. She has come immediately to our hut upon hearing that I had lost my job, with the intention of offering us shelter in her kitchen because otherwise as she says, "You will freeze to death." I am very touched by her offer and thank her for the kind thought but since we have enough kiziak to last us through the winter, I have no need to take advantage of her offer. I promise to let her know if the time should come when we shall really be in need.

She stays a long time, long enough for me to form an opinion about her life. She is married to a young Kazakh who belongs, as she does, to the Communist Party. Her husband is employed by the Party and earns a good income and she, as a teacher, is also paid not unreasonably. By local standards they are wealthy. They do not have to worry about food. For some time we talk about the feeding, the nursing and the bringing up of her little son becuase she is eager to bring him up as progressively as possible. It is obvious that she wants to imbibe as much Russian culture and progress as she can. She widens this topic to embrace the Kazakh race — she would like to elevate the standards of the whole nation and at this moment it becomes very apparent that she is primarily Kazakh and that Communism takes second place to the spirit of Kazakh nationality.

Waxing loquacious, she daringly broaches the question of religion and straightforwardly asks if, in my opinion, God exists. I can see that she must have been struggling inwardly with this problem which she cannot discuss with anybody here. Her question puts me in a quandary: if I say I believe God exists, I am openly contradicting the teachings of the Party, but to say categorically that there is no God, I simply cannot do. We theorize on this topic and eventually concur that there must be 'something' — perhaps that Allah up in the sky, as the Kazakh who sold me the kiziak, had said. I think that after talking with me she manages to reorganize her thoughts and doubts and becomes convinced that 'something' must be watching over us all. The word God never passed my lips because who knows — she might feel compelled to report my opinions to the Party? I do not ask about her husband's views.

From the subject of religion we move on to the theme of the fate of the Kazakh nation and this is when I discover that this Communist is in reality a fierce and fervent nationalist. We both tremble with indignation at the way in which the Russians are systematically destroying Kazakh culture. The Kazakhs used to have a European alphabet with some minor differences, such as accents, etc. I have seen school text-books which were written in Kazakh in their own language, whilst now the Russians have issued an edict that the Cyrillic alphabet must be used. The Russians have decreed that the whole world, that all civilized nations, use the Cyrillic alphabet. They have ordered all Kazakh books to be destroyed and have forcibly introduced the Cyrillic alphabet — thus 'culturizing' the Kazakhs. With this one sweep the Russians have destroyed Kazakh literature — books written in their language have been withdrawn from libraries and destroyed. I can no longer restrain myself and tell her that quite the contrary, the whole world in fact uses their alphabet and it is untrue that the Cyrillic alphabet is widespread, being used only by the Russians. The poor woman actually sighs — I have confirmed her fears that the Cyrillic alphabet has been introduced to denationalize the Kazakhs and not to uplift their standards of civilization and culture. As a teacher, she so much desires to be in a position to help her people but is instead completely impotent to do so. She is fully aware that the Kazakhs are being Russianized under the guise of being civilized.

I think of the schoolteacher's visit as yet another 'miracle' in Kazakhstan. She comes to my home during a time which is for me, a very dark hour indeed and raises my spirits, inspires me with hope and restores my faith in mankind. When I had thought the situation to be completely hopeless she appears and offers me her help. I shall remember her kindness always — I am very much in her debt and can never repay her. And to think that I have only known her from her visits to the Clinic . . . .

Unemployed I am left to face the winter months. I go round the Russian huts and essay to barter the remainder of our things for food. Only very rarely am I successful in obtaining a little brown flour, sometimes I get a handful of sauerkraut which in this environment is a blessing because it prevents scurvy. During the winter there is no nourishment which contains vitamin C and the milk which is unobtainable, would have to be boiled for fear of getting brucellosis. Many of the Poles suffer from scurvy which gives rise to haemorrhages under the skin, wounds, bleeding gums, and anaemia. I am proud to say that none of my friends have scurvy. I simply forbid them to cook the sauerkraut in soup. I explain that such a soup would have one effect: the destruction of the precious vitamin C which is present in raw sauerkraut. If they are desperate to have a hot meal, they can always wash down the sauerkraut by drinking hot water. Water because there is no tea — it is sometimes possible to buy a small piece of tea cube from the Russian Communists who come to Gieorgievka on business. I have never seen actual tea leaves in Kazakhstan — they are sent to the larger Russian cities, whilst Kazakhstan gets tea-powder which is compressed into flat cubes, measuring about 12 cm. by 6 cm. by 2 cm. in size. There is no question of being able to buy a whole cube. When and if the opportunity arises one can buy broken off fragments of a cube, which are then used a pinch at a time. Coffee substitute however, is always available in the shop — the ingredients are shown on the wrapping: roast corn, acorns, chestnuts and cocoa. It is quite good but most important, it provides a hot drink.

The frost exceeds -35°C and I sometimes feel it is just as well I am not working. It would be extremely difficult to get to work on a regular basis for eight o'clock in the morning in this frost, through snow-drifts and in the oft strong wind. And one could not afford to be late, not by one minute. Now I can leave home at whatever time I choose, depending on the weather. Only certain functions force me to venture outside, regardless of the weather conditions, such as emptying the ashes, fetching water and, of course, when nature calls. The last is the worst. When it is calm outside and the sun shines, I walk round the Russian huts looking for food — friends often let me know where there may be something to be bartered. I quite enjoy the walking when there is a crackling frost and when the air is still, clean and clear. The snow then sparkles and shimmers with all the colours of the rainbow.

One day I walk to that part of Gieorgievka which in the Tsarist times was inhabited by Russian voluntary emigrants. Their second generation descendants now live here. I know this settlement well but when I reach the place where I should come across the huts, I can see nothing but an immense snow-drift — the huts are nowhere in sight. Initially I think I must have lost my way, so to get my bearings, I start to scramble up the mountain of snow when I suddenly spot the top of a telegraph post and its wires protruding about a metre above the snow level. The huts are completely buried and I am walking over the roofs of the huts, stepping over the telegraph wires! After peering more closely at the scene, I can see that tunnels have been dug in the snow and that each tunnel leads to the entrance of a hut. I scramble down into one tunnel and find myself in an Alice in Wonderland world — the tunnels are propped up with everything and anything: sticks, boards, bits of furniture and everything is glistening and sparkling with an icing of frost. The tunnel slopes downwards gradually and as I walk along it the gloom envelopes me but now the door of the hut is close. It is warm, clean and bright inside the hut because they have dug steeper tunnels from the surface of the snow to the windows to let in the light. The housewife is baking bread and the delicious aroma fills the room; the walls are clean, having been freshly whitewashed and the floor is daubed yellow with dung. A homely air of prosperity and order pervades the room. The Russian woman is cleanly dressed, in valonki and with a white kerchief one her head, which alters not the fact that she is probably louse-infested. Even the wife of the KGB Superintendent in Gieorgievka has lice in her hair which I have seen for myself when she brought her child to the Clinic. I have become so accustomed to lice being commonplace that I am not in the least shocked. I watch as she scratches through the kerchief and take no notice. The housewife is very courteous and though she does not want to buy anything from me, gives me a small bread roll. I have been reduced to begging.

As I now have plenty of spare time on my hands, I 'cultivate' my social life and pay calls on my friends. I always have to take great care not to get lost because as soon as the buran begins to gust the landscape will change and where previously there had been a path, on my homeward journey, there can be a mountain of snow. One should never attempt to skirt round the snow-drifts because it is very easy to get lost and finish up walking out into the steppe. One has to plod through the drifts so as not to lose all sense of direction. It is essential to be particularly careful at night because the moonlight seems to change the landscape even more, throwing such peculiar shadows on the newly blown snow-drifts that the landmarks are unrecognizable. It is very exhausting wading cross-country through the drifts, which are often several metres high, even worse than scrambling up a sand-dune. To lose one's way may result in freezing to death on the exposed steppe.

The postman in Gieorgievka is a Pole, called Mundziu, who knows the village better than anybody else since he has been delivering letters and parcels for several months. One day, Mundziu too, gets lost and walks in the wrong direction out into the open steppe. He is fortunate enough to meet a Kazakh who turns him back because he was walking in quite the opposite direction. He is greatly disturbed that even he can get lost. We are all very fond of our postman, the lad is very likeable and courteous. He is our 'newspaper' as he goes about his work bringing us snippets of gossip. Mundziu is the first to know everything and is very useful to us all. He obtained the job at the Post Office because the Russians cannot read the addresses on the letters arriving from Poland — they know only the 'civilized and world-wide' Cyrillic alphabet.

When the buran blows, the temperature may rise to minus twelve or so degrees Centigrade but the wind is strong enough to blow people over and the ice-crystals lash the face, so then I do not leave our hut. When the sun is shining I enjoy walking about in Gieorgievka. The winters here are dry, which means that sometimes thick snow will fall but in the main there is a lot of sunshine and then, particularly at sunset, the snow becomes coloured. Too much so in fact, as on a sentimental post-card. The landscape turns pinkish-blue-green, almost sickly-sweet — these incredible colours are painted by the 'poor' artist — nature.

In the middle of winter we are all ordered to attend yet another census, just at the time when the buran is blowing. We dress as warmly as possible but I am anxious about my mother: the road is like a sheet of ice and the wind is so strong that one mightier gust can knock over a person. It takes an immense effort to walk into the wind, no less effort than climbing a steep mountain, and walking or relatively speaking, running with the wind is likewise a problem because one must brace the body with all strength against the wind to brake from being pushed. We manage to return home safe and sound.

One afternoon, I go to visit Mrs W. The snow glints colourfully in the sunset, the path is clearly trodden out and I thoroughly enjoy the walk. The buran blows up during my visit. On my departure the moon is shining and the landscape has altered drastically. In place of the path there is a huge snow-drift, several metres high. The buran is a 'warm', wanton wind, polishing the roads until they resemble skating-rinks, prickling the face with its icy needles, erecting snow-drifts in the least expected places and capable of doing all these things within one hour. I must admit I am scared of getting lost even though I know the way so well.

The buran can also lead to suffocation. Two of my friends, the daughters of Dr D., live alone in a small hut. One day they wake up to complete darkness and at first think that they have woken too early and that it is still the middle of the night: but then they notice that they can see nothing at all through the window and realize that the snow must have totally buried the whole hut. They try to get out but the door which is obstructed by the snow will not budge. They bang on the walls and shout. Their neighbours hear the noise and by ten o'clock in the morning manage to dig out the girls. The buran had been blowing hard during the night.

I often visit Mrs W. because I am friendly with her and also because her place is so comfortable, warm and homely that I can forget our terrible plight and can relax mentally. The bread which Mrs W. offers me also plays a certain role in enticing me. We often discuss cake and other recipes. Mrs W. was a cook in a restaurant in Poland and knowing more about culinary art than I do, teaches me all kinds of tricks in cookery which I shall find very useful in later years. People who are hungry spend all their time thinking and dreaming about good food. I learn this when I later meet men in the Polish Army who have been released from Russian concentration camps. They did exactly the same — 'eating their fill' on dreams of tasty dishes.

I smoke heavily to dull my hunger. Though we eat something each day, what we get is insufficient. There is nothing in the market. I once manage to buy a block of frozen milk and that is all. Sometimes they sell bran in the market. When I see Poles who live in a neighbouring Kazakh kolkhoz buying bran by the bucket, I am gripped by pity, pain and fear. In Gieorgievka the locals buy bran for their animals, for their cows and chickens, whilst the Poles are reduced to buying it for themselves. They go hungry in their kolkhoz so they are thrilled that at least they can assuage their hunger with the bran. Triumphantly they carry the bran away, pleased to have got hold of some food but the bran only accelerates their deaths. The human stomach cannot digest bran and most of the Poles fall ill. In the spring, I am told that during the winter, over half of the Poles at that particular kolkhoz starved to death.

The Russians who live in Gieorgievka have plenty to eat — the kolkhoz provides them with flour, groats, a little meat and pork fat from the pigs. They also have potatoes and sauerkraut. There is no milk for anybody — the cows are dry during the winter and if they do calf, the milk is saved for the calves which would not survive the winter on fodder alone. There are no eggs. As we now know that nearly all the cows are sick and that their milk will infect people, I even boil the block of frozen milk which I have bought after melting it, to kill the bacteria. By this means I also destroy all the vitamin C which is present in fresh milk. We have no vitamins in our diet — we must survive the hard winter without them.

I sometimes go to the one canteen which is to be found in Gieorgievka in the hope that perhaps after all I shall get a bowl of soup which though watery will have some nutritional value. They are reluctant to serve Poles in the canteen and we are usually told "nitchevo niet" (there is nothing). The Russians and Kazakhs who are on business always get soup, noodles and sometimes meat. One day I arrive at the canteen with two friends, the Misses O. We sit down and wait to be noticed. We cannot ask the waitress to serve us because from spite, she will give us nothing. We wait so long that we fear they will even run out of the soup. A young Kazakh in Red Army uniform is sitting at a neighbouring table, watching us — he must have realized that we had no hope of getting any soup because he invites us to join him at his table. The result is magic! We get a bowl of soup immediately! The Kazakh takes some bread from his pocket and gives us each a piece and eventually offers us some vodka which he also has in his coat pocket. We eat our fill, drink the vodka — and get drunk. The Kazakh watches us, smiling and politely bidding us goodbye, leaves.

At midday we set off for our homes, walking through the snow-drifts into which we sink amid much laughter. The day is beautiful, frosty, sunny and still and the snow is as soft as down — it is quite lovely to fall into its fluffy embrace and we giggle the whole way. We reach our homes with no further adventures. The Kazakh has not only fed us but has also given us a splendid treat! May Allah bless him!

For the first and only time during my time in Gieorgievka, the dispensary gets some saccharin. It is supposed to be for diabetic patients of whom there are none here so everybody who is able to, takes the opportunity of buying something sweet. The news spreads quickly and the dispensary is sold out of saccharin within a few hours. We all crave something sweet, later I get accustomed to being without sugar. Around this time I receive a parcel from friends in Lvov which amongst other things contains some pork fat. I decide to make some cakes for Christmas to send to my husband. I bake some shortbread on the griddle using dark flour, pork fat and the saccharin stead of sugar. I think the biscuits are excellent and my husband receives his parcel. I get letters from him each month and I write to him each week.

Christmas comes — a very sad and depressing Christmas. We have nothing special to eat on the traditional Polish Christmas Eve feast and have to make do with our everyday noodles. We spend the day sitting in darkness from three o'clock in the afternoon because we have just run out of paraffin for our small lamp and there is none in the shop. We are in a very negative frame of mind — it is interesting to note how much the human mind can be influenced by darkness. I cannot say that I relish the prospect of spending Christmas sitting in the darkness. Both my mother and I are very low until another Kazakhstan 'miracle' happens. At about nine o'clock in the evening, a Kazakh woman arrives, bringing a bottle of paraffin. She had suddenly required some ready cash and had quickly grabbed whatever came to hand, to sell us — it had happend to be the bottle of paraffin. I had never before been offered paraffin for sale and will never again be offered it. It occurs the once, on Christmas 1940. One cannot but help believe that there is 'somebody up there'. Once we have a light, our moods improve and I can even say we are almost gay because a miracle has happened, the world is lighter and the future is less hopeless than we had previously felt when sitting in our dark room.

We have a difficult problem in winter with bringing water for washing and laundering, though we can get the water from the kolkhoz well which is not far from the hut. I enjoy going for water in the summer: the well is deep and encrusted with ice all the year round so one can just see an 'eye' of water at the bottom surrounded by a white rim. The water is sweet, clean and ice-cold — fine in the summer. Now during the winter I carry the buckets on a yoke and go to fetch the water twice a day but have to make twice as many journeys if the buran is blowing. The wind swings the buckets on the yoke, tossing them around and spilling the water. I cannot carry the buckets by hand because the water would be blown over me. If we need four buckets of water each day for household chores, I have to go to the well at least half a dozen times. Each time I return there will only be a little water left in the bottom of the buckets.

I have the 'veterinary' soap which Mrs W. had given me, we keep the stove burning all day and always have hot water. I borrow a tub from our landlady and can easily do all our laundering. It is quite a different matter to dry the clothes. I have problems with hanging out the articles because the wet clothes freeze before I have had time to fasten them to the clothes-line with safety pins. I cannot straighten them out and find myself handling stiff, creased and crumpled pieces of 'cardboard'. It cannot be helped and I have to be satisfied to leave the frozen washing as it is. When the clothes become pliable and can be seen to flutter in the wind it is a sign that they are dry and can be brought inside. I have to be careful when hanging up the wet clothes not to let my hands become frozen to them and frostbitten — I dislike the chore. Washing oneself can even be a pleasure. I stand the basin beside the hot stove and can easily wash all over, piece by piece, with the hot water. Though we have to go outside the hut when nature calls for 'No. 2' and it is quite a hardship in the freezing temperatures, the area round the huts is quite clean and there is no stench because everything is frozen and covered by snow. When the snow melts in the spring all the dirt is washed away.

The kiziak burns well and our room is warm. We have no need of matches because we keep the fire glowing all night.

I have the good fortune to get a 'chugun' which is something no Kazakh household can manage without. I am indeed very pleased when the chance comes to buy a second-hand chugun because I have never seen any for sale in the shop. A chugun is a kind of cooking pot made of heavy cast iron, glazed with thick white enamel on the inside and tapering towards the base. It can be placed into the hole in the griddle top of the stove so that the flames surround it on all sides. The pot is very quick to come to the boil. The exterior of the pot is thickly coated with soot which is never cleaned off whilst the enamel on the inside is easy to keep clean. I should think a chugun will last a very long time because they all have them and yet I have never seen one for sale. They are probably handed down in the family. It would be difficult to cook here without a chugun — hard to exist.

The Poles in Gieorgievka are laughing: the shop has received a consignment of excellent 'pots with handles' — chamber-pots! The Russian women immediately buy the shop out of them and it does not even cross their minds that the pots are meant to be used for other purposes than for cooking. I suppose they are unaware that potties exist. I also expect they become disappointed very soon because their new cooking utensils are made of very thin metal which will soon burn through and the enamel will crack. Still they will be able to use their purchases for making yoghurt in — so perhaps the 'pans' will come in useful after all!

Our hut stands next to the kolkhoz buildings: the byres, the stables and the 'bania' (public baths) where the kolkhoz workers bathe or rather wash once a week. The women use the bania on certain days and the men on others because the bathing is communal in one room. On the days during which the bania is open, the activity starts early in the morning — the men fill the cauldrons where the water is heated, and the women light the stoves. Each kolkhoz worker has to do a spell of work at the bania on a rota system. Inside the bania it is hot and there is always plenty of hot water. People leave the building warmed through and well-scrubbed — I do envy them — I am not allowed to use the bania because I am not employed at the kolkhoz.

Half-way through the winter I receive a letter from Lvov from Professor L., who is the father of an old school friend of mine and with whom my parents used to socialize. Professor L. has known me from childhood and upon hearing of my fate has written to me to help me. He writes that he is in a position to have me brought back to Lvov — only I must accept USSR citizenship. It has never even entered my head that I could escape from Asia by paying such a price. I cannot accept the conditions demanded beyond any shadow of a doubt. I do not reply to the letter and the Professor's good intentions miscarry. Here, I have to remove any doubts whatsoever which may arise as to the Professor's loyalty and patriotism because of his Jewish blood. He is a good man, an intelligent man, and if he is able to bring me back to Lvov it will be thanks to his intelligence, his ability to deal with people, and luck. There can be no doubt that he is a good Pole. I will later meet him in Britain, a few months before his death.

It is becoming more and more difficult to obtain food. We are told that they mine gold in the Altay Mountains, which are about forty miles away from Gieorgievka and that there is a shop, a 'gold mart', in the mining village where one can obtain provisions in exchange for gold. Several of the Poles have already been taken to the village by a Kazakh with a sledge and have exchanged wedding rings, bracelets and other gold articles for coupons and then the coupons for flour and sugar in the shop. Gold can also be exchanged for clothes and shoes. One cannot always get what one wants for the coupons in the shop and the coupons are only valid for a period of three months. My mother asks a Polish lady who is going to the mining village, to take her wedding ring and exchange it for some coupons. Then later, I would go myself to the village which is called Altay Zoloto (Altay — Gold) and exchange the coupons for provisions. The days are now very short so it is a question of time to fit in the journey and transaction because they are in no hurry to exchange the gold for coupons in the gold mart and it could happen that they would close the shop before one received the coupons. The risk of this happening would be lessened if the transactions took place in two instalments.

On her return journey from Altay Zoloto, the lady stays the night with us because she lives in a kolkhoz beyond Gieorgievka and it is too late for her to reach her destination that day. We treat her sledge wagoner, a Kazakh, to some tea, we give her supper (noodles, of course) and the next day, breakfast. Her two sacks of sweets — fruit drops — have been standing in the corner of our room. She had wanted to exchange her coupons for sugar but there had been none. In the morning as she is getting ready to leave us, she shows no inclination to reciprocate our hospitality of the night, not even as much as by leaving us a handful of the sweets. I help myself to two fistfuls of her sweets when she leaves the room for a moment. I am only reclaiming those calories which she had eaten whilst with us. I will not call it theft and am not in the least ashamed of my deed. She departs without even leaving us a couple of sweets — we are not only undernourished but are also craving for something sweet — our mouths fill with saliva.

We have the coupons from Altay Zoloto but somehow nobody goes there now because we are in the depths of winter and the snow is very deep. I cannot find any Poles who would be willing to hire a Kazakh sledge jointly with me so I shall have to organize the proposed trip by myself, quickly because the validity of the coupons will shortly expire. The buran continues to blow and though sometimes there may be several days of calm, before I have had the time to find a driver the peaceful spell will probably end and the wind will blow again.

The Kazakhs are reluctant to travel far unless they have business to attend to themselves, so my chances of realizing our coupons diminish with each day. Eventually I manage to contact a Kazakh who is planning to go to Altay Zoloto and who agrees to take me with him if I pay him. The weather is fine and calm. The Kazakh arranges to pick me up at six o'clock in the morning. The whistling of the wind wakes me during the night — the buran has returned. I lie in bed and begin to dread the pending expedition: there will be snow-drifts and wolves on the steppe, I shall be starting the journey at night, a few hours before dawn and shall not return until a few hours after sunset. I know my mother feels I should go but I become more and more frightened as I hear the wind howling and raging and the noise of the ice-crystals tinkling against the window panes. I turn coward and decide against going. I feel very humiliated because I have been unable to control and overcome my fears but there is nothing I can do about it. The Kazakh goes alone and returns safely but we have forfeited my mother's wedding ring — we have been unsuccessful in 'eating it'. Though the Kazakh completed his journey safely there would have been no guarantee that the trip would have been as fortunate had the two of us gone — my fear might have attracted a disaster. I do not regret my decision because I have never been so frightened as then.

When I eventually come to leave Gieorgievka, I travel through the Altay Mountains and the settlement of Altay Zoloto, on my way to the railway station at Zhangistobe. The area is very depressing. The mountains are completely bare, nothing grows here and the landscape is lunar with the difference that instead of craters there are hillocks. Water is absent and has to be brought in from a distance of several kilometres and is bought by the bucketful. The gold mine is worked by deportees who spend all their earnings on food and water. They have to buy all their provisions from the one existing state-owned shop. As there are no settlements in the area within a large radius, nothing can be bought privately. The water is rationed officially, but the free rations which are so meagre, will barely sustain human life. For washing and laundering the water has to be bought. In the winter it is easier in this respect because snow can be melted down for water.

There is plenty of gold in the locality, some nuggets as large as hazel nuts, and the deportees devote each free hour to scrabbling in the waste heaps where they often find fragments of the precious metal, even though the soil has been panned officially. Workers queue outside the gold mart clutching pieces of gold in their hands. They receive food and clothing coupons for their gold after it has been weighed. The whole area and the miners' settlement is spectral in appearance.

All the Poles in Gieorgievka, which can be considered a relatively wealthy village, go more or less hungry, depending on whether they receive parcels from Poland with food and embroidery threads or whether they are left to their own devices completely. Everything here is dull, nothing has any colour but the Russian women are crazy about the gaily embroidered blouses and the Polish women get down to the embroidery so that a whole industry flourishes which proves very lucrative. Some ladies become so expert that they can work like greased lightning on the embroidery. From the Kazakhs they have learned to hold the needles in a fashion differing to ours, which enables them to embroider much more speedily than by our method. The ladies become adept in economizing on the coloured threads and use or draw their own patterns, which though very effective are such as to use up little thread, which makes their supplies go further. Those ladies who receive coloured threads in parcels from Poland are well off and go less hungry than the ladies with no parcels.

In March there is much bustle in the kolkhoz in Gieorgievka — spring will soon be here and the machines have to be got ready to start cultivating the soil. And there's the rub because nobody knows where the machines are to be found. Nobody can remember where they were left over the winter — they have disappeared. After lengthy deliberations somebody remembers that the machines were forgotten about somewhere along the road, they were not taken inside and must be blanketed 'somewhere' by the snow. There is nothing to be done but to wait for the snow to thaw. Nobody shows undue concern about this state of affairs. It seems highly improbable that a large group of people could forget not only to put the machines away for the winter but also to forget where they had been abandoned. Nevertheless that is the way of things here as I witness the unbelievable negligence. Naturally the machines become rusty.

With the beginning of April it suddenly gets warm. The snow thaws before our very eyes and there is water everywhere, which is soon absorbed into the soil or which evaporates and disappears. Spring lasts three weeks and summer is in full bloom by the end of April. As soon as the snow starts to melt, people hasten to sweep it away from the walls of their huts. Not I. The result is one very wet wall in our room and a pool of water on the beaten earth floor — I have almost been instrumental in 'dissolving away' the hut. Now, as quickly as possible, I tackle the task of clearing the snow away from the hut but I have delayed too long and the snow is wet and sticky. I give myself a great deal more trouble than I need have done, had I cleared the snow sooner with everybody else, whilst it was still dry and powdery. By the time I have cleared a narrow track of snow away from the hut wall I am perspiring profusely. The snow will stick to the shovel and will not come away when I try to throw it off. The wall dries eventually, but quite unnecessarily we live in the meantime for several weeks in a very damp room.

I have also been negligent in the care of the floor of our room. I have regularly swept it with a home-made broom of twigs and grasses but have not put myself to the trouble of regularly painting the floor with the cow dung. With use, the broom has lost many of its 'bristles', so that eventually I had been scratching the floor and not sweeping it and had scored out a large hollow. I fear I have ruined our landlord's floor for good because even though I try to level and smooth it over, I never succeed totally. From now, like everyone else, I smear the floor each week with the mixture of cow dung and water to produce a hard and smooth surface. I also make myself a supply of brooms.

As it gets warmer, I start looking around for some work, so as to have at least the right to buy bread. I learn that they are supposed to be building a dairy and so I apply for work there. And now the pandemonium, which could only happen in the USSR, begins. The work gives me many occasions for laughter and even at this moment as I write, I must smile. One must actually be there and see what takes place to appreciate the comicality of the situation and to realize to what Communism can lead. From the point of view of my work on the construction of the dairy, Communism leads to scenes which would not be misplaced in a farce.

A dozen or so Polish and one Russian woman apply for the work. The Russian is elderly but wiry and has, I expect, been drafted here from the kolkhoz because they do not want it said that Poles alone have built the dairy. The Russian peasant woman is sullen, keeps herself to herself and silently glowers at us from under her brows. Presently she produces a rag and blows her nose on it with refinement. In the next moment I see a Polish woman adroitly blowing her nose through her fingers — the roles have been switched. I feel sorry for the Pole and want to laugh at the Russian because she is quite obviously using a 'hanky' for the first time ever. Apparently she has been briefed to demonstrate to us that the Russians are cultured too but in the meantime, contact with them has 'decultured' the Poles.

Before setting off to the building site we hold a meeting with our boss — the tall, thin peasant lectures us that he who works not eats not, "rabotat nada" (we must work), that all people in the USSR are equal, that men and women are one and the same thing. Immediately somebody from the back calls, "Then why don't men give birth to babies?" And we all burst into laughter. He lectures us no more. As a matter of fact I feel slightly sorry for him, because he had been speaking as instructed probably, trying to spread the propaganda, but instead has covered himself with ridicule.

Stacking stones which are to be used for the foundations is the first job allocated to us. We are taken quite a distance beyond Gieorgievka, to where there are piles of stones which have been lying there for years, previously neatly stacked but now scattered in a disorderly fashion. They explain that several years ago the stones had been brought here in readiness for the construction of the dairy. However, the plans have been changed and the dairy is to be built two hundred metres away from the old site. We are to transfer the stones to the newly designated site. We start carrying the stones one by one and if the stone is a very large one it takes two of us to carry it. This makes for very slow work so our boss had a better idea: we will form a line of people and will pass the stones along the line. We duly line up but there are positively not enough of us to span the distance involved and to organize the work in this manner. I am surprised the boss does not see this immediately. The peasant scratches his head, muttering "nitchevo" (never mind) — he has a new idea: he stands us in pairs, spread out evenly between the old and the new site and tells the first pair standing by the pile of old stones to throw the stones into a pile towards the second pair. The second pair is to throw the stones to the third pair and so on until the last pair throws the stones into a pile on the new site. The larger stones have to be thrown by both partners of a pair but even so go nowhere near the next pair. We get down to the job but after the first half-hour we start to laugh: the stones are weathered and friable having lain exposed to the sun, frost and snow for several years and crumble into fragments as they hit the earth. The stones reach the newly designated site in the form of large gravel. This last useless pile of 'stones' amuses us so much that tears run down our faces from laughter. At the very beginning we had drawn the foreman's attention to the fact that the stones were breaking up into pieces where they landed on the earth but he had said "never mind" and had told us to continue. He now has the first portion of stones on the new site in the form of dust. The stones had been unsuitable for foundations before we had started moving them but — the foreman had been told to have them moved and move them he does.

After conferring together we ask for a wheelbarrow. There is no wheelbarrow. We suggest getting some planks to use as a hand barrow so that the stones can be moved without fragmenting — the idea appeals to the foreman. He goes to the kolkhoz and brings back some genuine wooden hand barrows. Consequently the work now starts to progress. We pair up, matching our physical strength because we are to be paid according to the number of stones moved, so each of us wants to transport as many stones as possible within the limits of our capability. I find a partner who is as strong as I am and we start to carry the stones on a hand barrow. We can take a few stones at a time and carry them at almost a trot or we can take more and heavier ones and walk slowly with the burden. Legs become leaden under the weight and with each step it is difficult to lift the feet off the ground. We try both methods and find that it is to our advantage to carry the lighter loads and to trot backwards and forwards quickly. Less exhausting also than carting heavier loads slowly. Some of the stones are so large and heavy that we can barely lift them on to the hand barrow and when we carry these we can only walk very slowly; however most of the time we are able to run with the lighter loads. Once we have moved the stones we have to stack them up into a cube shape of given dimensions so that when the work is finished the foreman can measure the cube and pay us according to the volume of the stones. The foreman is very indulgent and pays everyone the same amount.

At midday we go to get our free lunch which has been cooked by a Polish woman. We are given a bowl of hot skimmed milk with noodles. In the evening I buy the ration of bread to which I am entitled but I feel hungrier now than previously when I was not working because now I expend more energy in hard labour. Our cook is well-fed and carefree. She has made herself quite at home here.

And so we continue moving the stones for approximately twenty days until they have all been shifted from the old to the new site. The time has now come to start digging the foundations. The ground on which the dairy is to stand appears level to the naked eye but after measurements have been taken it is found to be not quite flat. So we start the work by levelling the area using spades to eliminate the humps. The soil from the humps is carried on the hand barrows to fill in the hollows. Anyone who has had no experience of this task will not appreciate how much soil it takes to fill in a barely noticeable hollow. The soil seems to disappear and the indentation remains an indentation. It is simply incredible and most irritating.

At last we start to dig the foundations. I make hard work of it and feel humiliated when I see other frail looking women digging far better than I do. I find it easy to hoist heavy weights but seem completely incapable of digging the spade into the hard and heavy soil. It takes us about two weeks to dig three-quarters of the required foundation trenches, when we suddenly hit gravel one day. The gravel falls back as quickly as we dig it out. It proves impossible to dig out the trenches for the corners of the proposed building because one finds oneself sliding down, spade, gravel and all. We have discovered the bed of a prehistoric river! The small round river gravel is more than two metres deep here. We call the foreman but he is not perturbed and says "nitchevo" (never mind) and "carry on digging" — but we cannot because how can one dig deeply into dry sand? We don't know whether to laugh or cry. As it proves however, the foreman must have stopped to consider the problem because a few days later a committee of engineers arrives from Semipalatynsk. After inspecting the site and the results of our efforts, they call a halt to further work on the proposed dairy. The young and pleasant Russian engineers are so horrified with what they see that they will not allow us to lift our spades again. Kolkhoz money has been wasted in paying us because the work was rashly commenced, without prior consultation with the specialists, on an unsuitable site — in other words — sabotage. I am ignorant of the final outcome of the affair and whether anyone is held responsible. It is hard not to laugh at the project of the dairy.

Whilst I was still working on the dairy construction we were taken on a very pleasant outing. Certain people specializing in clay and stones arrived and took us in lorries into the steppe to search for 'minerals'. We were given a day off from the digging and were sent into the steppe to look for clay. We were armed with spades and pickaxes which we could not even lift but the trip was a great success! It was most enjoyable driving across the steppe, as was enjoyable the company of the young experts who were searching for building materials.

When digging beneath the grass on the steppe we had found many clays of differing hues; pink, blue and green; beautiful, 'oily' superior quality, pure clays. The boffins were pleased with our samples. We were not as successful in collecting samples of stones because none of us had the strength to break open the larger stones with our pickaxes. The good-natured experts only laughed and broke open the stones themselves. We had spent the rest of the day resting and talking — yes, the trip had been voted a success!

After the building project literally collapses, I am again left without work and shall have to look for another job. I discover that they require labour in Gieorgievka in the saman 'factory'. The samans are those huge, unfired bricks or building blocks which they use here for building houses. I apply for work and am employed. The samans are made in the open, by the stream, or perhaps it is an irrigation channel — I cannot tell, where the water runs slowly and the banks are high and steep and almost pure clay. All the workers here are Polish women. Our first task is to dig up large amounts of clay from the banks and to carry it up above the stream to where the terrain is flat. It is very hard work and one has to be very strong to be able to dig the spade into the solid, sticky clay and lifting the spade with its heavy load of the clay, to carry it a few dozen metres, requires an even greater effort.

After several days of this hard labour, I develop a pain in my stomach, in the region of the navel. I think it will probably pass, that it must be the strained stomach muscles which I have not been accustomed to using, which are aching. However, a few days later still, I realize that I am well on the way to developing an umbilical hernia. The thought of what will happen should I become unfit for work, bathes me in a cold sweat. As yet I am not an invalid and have inadequate reason to take time off from work, so I console myself with the thought that the clay-digging will not go on forever. After we have dug up a suitable amount of clay, we start adding the straw and water to it as a preliminary to making the samans. We are given a horse, which tied to a stake, walks round and round treading the mixture into a pulp, whilst all the while we have to keep adding water. We get the water from the stream: one of us draws it, three of us pass the bucket up the bank standing on its steep sides, the fourth person pours the water on to the mixture. Three more of us run back to the stream with the empty buckets to supply the person drawing the water, with the next bucket. The clay and straw mixture becomes homogenous after a few hours of treading and adding water and is then ready for shaping into samans. We are given wooden moulds which must be dampened and then filled by spade with the clay mixture. The mixture is levelled with a small plank. We have to move the filled moulds a few dozen metres away where we shake the shaped saman out of the mould with one quick, deft movement. The newly moulded still soft clay disintegrates easily at this stage and great care has to be taken otherwise it is back to square one. The wet clay is heavy, the moulds are large and it is very hard work carrying and emptying them. The samans dry quickly in the Kazakhstan sun but we have to turn them carefully every so often to allow all the surfaces to dry as evenly and quickly as possible.

We work like this for several weeks and all the time I feel I am getting worse because I get an abdominal pain each time I have to lift a heavy weight. On top of everything else I am very hungry, so hungry that I keep going dizzy and I am rapidly losing weight. I shall soon look like a skeleton. I am scared at the prospect of developing a hernia and decide to attempt to terminate my employment. In Russia it is not possible to finish working at one's whim — once employed one has to continue until the job is completed. I calculate that it will be more economic not to work and thus to eat less than to work, lose weight rapidly and possibly get a hernia. I see our felcher, Anna Sacharova, who is kindly towards me but am not certain if she will help me to quit work since she has herself to think of — she cannot risk being accused of favouritism towards a deportee Pole. Anna Sacharova understands my situation, sympathizes that I am having to work so hard, and gives me several weeks' release from work. I do not know what will further happen to me but in the meantime I pluck up my courage, I shall manage somehow and later — well I shall have to see 'que sera sera'. As yet I do not have a hernia and am not dying from hunger, so I must not cross my bridges before I come to them. In spite of trying to comfort myself this way, the prospect of the future scares me more and more. I stay at home and take things as easy as possible to conserve my energies but I am continually very hungry and my bouts of dizziness get worse. My mother is also hungry.

It is now June 1941. The summer is in full bloom and it is hot and sunny. Hoping to keep up my spirits, I set off to pay a call on my friend Mrs W. who is always full of optimism and energy. She also has the radio — I need a change and perhaps my visit will give me the energy required to fight on for life. We chat and listen to the radio when suddenly the programme is interrupted and it is announced that Stalin himself will now speak. We are flabbergasted! We hear 'Batiuskha' (Daddy) Stalin saying: "The Germans have basely and deceitfully invaded Russia — the fatherland needs you" — in Russian this comes across as 'Mother Russia' and 'one and all to arms', etc. Mrs W. and I react childishly and ridiculously: we hug each other and prance around like children. We are so thrilled that at last something will be happening. Now Russia will have to go hand in glove with the decadent West — for this is how the Russians refer to Western Europe and we will no longer be the People's Enemy and deportees but must become the allies. There has been enough time for me to realize that we can never be the Russians' comrades, but it will suffice for us to be united against the Germans.

I rush back to my mother with the joyful news and we both practically weep with happiness. The news that Russia is now at war with Germany spreads through the whole of Gieorgievka like wildfire. The locals, Kazakhs as well as Russians, are scared and worried — I am hardly surprised. We stay indoors to avoid broadcasting our joy, whilst they are saddened.

When night falls, Ivan Siemionovitch comes to see us, but before knocking on our door, he walks round the whole house and even once inside our room, peers through the windows and also opens the door again to check that nobody is eavesdropping. He begins to speak only when he is convinced that it is safe to talk. Ivan Siemionovitch is also pleased at the outbreak of war and thinks it likely that now Communism will collapse. For long, apparently, has he been awaiting such a moment, a time when Mother Russia would be liberated from Communism. Poor Ivan Siemionovitch is very agitated because of his conflicting emotions: he wants Germany to win and Communism to fall but he does not want Mother Russia to suffer for it. He is ashamed of himself for rejoicing at the state of war. He asks for our opinion point blank because he so much needs a confirmation of his supposition that the Germans will win. We dare not be frank and open with him in case he is an agitator. And besides even if Ivan Siemionovitch is not an agitator, he may sometime in the future blab and land us all in the soup, not excluding himself. It might also be feasible that he could be placed in such a situation by the authorities that to save himself and his son he would be forced to tell what he had heard from us. In the USSR one becomes so guarded and suspicious that even with the most decent of people one lacks the courage to be candid. We do not therefore agree with his views — we only speculate on the possible outcome of the war and even then, very warily, letting it be understood that we had not even imagined that Communism in Russia could possibly come to an end. We hide our joy. Perhaps it is just as well that we do not promote his dreams — later his disenchantment will not be as great. The poor, elegant, old-fashioned, elderly gentleman could already rot in prison for the things he has been saying.

The following day all the Poles parade in Gieorgievka with radiant faces and I make my way to the Clinic because perchance they will now be prepared to re-employ me? They do — and with open arms because I have now become an ally and they also know that they will be needing doctors because their own will probably be sent to the front and there will be a lack of medical care behind the lines. I begin to discharge my duties — the making of samans can be forgotten.

Our Rajzdrava trembles with indignation at the German outrage. She is a zealous Communist — also a Russian nationalist, a dichotomy which is quite possible within the Russian mentality. I fail to see how the two conflicting ideologies can be conciliated because Communism recognizes no country boundaries — all people are the same and equal. However, the Russian personality is complex and agile so that there is room for both systems to co-exist. The Rajzdrava is eager to do something for the 'family' — that is the fatherland, immediately and that same day in the late afternoon, a public meeting is called in the market-place. She takes the platform herself, the platform in this instance being a few crates, and begins to speak to the crowd. Everybody with the slightest connection with the Health Service has turned up because they dare not do otherwise and also, many of the locals help swell the numbers of the general mob. The Rajzdrava speaks but in her agitation gets confused and produces a speech which had been prepared before the outbreak of war between Russia and Germany. Like a well-schooled parrot she talks about the decadent West, about those enemies of the USSR, Britain and France. All of us on the staff of the Clinic become paralysed with fear and feel extremely sorry to hear her talking such nonsense publicly, condemning the allies and making a fool of herself, when in reality she is a good and wise superior. She has quite obviously forgotten that the general situation has completely changed in the last twenty-four hours. What would happen to her should someone report on her? Our skins crawl at the thought of what she may say about the 'brave German nation who is helping Russia to fight the decadent West.' It is impossible to interrupt her but she herself notices the commotion and our horror-struck faces and realizes that her memorized speech is out of date. She does not, however, lose her head and adroitly manoeuvres the rest of her speech on to the right tracks, begging people to give donations to the Red Army which is fighting Germany. We release a breath of relief.

The next day our young nurses start to talk and laugh loudly about her slip, but nobody takes them up on it and none of us 'notices' it. They see that they are without sympathizers and never mention the topic again. What is this system which can turn a young intelligent woman into a parrot who will automatically recite a memorized lesson? There has as yet been insufficient time for the Party to write and hand her a new speech to memorize.

At the Clinic they are organizing a collection of winter clothes for the Red Army even though it is only June but the Russian winter will be coming and it is wise to start preparations now. I too, make my donation — my ski-socks. As an employee at the Clinic it would not do for me to give nothing. The nurses are awaiting their conscription into the Army. There is also talk of the doctors being called to the front. As for me, the nurses laugh into my face because I am not deserving of the honour of being conscripted into the Red Army — it is a well-known fact that I am the People's Enemy and a deportee. As if all I needed now was the 'honour' of serving in the Red Army — thank God I am unworthy of it! Because what would happen to my mother were I to join the Army? She would die in Kazakhstan. Will these naïve girls survive the war? So young and truth to tell good lassies. They are honest and moral girls, brought up without religion but able to distinguish between good and evil. The system may be blamed for the way they enjoy themselves at my expense for that is how they have been brought up. They have excellent singing voices and an extraordinary ear for music. When out walking in groups, one will begin to sing and the others will soon join in descant creating a choir. They sing in tune and without the slightest effort. What will become of them?

We are very busy at the Clinic because as always each summer there is an outbreak of dysentery. But this time Moscow has sent us medication in advance. We receive a huge quantity, almost a barrelful of bacteriophage, which is a new thing in these times and the treatment is made easy, quick and effective: this year the mortality rate due to dysentery falls and the children do not die like flies, as last year. Treatment with bacteriophage is later to be abandoned, to be rediscovered again in the West.

It must be admitted that the dispensary is well stocked which is not an easy feat to achieve, taking Russian distances into consideration. The only thing is that we have no surgical spirit, but then what are the perfumes for?

A man who works with sheep's wool and is ill with anthrax, popularly called here Siberian ulcer, comes to the Clinic. The patient is very ill, running a high temperature, oedematous and barely able to stand on his feet. He is immediately given an injection of the necessary serum and the Rajzdrava, fearing that the Clinic's staff may become infected, will allow no one to touch him, changes and burns the soiled bandages herself. The peasant recovers and nobody becomes infected even though he is treated as an out-patient and is not isolated. In Poland nobody would expect such a seriously ill man to walk to a Clinic.

We commence to inoculate the children against diphtheria and when all the local children have been given their injections, I and one nurse drive out by cart into the countryside to inoculate children in outlying kolkhozes. I am worried because I know that our quarters for the nights will be the one bed for the two of us in some Russian huts and my sixteen-year-old nurse has nits in her hair which means she must be absolutely louse-ridden. I sleep with my head so tightly bound up with a cloth that the material digs into my skin but I prefer this to becoming louse-infested. We carry a spirit-lamp with us and boil the syringes on the ground, not having a table. We are away five days and all would have been well had it not been for my fear of the lice. We inoculate several hundred children.

An elderly lady and her daughter come informally to see me at the Children's Clinic because they are Poles and ask me to examine the mother's head which is eczematous. I look at this eczema and cannot believe my eyes because on the patient's head there is a weeping, writhing mass, the size of a walnut. In Polish medicine there is a specific term for this degree of lousiness but I have never before seen it in reality, until now in Kazakhstan. I am very sorry for her because when she is told what the 'eczema' is, I know how she will feel. I tell her the truth and describe exactly how it can be cured by using home remedies. Both mother and daughter impress me: rather than tolerating the abomination on their heads for the next several days, upon leaving me they go straight to the barber and have their heads shaved. Then for the next few months, whilst the hair is regrowing, they go about with their heads covered with kerchiefs. The steps they have taken do not surprise me, their treatment is instant and radical but one has to have a strong character to come to such a decision on the spot, especially in the case of a woman.

Since felcher Anna Sacharova is on leave, I see to her patients. One day I am called out to see an old peasant and his wife who live in a large and beautiful hut which is shaded by a veranda on all sides. The hut is old and neglected but one can see that once it must have belonged to a wealthy owner. The man is seriously ill and suffering because his abdomen is distended and he is too embarrassed to pollute the air in the room in which they sleep. Old Gran, his wife, tells me their story. They came here voluntarily in Tsarist times because they had heard that there was plenty of fertile land in Kazakhstan. They had built the beautiful hut, had seeded the huge fields with wheat and had kept a large herd of cows and had been very wealthy. Their circumstances changed with the birth of Communism: they had been 'de-kulaked'. A kulak in Russia is a well to do peasant and what had taken place was that the kulaks had been reduced to beggars. The kolkhoz which had been formed just after the Revolution had taken all their fields and all of their cows, except for the one. They were allowed to keep only their hut and a tiny garden. The methods of 'de-kulaking' had been brutally cruel: all the kulaks and their families had been driven out into the steppe in the middle of the winter and had been abandoned there, leaving them to God's mercy. Those who were young and strong had returned to their village on foot — the old, the weak and the children had died in the attempt to return. The couple had been young and strong at the time and had tramped through the snow and in the frost for two days to return to their hut. The one and only pride and joy of their lives now is their tiny garden. As the ultimate peak of kulak 'profligacy', Gran grows the Siberian berries and shows me these small shrubs which bear fruit similar to the bilberry but without its flavour. However, as there are no berries or fruits here, Gran is very proud of her Siberian berries.

I cope with the children far better than last summer, having had time to teach myself paediatrics on my patients. I have gained self-confidence and am no longer scared of my small patients, since I see that not only do I not harm them but am even able to help them. I do not know how much credit I can take and how much must be given to the drugs which we had received but the mortality rate falls drastically.

My other problem still remains: pregnant women under my care are entitled to four weeks off from work before and after labour. I may not err by more than two weeks either way. If the maternity leave I give them is too long, I can be accused of sabotage — depriving the State of its workers. If the maternity leave I give is too short, I can be accused of making the woman stay at work too long 'inhumanely' into pregnancy. It is not so bad with the Russian women who are able to give me details and usually make no mistakes but I have no end of trouble with the Kazakh women. They are unable to give me any particulars, do not remember any dates and come to see me with their large bellies, simply expecting me to tell them when the baby is due. And of course they demand their four weeks' maternity leave. I make mistakes continually and keep them at work too long — they give birth sooner than expected. Abandoning professional pride, I ask felcher Anna S. for help. Anna S. is very experienced in these matters and makes no mistakes with the dates, so I call her to each pregnant Kazakh woman I see and rely on her verdict. And so it remains until the end of my stay in Gieorgievka.

The mystery of my errors is solved much later in Teheran where I meet Dr Duczyminska, a gynaecologist from Lvov. I relate my difficulties and learn much to my delight that she had experienced similar problems in Kazakhstan, until she realized that Kazakh women have a shorter pregnancy. Their pregnancies last nine lunar months and not the usual ten lunar months. From the time she started estimating the expected dates of deliveries on this basis, no more mistakes occurred. I am not an expert in this field of medicine and would never have hit upon such a daring and original theory. Dr D. restored my professional honour. I am curious to know whether there may be other tribes in the world where pregnancy is shorter than the normal. The experience with the Kazakh women is quite enough for me.

In one of the Russian villages where I had been inoculating children against diphtheria, I had noticed that all the inhabitants had damaged tooth enamel and the children's teeth particularly presented a sad picture. Their teeth were opaque and eroded but without caries. The puzzle became clear when I learnt that they kept bees in the village. The settlement was wealthy, the fields well tilled and they could afford to install hives from which they obtained sufficient honey for all the inhabitants for the whole year. They ate it continually and the children sucked rags which had been soaked in honey. The enamel on their teeth was destroyed by the acid produced from the honey.

A different medical curiosity was a village where the majority of the people have a thumb and five fingers! I had come upon the village during the occasion of the inoculations. Their hands were in no way deformed being just broader than usual and having six appendages. The stump and the five appendages in a row, evenly and normally spaced. This village is very isolated from other settlements and there are many intermarriages. Somebody at some time had introduced the abnormal gene which in time became rampant and a race of people with six appendages had bred in the village.

As always, the summer here is very hot and I, as all women always, have nothing to wear. Day in day out I wear the woollen dress in which I was deported and in my suitcase, put away as reserve, I have a woollen skirt and jumper. So I am more than pleased when I learn that some summer dress materials and plimsolls have come to the shop. They have just received their quota of summer clothes. I hurry along immediately to see what there is — the quota consists of several dozen pairs of plimsolls and a roll of material, possibly a few dozen metres of yellowish calico with a nondescript pattern of greyish flowers. How pleased I am to have been told in time by my friends to be able to buy some material and a pair of plimsolls. My friend hand-sews me a dress in the most simple of patterns possible. I dry the dress in the sun after washing it — I have never yet seen an iron in Kazakhstan. The shoes which I wore when I was deported have disintegrated, thanks to often having to prise the kiziak away from the grass by kicking it with more or less force. So I had been left with no footwear either and the plimsolls come in very useful. The problem of how to cope with the feet sweating in the rubber sole now arises. There are no socks here. I find a simple solution: I steal some thick bandages from the Clinic and use them to bind round my feet — the bandages also launder well. It cannot be said that people are not provided for in the summer by the authorities! Now, during the summer, life is easier and can sometimes be even pleasant, for example, when washing clothes outdoors in a bowl of warm water, in the sun. Even drying the washed clothes is now almost child's play compared to the same chore in the winter. Everything dries instantly and the clothes can be spread out to dry flat on the grass so that an iron is not even necessary.

Butter for sale appears on the market. It is well wrapped and packed in large crates which are labelled 'Germany'. Evidently at the last moment, the butter had been stopped from being sent to Germany and instead had been distributed within Russia. We in Kazakhstan get the butter instead of the Germans! The Russians talk about the ungrateful Germans bitterly: "We send them butter and they attack us" — whilst the Poles are delighted that the Germans have got one over the Russians.

It is likely that a similar thing happened with the honey because although there are no labels of 'Germany' on the barrels, suddenly and unexpectedly and for the first time since we have been in Kazakhstan, we see honey at the market. We have seen no butter or sugar for over a year and a half so we are very eager for both but the prices are exorbitant. It is going to be a luxury to get either. None of us can afford to buy both — we have to weigh up which is going to be more worth while. I compare the prices of the honey and the butter, I calculate the number of calories in each and discover that the prices are so calculated that a given number of calories in the form of either butter or honey will cost the same amount. They are not stupid unfortunately and have thought it out well! Honey would be nicer to have because of its sugar but it is the butter which contains the vitamins. We therefore buy some honey, just once for flavour, and later solely butter as often as we can obtain and afford it.

As last year, social life flourishes in the market. The Poles exchange news and gossip amongst themselves, learn of friends in distant kolkhozes and are either gladdened or saddened, depending on the news received. My friend, Mrs S., points out a young bearded man. I know him but now fail to recognize him. He is unshaven, dirty and ragged. We travelled in the same wagon but he is completely altered in appearance and now looks plainly abnormal. It is the student from the Lvov Polytechnic. In the atrocious conditions he has gone to pieces and is mentally ill. Turned wild, shunning people, he has become a tramp who trails round villages begging. He will sometimes do a little work and then will get fed. Mrs S. pities him, feeds him when he comes to her, cuts his hair, washes his rags and attempts to rid him of the lice. He has to be driven to get washed and watched to see that he scrubs himself. The young, stalwart, physically healthy human is a doomed man.

One day at the market, I meet an intelligent Russian man, a Communist, who had been up to something and as punishment has been sent to Kazakhstan for a year. He is a confirmed Communist, admits to having strayed off the Communist straight and narrow path and is repentant. Like a child he accepts his punishment with humility and resolves to behave better in the future. We discuss his problems but I am very careful in what I say in case he wants to provoke me into saying something anti-Communist so that he can report me and get his sentence reduced as a reward. What he says is correct in theory but impossible to implement practically. I find conversation with him interesting if only for the sole reason that it gives me an insight into the mechanics of the Communist brain. He would so much like to convert me.

At the market I also meet Mr L., who works in the production of dried milk. I did not even know that dried milk was make in Gieorgievka and am very willing to have him show me the plant. On the outskirts of Gieorgievka stands some low, eye-level scaffolding and on it lie the flat trays of fresh milk. The milk has to be stirred frequently with a spatula and dries quickly in the sun and heat. In about a fortnight the trays will be full of white, fluffy powder. The milk dries so quickly that there is no time for it to turn bad. What a simple and productive dried milk 'factory' this is!

There is also an ice store in Gieorgievka where the ice keeps all summer: the store looks like a huge barrack, without windows and with only one entrance. They cover it completely with a thick layer of clay, then straw and then clay again — good insulation. In winter, blocks of ice are hacked from the river which flows some kilometres beyond Gieorgievka, transported to the village and then stacked closely and tightly together to form the large barrack shape. The ice is then covered over with the clay and straw and finally with cow dung. At last I know the canteen's summer source of ice.

It is easier now to get food. I have my salary, the right to purchase bread for myself and my mother, am able to buy various extras and also put away a certain sum of money, without my mother's knowledge, for any unforeseen expenses which may arise. My mother is a little surprised that I economize on the food as much as I can but we must have some ready cash. I have no idea what may next happen to us.

To save on the food, I have my lunches in the canteen where they sell cheap soup. It is not always that I can get something to eat — they sometimes shut the counter because everything, that is the soup and noodles, is finished. All is well until one day a row blows up — or rather I make a scene. Many Party members, on 'business', are present in the canteen and naturally they are served first. I have no choice but to wait meekly until the waitress should come to serve me. Time elapses and I know they will soon run out of the soup, so I turn to the waitress, tell her I work and ask for some soup. The waitress has her hands full of plates, laden with meat and noodles for the Party members but says churlishly that there is nothing for me. I now demand food within my rights as a worker but it does no good and after waiting another hour and a half, I return home with an empty stomach. I consult with the S. family and Eddy S. digs out the Constitution of the USSR and we find the paragraph which refers to my rights to obtain food. I learn it by heart and thus armed return to the canteen to speak to the manager who takes sides with the waitress against me. However, his face falls when I begin to quote the memorized paragraph regarding the rights of the 'working intelligentsia'. He gets scared and is speechless. From this time on, I always get food at the canteen.

I learn from some Russian women that there is another Polish woman doctor in Gieorgievka. I ask for her name and address and am given the address of a colonel's wife. I am in a quandary because medical ethics will not allow me to tolerate the practice of medicine by an unqualified person but on the other hand the person in question is a Pole and she too wants to live. I am sorely tempted to notify the Health Department because this lady apparently demands payment for her consultations and 'treatment' and fraud of this kind is punishable in Russia, as elsewhere in the world, but somehow I cannot bring myself to do so. I confine myself to assuring the women that this person is not a doctor and mention the matter to nobody. I am later to have the misfortune to meet her again in Buzuluk under circumstances where she is at the 'top' and I am at the 'bottom'. Her behaviour then does nothing to testify well of her character.

The German/Russian front moves eastwards and the Germans living in the German settlement on the Volga are evacuated to Kazakhstan. Some of them are destined for Gieorgievka. There has already been some commotion in the village, well before their arrival — huts are having to be made ready for them, they have to be painted with the cow dung, whitewashed and furnished. The whole population awaits their arrival with great respect since it is well known that the Germans are good and hard workers. These Germans evoke esteem in spite of the war with Germany. I am an eye-witness to their arrival in Gieorgievka — they have brought everything with them apart from their cattle. There is a procession of carts loaded with furniture, bedding, cooking utensils and the Germans themselves look prosperous and well dressed. Their evacuation has been well organized and the authorities have gone out of their way to help them. Almost at once the Germans start work at the kolkhoz but they keep to themselves, do not mix with the locals, and I have no opportunity to come across them again.

For several weeks there have been rumours that a Polish Army under Polish command is being formed in Russia, so I impatiently wait for a letter from my husband. In the meanwhile here the Siberian autumn comes upon us quickly — the steppe has already become colourless, the wind rages across it, winter is fast approaching and I dread to think how we are going to survive it this time. My salary allows us to live but very frugally and I have nothing left now to exchange for the kiziak necessary for the winter. My husband's letter is late but arrives at last with the news that my husband has been released and is in Tatischevo with General Anders's Polish Army. My husband writes telling me to come to him as soon as possible.

There is unrest at the Clinic, the Rajzdrava expects to be called up to the Red Army at any moment, as does Dr Kuzienkov. In the situation which exists now, I can be assured of my job at the Clinic because they will be left without doctors and I am not 'deserving of the honour' to serve in the Russian Army, so I shall not be called up. Nevertheless, I am anxious to leave this place as soon as possible since I do not know if in the future I shall ever again have such an opportunity. My mother and I are about to leave on a journey, which as the crow flies is only 5,000 kilometres long!

There are no problems with leaving my job and Gieorgievka. I now awaken respect and jealousy because I am about to go and fight the Germans. The young nurses at the Clinic look sheepish — I have become 'deserving' of serving in the allied Polish Army and they can no longer sweep the floor with me. The silly girls are taken aback by my sudden 'promotion' and with each moment I gain importance in their eyes. Felcher Sacharova begs me to enquire amongst the Polish men, released from concentration camps and prisons, if they have come across her husband. I later do what I can but it is impossible to question everybody because the whole Polish Army consists of Poles from concentration camps and prisons. I do not find her husband.

For the last time I walk out into the steppe, strange how attached I have become to the steppe. The land now looks sad and a little formidable, dull and lifeless. The whistling wind carries dry dead fronds of grass, there is no longer any water in the irrigation ditches to bathe in, the sun only shines and gives no warmth, the steppe is no longer fragrant. Lifelessness prevails.

We pack in haste and things we still have left we throw into our famous 'cockroach trunk', leaving ourselves with a small suitcase each for personal belongings. There is agitation amongst the Poles in Gieorgievka — the young men are planning to join General Anders's Army but I outstrip them all and we are the first to leave. It is very hard to say goodbye to friends we are leaving behind in Siberia — I may never again see them. Subsequently most of them are to follow in our footsteps.

We leave Gieorgievka in a horse-drawn cart driven by a Kazakh. Luckily I had managed to save some money in secret, to pay for our journey to Saratov so I am light-hearted and happy because we have wrenched ourselves out of exile, though goodness knows what the future holds for us and I am also more than a little scared.

En route to the railway station at Zhangistobe, we travel through the Altay Mountains and the gold mining village of Altay Zoloto, where my mother's wedding ring had disappeared. The settlement looks weird: bare rocky hills, the one road covered with a thick layer of dust, running between the huts and no vegetation whatsoever, not even any grass.

We must have travelled a different route when they had brought us to Ak-Buzal from the train because we had not seen Altay Zoloto but now on our departure from Kazakhstan I see it for the first and last time. At Zhangistobe railway station we buy tickets for Saratov and I load our large trunk on to the train myself, putting it in the goods wagon. I shall never know how I managed to lift it but my efforts are to be wasted because we never see the trunk again — it is to disappear and never gets to Saratov. We are to be left without bedding, without any cooking utensils whatsoever, without various odds and ends which help to make life easier. We are to be left with only the two small suitcases but then we are on our way to Tatischevo to join the 5th Division of the Polish Army.

JOURNEY ACROSS RUSSIA

I feel different from the very moment we board the train at Zhangistobe because as an ordinary passenger and no longer a deportee, I have been restored to the ranks of free people. We sit in the train, which as all trains in the USSR has only the one class and talk to the Kazakhs who occupy the whole compartment. A Kazakh and his pregnant wife board the train at one station — he fights and jostles his way through to find a seat for her and once again I am struck by how well the Kazakhs look after their women and children. They make very good fathers and in the majority of instances, good husbands. They do have some certain manly charm because several Polish women stay behind to remain with their Kazakh men and a few more, though they leave Kazakhstan, proceed to give birth to 'Kazakhkets' in Teheran. I later work in the Polish Hospital in Teheran and am able to see these offspring of the Polish women and their Kazakh men — their parentage can hardly be concealed. Polish blood receives yet another, after the Tartar, dash of Asian blood. I wonder what will happen to these 'Kazakhkets'?

Slowly, but without any hitches, we reach Novosibirsk, where we have to change trains for Saratov. The station at Novosibirsk is magnificent, being one of the main stations on the Trans-Siberian railway line. It is sumptuously fitted out on the grand scale of the heavy 1910 style. There are several waiting-rooms — practically grand halls — and each one is decorated with marbles of different colours. Monumental staircases, also of marble, link the various levels. There are also several restaurants — canteens — and a separate 'village' built on the lines of a quadrangle, with shops, hotels and hairdressing salons. It is out of the question to get in here because the whole precinct is full of Party members and the military. This enormous station is packed with people — thousands of human beings! Some are journeying to join-up, others already in uniform are travelling to join their units and the others are a mass of refugees fleeing to the east, away from the Germans — just as I am about to journey to the west to Saratov.

The toilets at the station are large and clean and are provided with running hot water, so one can get washed and cleansed of vermin. And as in all the larger USSR stations, there is a 'Nook for Mother and Child' — a small separate room, where there are some freshly made up cots, basins and hot water. This room is reserved for the sole use of mothers with babies or small children, where they can be bathed and put down to sleep, if only for a couple of hours. Also it is obligatory for there to be a 'Red Nook' at each station and here in Novosibirsk it is a smallish room, furnished with chairs and tables, cluttered with Red literature. The room is not to be used as a waiting-room, one must not spread out here and rest or sleep. The nook is for the purpose of steeping oneself in Red Culture. It is usually empty.

On the platform there stands, as in even the smallest stations at present, a larger than life-size, cement and gilt monument, which depicts Stalin and Lenin sitting on a bench, conversing. They sit here, golden, smiling benignly and chatting about the future of the nation — Lenin and 'Uncle' Stalin.

Inside the station buildings there is pandemonium — thousands of people crowd and push and spill from hall to hall. There is nowhere to sit, not even on the floor. Nobody knows when and what train departs from which platform. As soon as a ticket-box window opens, the crowd surges forward towards it but most people fight to get to the window only to discover that it is not for their train but for one which is going in the opposite direction. Even supposing one eventually buys the correct ticket, new obstacles immediately loom on the horizon: there appears to be no way to find out when and from which platform the train will depart.

One has to have one's wits about one to get something to eat because although the canteens work with full speed, they are unable to supply the required amount of food to cater for the thousands of people who find themselves stranded here. These thousands have already been dossing at the station for a week or more and it is beyond the means of the canteens to cook even the simplest of food for such numbers. It is best to stand close to a canteen door, watch without taking one's eyes away and run and push the moment the door should open. Once the cooked food has been served, the canteens close their doors for a few hours. In time the doors open again and the whole mad scene is repeated and so forth for twenty-four hours of the day, except that the canteens are shut for longer periods during the night. We once get a plate of sweet semolina garnished with sunflower oil, which we find delicious. Then after the dessert, a bowl of soup which is the standard dish served in the canteens. From the moment of tasting the semolina I come to the conviction that every meal ought to begin with the dessert and in years to come, whenever I am able, I do this.

We are completely swamped in this crowd and I cannot visualize us ever getting out of this place. I am overcome with fear because we are running short of money, we could be dying from starvation here and nobody would take any notice. I rack my brains to find a means of getting us out of Novosibirsk. There is a large Clinic at the station, so my first idea is to turn for help to a fellow doctor there and ask him to aid us in getting out on the grounds of my mother's ill-health. My mother has had heart trouble since early youth but with medical attention and with the experience of a lifetime in managing her handicap, copes extremely well, occasionally resorting to tablets and avoiding any great strain. Having now spent several nights in an upright position, her legs are swollen and as thick as tree trunks. I realize she needs only to spend a couple of days in bed to return to normal but I hope the Russian doctor will not realize this, or if he does, will be willing to help us nevertheless provided we can give him the pretext. He proves to be too good a doctor because he grasps the true state of my mother's condition — tells me there is no need to worry because my mother, even with her heart condition, will live yet for many years, which later is to prove true. There is no question of getting any backing from him on the grounds of our mutual profession — we get no help from my medical colleague which could have been given, had he wanted to, without any fear of recrimination. So my first idea is a flop — I shall have to find another solution to the present impasse.

It now crosses my mind that it is always best to start by going straight to the top, but usually people are reluctant to do so. Alone this time, without my mother, I decide to see the station-master, who being in charge of as large a station as Novosibirsk is too important a figure to be pestered by people and there is nobody outside his office. Perhaps my attempt to see him is too daring and will backfire, but I have nothing to lose and he can only show me the door. I ask some clerk who is sitting in the vestibule if I might speak to the station-master and am admitted without any objections. Without any reference to my mother this time, I put my case to him saying I cannot wait to get to the front, there is nothing I want more than to be there treating the wounded at this very moment and helping in the war effort against Hitler. My fighting talk must have got through to the station-master since he looks very pleased. "Harasho" (good) he says and hands me a piece of paper authorizing me to obtain two tickets, out of turn, as I had asked at the very last moment. I can breathe a sigh of relief. I snatch the slip of paper on which he had written that I was on my way to Saratov to join the Polish Army and must be given two tickets immediately. I am now emboldened to well and truly push towards any ticket window which may be open. Waving my chit, I push, elbow, kick a little and in this way reach an open window out of turn, all the while shouting that I am a doctor and must instantly reach the Polish Army. People do not actually make way for me but neither do they dare to shoulder me away or curse me. In the USSR, any official slip of paper or 'bumaga' as it is called, possesses magical qualities. I buy my tickets out of turn and nobody even asks why I need the two tickets. Now it only remains for us to wait for and catch the appropriate train, without knowing when it will be departing and from which platform. I worry that we might board a train which will take us to God knows where. For the time being we are stuck in the station and spend yet another night sleeping upright on a bench. The next morning, I soon discover that my ankle is so painful that the leg will not stand my weight and there is no question of being able to walk let alone struggle and jostle through the crowd to board a train. What a calamity if I am immobilized in this throng of people! I must have torn or sprained something when I had been pushing to get to the ticket window. I am extremely worried but however luck does not desert me because in the crowd I suddenly spot an older friend from Medical School, Mira Z. The chance meeting is a thrill for us both, especially for me. Mira examines my foot, declares that she can see nothing wrong with it and expects it will soon get better. She bandages it tightly and after a few hours my foot improves so that by the next day it is as good as new.

We have already been stranded on the station for six days. On the seventh day there is a general commotion and I hear it being said that the train to Saratov will depart tonight. I ask around and get a similar opinion from an increasing number of people. There are no official announcements, no loudspeakers and all the while daylight is fading whilst the platforms are unlit so it is impossible to see where the train may be waiting. In any case it is by no means certain at which hour the train will leave, assuming it is true that there is a train going to Saratov! Finally the crowd starts to move towards a platform and we join the river of humanity, still unsure if we are going to the correct train. The total blackout exacerbates the general confusion. The jostling, the turmoil impregnates me with terror but somehow or other we manage to board the train still being uncertain if this is our train when it moves off. There had been no official announcement nor had there been any station staff on the platform whom I could ask to reassure myself. It is only after some time has elapsed that I realize that at least we are travelling in the right direction — if not to Saratov itself.

The train crawls along slowly, sometimes coming to a stop in the open fields and halting at every small station. At one such station we are told we shall be here for some time since this is where we can get 'kipiatok'. Kipiatok is the name for the boiling water which people use to brew their own tea. This custom is a generally accepted one in Russia, particularly on the Trans-Siberian route. We get some kipiatok and next go to the toilets. And I have never seen anything like it in all my life! A long rectangular room, a raised wooden platform running the length of it on one side, on the platform a long wooden seat and on the seat, holes every metre or so — about twenty holes in all. And under the holes a stinking trench. Men, women and children, all sitting together, contemplating nature and observing each other mutually. There is no toilet paper. The complete scene, with its corresponding smells, its symphony of noises and apt expressions on the faces of some of the occupants, is to haunt me for many days to come.

In the compartment there are rumours that this train will not be going to Saratov itself and concurrently I hear some Russians saying that we are close to the Volga and that from where we are, one can get to Saratov quicker by going on the Volga than by train. At dawn, after our two day journey, some of the Russians decide to continue the journey to Saratov by boat. We come to the same decision and join them when they leave the train at some tiny station. We hope to reach Saratov sooner this way and without eventually having to change trains. We get down from the train but before I realize what is happening, the Russians have hired a cart and have driven away. We are left alone in an unknown place at the mercy of another wagoner from whom we hire a cart. I suppose it could have been worse — there might not have been any more carts.

We reach the landing-stage on the banks of the Volga. Words fail me when I see the mighty Volga. The far bank is barely discernible, the water is as blue as the bluest sea, flowing slowly, waves rippling in the light breeze — the majestic river in all its glory. Little wonder that the Russians sing 'Volga, Volga, our own Mother' — a river which is a giant, a river which is mother, giving life to verdant villages along its banks. The landing-stage and the ferry-boats are small but one can sail to various destinations from here. There is a crowd of people round the ticket-office and I join the fray. I am aware of kicking and elbowing somebody because otherwise I shall never get our tickets. I buy the tickets and we board the ferry — what a marvellous feeling! The calm, the quietness, the clear air, the smell of water, even though there are many people on deck. The sun is shining and there is a holiday feeling to the day — I have forgotten the existence of such simple pleasures. The boat is clean and one can even buy buns on board! We sail off smoothly, the boat barely rocking and there are magnificent views on either side. We sail past villages clustering on the banks, which look clean and prosperous, where the houses are whitewashed and surrounded by gardens and orchards. At times the river banks disappear from view and it is almost possible to imagine one is at sea. I am in good spirits, I shall soon see my husband, the day is beautiful and everything is rosy.

I spot a shabbily dressed Kazakh carrying a bundle thrown over his shoulder, who apparently sensing that I like and am in sympathy with the Kazakhs, comes over to talk to me. He needs somebody to talk to and share in his joy: he has just been released from prison, having served several years, and is returning home at long last. The Kazakh is very isolated because the Russians will not go near him or talk to him — I think they can tell that this is a man who has just been in prison and will have nothing to do with him, all the more so since he is a Kazakh. In his loneliness he has turned to a non-Russian since he had heard us talking in an alien language. I learn that he has spent several years in prison but has just been released with the announcement of the general amnesty because of the war. Little does the poor Kazakh realize that he has been released so that he can be conscripted into the Red Army and sent to the front. He is only thrilled to be going home at last but I very much doubt whether he will be allowed to remain there for long. The Russians are forming platoons, consisting solely of Kazakhs, who after being given a short training are sent to the front. I take pleasure in talking to him, the kind of pleasure one can experience in the company of an intelligent and cultured person. After a while the conversation turns to religion or rather to a belief in God, as usual. The Kazakh now knows that I am Polish, so does not scruple to talk openly on this matter. However I cannot be a hundred per cent certain that he is not a provocator and therefore give evasive answers and am ashamed of doing so but dare risk nothing.

Looking back, I do not think any of the Kazakhs I had spoken with, had in fact been provocators, but had merely raised the subject because of a need to discuss their spiritual experiences with an outsider. They are desperate to resist the atheistic attitude of Communism and seek support from anyone who can sympathize with them.

I also get approached by a young Russian engineer and the conversation again turns to religion. Can the whole of the USSR be rife with provocators in many guises or can it be that people cannot exist without a religion of some kind, think about it but fear to discuss the existence of God with their own, so make most of any occasion to talk with a foreigner?

I should have to live in the USSR for a good few years to find my answer but as like as not, even this would not help since I should be certain to come across a provocator sooner or later, which would result in my arrest for 'religious propaganda' before I had had the time to conclude my 'research'.

We had left the landing-stage at nine o'clock in the morning and by the afternoon we arrive in Saratov. The weather here is different, there is melting snow everywhere, it is very damp, cloudy, windy and cold. My felt boots, from Zakopane, which I have been saving for just such a time as now, because they were useless in Kazakhstan, quickly become sodden. My feet are cold and wet, I am cold all over, all the more so since my cap is a thin woollen one and I am not wearing my trousers or gloves. The home-made Kazakhstan fur cap and gloves are packed away in our wicker trunk. I am wearing my 'elegant' outfit and suffering. The trunk contains all my warm clothing and the trunk has not arrived in Saratov with us . . . .

TATISCHEVO — IN THE 5TH DIVISION

Polish uniforms are in evidence here in the port of Saratov so I ask around for the whereabouts of Tatischevo, since that is where I shall find my husband. I am told that Tatischevo is quite some distance away from Saratov but some helpful Polish soldiers offer to give my mother and myself a lift there by army lorry. We arrive safely in Tatischevo and since most of the officers know each other, my husband is soon informed of our arrival.

The Polish Army camp in Tatischevo is located on a firing range, which the Russians have handed over to the Poles, to be used for the formation of General Anders's Army. The camp had been used by the Red Army for its summer manoeuvres and is thus fitted out accordingly. It is large, situated amidst open fields but the officers' quarters are wooden huts which resemble summer holiday cabins, in fact quite attractive and fine for summer weather — the water taps are out in the open on the grass. It must be lovely here in the summer but not now that winter is approaching. There is also a wooden built canteen, mess, clinic and hospital. Our commanding officers have installed themselves in one of the larger wooden huts whilst the rest of the huts have been allocated for the use of the army families, who have come here. There is snow on the ground, the temperature is beginning to drop and the soldiers have to live in tents. My mother and I are directed to a hut where the women sleep on palliasses, side by side on the floor. We have no heating whatsoever, everything is so damp that it is impossible even to dry a towel after having washed outside in the ice-cold water. We are very cold here. The army shares its rations with the civilians since the Russians have made no allowances for them. It is most unpleasant to think that we, the army families, are eating the soldier-starvelings out of hearth and home, in the strictest meaning of the expression. I went hungry in Kazakhstan but never sponged off anybody.

We are given soup, three times a day, from a communal cauldron and have to carry it in mugs or billy-cans, back to our hut. As the kitchen is some way off, the soup is cold by the time we reach our hut. The soldiers also share their bread ration with us.

Some friends from Medical School, whom I meet here, are astounded that it has only taken me ten days to cover the distance from near to Semipalatynsk to here because the journey usually takes up to three weeks to complete. It seems I have broken all records whilst I had thought my journey to have been exceptionally lengthy!

Unfortunately, there is nowhere one can talk, even with one's own husband. Outside, it is freezing and the days are short. We have no access to the canteen because although my husband, as a doctor, is a second lieutenant, he is not allowed to bring in a civilian. I am not allowed to bring a man into our strictly female hut. There is discipline! We may be starvelings and poor wretches but discipline must be maintained. As though it was of prime importance! And so my husband and I can only meet outside where we walk around, frozen and miserable because it is suddenly winter; we are in the grip of freezing temperatures with the wind howling and snow falling. We usually take our walk in the dusk because my husband is occupied during the day but they even try to make this impossible when I am told that it is forbidden to walk out with a man at night. And we have so much to tell each other. We continue our walks occasionally but I feel like a hunted animal.

Our small huts are unheated, the water from the outside taps is ice-cold, there are no bowls for washing in and even if we had them, there is nowhere to put them down. There are only narrow passageways between the rows of palliasses which cover the floor. In spite of our jubilation and joy that the Polish Army is forming, life is very hard and sad.

Starved, ragged Poles are arriving all the time from prisons and concentration camps, covered with sores and ulcers due to lack of vitamin C, with frost-bitten feet, without shoes, their feet wrapped in rags.

Skeletons, wearing tattered remnants of army uniforms, bustle about the camp. The majority of them are fit only to be hospitalized but they are the Army, living in unheated tents and coming under army discipline. My morale gets worse with each day.

The winter becomes so severe in the beginning of November, 1941, that the life of the soldiers in the tents becomes impossible without any form of heating. Columns of soldiers are sent out into the nearby forests to fetch wood. They attempt to cut a dash as they march but most of them are barely able to drag their feet. They return with the wood but their bare hands and feet clad in torn 1939 boots, are even more frost-bitten. It becomes a vicious circle: they either freeze in their tents or have a little warmth at the cost of more frost-bite, colds and bronchitis.

The situation is tragic — to improve the living conditions of the soldiers, even if only slightly, the command orders the soldiers to dig themselves in. They will be warmer in the dug-outs because at least there will be no wind or draughts and the tents can serve as the roofs. So the soldiers start digging the frozen earth with their frost-bitten hands, with visions of kindling fires in the dug-outs to warm themselves by!

When my husband had written to me in Gieorgievka telling me to make all haste to come to Tatischevo, he had done so on the recommendation of

General Boruta-Spiechowicz, who had advised the soldiers to 'gather in' as many families as possible to the army. Later the situation changed. The Russians did not provide any food rations for the civilians who were attached to the army, nor did they provide any suitable quarters for them. Soon after my arrival in Tatischevo, the attitude towards the army families underwent a radical change: the families were seen as a ballast for the army, which was supposed to be leaving for the front. A most unpleasant situation indeed for the civilians. I have moments when I regret leaving Gieorgievka.

Rumours circulating round the camp say that the civilians are to be evacuated to a camp in the south of Russia. I have to decide: do I stay with the army and send my mother alone to the camp or do I stay with her and get myself sent with her to the south? Youth, fervour and even perhaps egoism wins and I decide to stay with the army and to dispatch my mother alone to the civilian camp in the south. How bitterly am I later to regret this decision! My mother is to survive in the non-existent camp, only by a sheer miracle!

A special train is laid on and during the night on the station in Tatischevo, my husband and I load my mother on to it. Everything happens in complete darkness and creates a most painful impression upon me. My heart bleeds when I say goodbye to my mother. Just behind the locomotive there is the provisions wagon, crammed with tins and food-stuffs, overseen by the train escort of a few military men. My only consolation is that it will be warmer in the south and my mother will be well cared for in an organized camp. I have no idea how long we shall be separated. I am not to see her again until September 1942, in Teheran. I return to the camp with my husband and, although I want to participate and fulfil my duties in the army, I feel dreadful.

In the meantime we hold soirées in the presence of General Boruta-Spiechowicz. Women soldiers of the highest rank, drape themselves artistically at the General's feet, the rest stand or sit wherever they can, and sing. We sing sentimental and aggressive soldiers' songs — we might be Girl Guides — what am I doing here? These women appear ridiculous and infantile — they sing of 'honour' in the battlefield, of 'glorious' death in action, with great enthusiasm. In simple words, we wallow in cheap sentimentality. To this is added a most discordant note because we find there are quite a lot of professional prostitutes amongst us. Upon their invasion of Poland, the Russians had hunted out as many prostitutes as they could and had deported them into the depths of Russia. Hearing that the Polish Army was forming in Russia, these prostitutes had filtered through to Tatischevo and had immediately found themselves protectors. They acquired a status of some importance and were immune. Perhaps this was why the woman commanding officer had issued the order prohibiting us from walking round the camp at night in the company of a man? Since night falls very quickly now, the order has deprived me of the one opportunity of talking with my husband who is tied up in the Clinic until five o'clock in the afternoon. The prohibition is, in my case, an inhuman order — thanks to the 'ladies'. Whilst they, in spite of orders and prohibitions, manage anyway.

I continue to suffer qualms of conscience — was I unfair in sending my mother alone to the south? But I keep my resolution and as soon as my mother has left, I join the Women's Auxilliary Service as a doctor. Unexpectedly, one day we are called together by the woman commanding officer and are made to swear an oath of allegiance and loyalty to the army. It is impossible for me to back out because I have nowhere else to go but I hope the ceremony is a formality only, since I have no intention of being a soldier.

The commanding officer gives me my first job, which is to distribute one jar of jam amongst the children of whom there are many here: I have to share out the one jar of jam between about thirty children. They receive less than a teaspoonful each and I have to exact all my will-power to stop myself from licking the jar clean, giving some child the last scrapings. I even manage to stop myself from licking the spoon!

Since there are fewer and fewer remaining civilians here and since I am now officially in the army, I am no longer entitled to live in the hut with the women civilians. After my experience with the task of sharing out the contents of the jam pot, I turn to the major, who is a doctor, ask to be engaged in some work as a doctor and to be allocated quarters. The major is very friendly and offers me work and a corner for my bed, in the Clinic. The woman commanding officer refuses to agree to the arrangements. I am told I am a woman soldier, I must live with the rest of the volunteers, must attend drill and must learn to shoot! I know myself and I know that I would never be capable of shooting anybody — in my case my vocation is to save life and not to kill. Unfortunately I had been placed in a situation where I had had to swear the oath of loyalty to the army. My situation is frankly incredible: I had volunteered as a doctor but they want to make a soldier of me. I know that this business of shooting is only theoretical, that nobody will ever expect me to go to the front with a rifle in my hands, but the circumstances are enough to repel me from serving in the army. And why should I, a woman, have to learn to shoot? After all, the army doctors do not carry arms. I am aware that all the male doctors from the rank of second lieutenant upwards, have been through basic training but I am a woman and the circumstances at the present moment are exceptional: we are at war. It seems that rules and regulations and equality do not take circumstances into consideration.

For the time being I must sit tight and await my future fate. I can see soldiers bringing in freshly cut down spruce trees, covered with frost and snow, from the forest. They build a large fire on the construction site, from the sawn off branches and commence to build a barrack from the soaking wet logs, for the women soldiers. We are to move in as soon as the roof is finished. About a hundred women are to live here, sleeping in tiered bunks, washing in the ten basins provided, keeping warm in the heat from the one stove.

Finally I come to the end of my tether and tell my husband that I refuse to live in the women's barrack, will not be drilled or taught to shoot, and will never again attend any soirées, since I refuse to make a fool of myself. After conferring with colleagues and with the permission of his direct superior, my husband decides to shelter me in the barrack where he lives. We are playing for time. I become another of the ladies who hide away in the barracks. My hiding place is an officers' barrack where doctors alone live. The room is tiny and has four bunks. I make the number of people living here up to five and sleep with my husband on one of the bottom bunks. There is only a very narrow space between the bunks and when all five of us are here, there is no room for us all to sit down on the sides of the two bottom bunks. My fellow doctors tolerate me but the situation is very unpleasant and awkward for us all.

I cannot leave the barrack during the day, in case somebody should see me. What shall I do when nature calls? I have a tin mug for drinking from and so I use it for the other purpose also — just as well my aim is good — and then I empty the mug's contents through chinks in the floor-boards. The second call of nature has to be postponed until it gets dark, when I use the outside convenience, worrying about being seen or meeting somebody there. One can see the funny side of the situation but I am afraid I cannot laugh. I can only get a cat-lick at night, in the corridor, using a basin of luke-warm water which I manage to heat on the only stove at the end of the corridor. The worst of it is that most people have to get up three or four times during the night to go outside. I do not know if this is a direct result of the cold or infections but our kidneys produce unheard of amounts of urine. Naturally, going outside intensifies and hastens the next call of nature and so on, in a vicious circle.

My husband and our colleagues feed me with soup which they bring across and also share their bread with me. Sometimes, when I can make myself some tea during the night on the stove in the corridor, I drink it from the same mug which I use for the other purpose. What a good thing that one is not sickened by one's self. I wonder how many other people are forced to such abhorrences by circumstances?

I am very bored, there is nothing to read and I must not leave my little prison. In the mornings I wait for my soup, then I tidy up a little and again wait for the food my husband will bring me. The afternoons also, I spend by myself. It is only in the evenings with the return of my room-mates that I get to talk a little. How long must I live like this?

The whole barrack is crawling with mice. Fortunately, I rather like mice. I sometimes sit and watch the antics of whole families of them, as they search for food but sadly they are very timid and will vanish at the slightest movement. Till one day, the mice disappear, for no apparent reason, as though they had been swept off the face of the earth. I miss their company and practically worry what has happened to them. There is a deathly silence — no scrabbling or rustling. Then on a certain day I hear a vigorous scratching which alarms me. That night I see the first rat — and this is enough to terrify me! I loathe and fear rats because they are aggressive, will bite and at the same time, are very intelligent, so as opponents, cannot be taken lightly. I sleep uneasily, I worry they will bite, because they are into everything and even scurry over our bunks. The rats are a threat, they evoke repulsion and fear in me and also a grudging admiration. Their shrewdness and physical agility is fantastic — I had dried some bread for a dark hour of need, had placed it inside a leather brief-case which I had hung on a nail high up on the smooth vertical wall, so high up, that I had to stand on tip-toe to reach the brief-case — in the morning the brief-case is still there but the bread has gone! The rats have bitten a hole through the side of the case! I cannot imagine how a rat could have climbed up the sheer wall to a height of about two metres.

There will sometimes be a lighter moment: my colleague, a friend from University, Dr J. K., gives me a magnificent present: namely a piece of loaf-sugar. He has had the sugar for some time but saved it for me when he heard I was coming to Tatischevo — I should not have been capable of so doing. The present gives me tremendous pleasure, not only spiritually but also gastronomically and my friend's unselfish kind heart inspires me with renewed faith in people and hope for a better future.

One of the doctors in our room remarks that my husband could face difficulties through concealing me here. I am well aware of this but somehow it particularly hurts me to hear him saying so. I am very worried because where can I go? The colleague advises me to go into the village to ask for lodgings. I set off in the frost, in the snow, in my lightweight Zakopane boots, to look for a place of my own. I walk from hut to hut but nobody will have me. One peasant woman takes pity on me, although she is not prepared to offer me lodgings, and seeing that I am frozen, gives me a dish of hot marrow and millet, which I find delicious. Once again in Russia, I am out begging — and what can possibly come of it? Even were I to find lodgings, then when the Polish Army moves, I should be left here, completely alone, without any means of supporting myself, severed from the group of Poles, lost in Russia. In this moment, I decide to leave Tatischevo and seek out my mother. I return from the expedition with a firm plan formulated in my head — I have had enough of hiding like a criminal, of begging like a beggar amongst the Russians, I will not be a soldier but will be myself, a doctor. I am young and adventurous and believe that I can manage to take care of myself. Admittedly, it may be virtually impossible to trace somebody in Russia but I have confidence that I will find my mother, that nothing is impossible. I feel better as soon as I make my decision because the thought of doing something concrete and useful immediately gives me a lift. I shall look for the civilians' camp in the south of Russia. I return to the barrack in a completely different mood — I can see an end to my passive waiting.

The next day, on the 15th November, 1941, my husband drives me to the railway station in Saratov.

DEPARTURE FROM TATISCHEVO

There are masses of people on the station: the local Russians, who are going east to flee from the Germans and the Red Army soldiers who will be going in all directions to join their units or to the west, to the front. In the throng, I find a group of Polish soldiers from Tatischevo, who are going to Koltubanka where they will be training as pilots. It is precisely this group of young men who later get to Britain and take part in the Battle of Britain.

I attach myself to this group and tell them of my intentions, which they consider to be impossible to accomplish. They convince me — and at this moment my plan to look for my mother, collapses. I have nowhere to go. I will not return to Tatischevo, so I can only go with them to the headquarters in Buzuluk — I do not know what will happen to me later on but I have to leave here for somewhere.

The Russian trains no longer run according to a timetable — the trains come and go without prior announcements, at all times of day and night and the young soldiers have already been here for several days, waiting for a train to Buzuluk which is near to Koltubanka. It makes sense for me to get to Buzuluk because I know that the Chief of the Medical Corps there is General Szarecki, with whom my husband was in prison camp in Starobielsk, so I shall be able to turn to him for help.

The future pilots take me under their wings as though I were their sister, sharing their bread with me, trying to make it possible for me to bed down and get some sleep, I could say they are too good to me. Every few days their liaison officer comes to see them from Tatischevo, bringing their ration cards and various news.

We are on the station for about two weeks, squatting on the waiting-room floor, on our suitcases and bundles. We have to watch our luggage most vigilantly because the crowds pass by us all the time, a river of humanity — and if a suitcase were to be nudged, it would move along with the crowd and would flow out of sight. It would be out of the question to attempt to retrive it because even if one managed to grab it, the crowd would not allow one to return 'against the current' — one can get lost amongst the masses on the station and be left completely alone, helpless, with the suitcase in hand. This situation applies to me only because the young strong soldiers would be able to manage but I am nervous and do not take my eyes off my suitcase when I am not sitting on it.

We smoke cigarettes — one between a few persons, passing it along after a few drags each, and talk of the past, the present and chiefly the future — we never run out of topics. We have a marvellous arrangement to secure a place at a table in the canteen. The table is always occupied by some of us and when a meal is served and eaten by the people already at the table, we change places and the next group of us gets a meal. In this way, we all get something to eat, three times, every twenty-four hours.

My husband comes to the station to see me. With his first visit he brings unpleasant news: I have been expelled from the army for desertion. The edict has been read publicly and loudly. I suppose I ought to be grateful that I have not been arrested and court-martialled! That could have happened because I had been sworn into the army. I am very sad that I have placed my husband in such a 'dishonourable' position — "Have you heard about his wife? — A deserter, what a disgrace in the family!" Although my husband does not adopt this attitude towards my escape, I know that other officers do.

Apart from the sadness, I experience shame, not on behalf of myself but for 'mine', that they should have felt it necessary to find fault in discipline under such atrocious circumstances and from whom? A woman, who is a doctor and who wanted to execute her duty as a doctor in these times of war. My intuition tells me that some female had been jealous of my profession and had taken revenge. But that she should have been allowed to get away with it?

My husband's next visit is the cause of a nightmarish experience. He hears that there is a hotel near to the station and thinks that having spent so many nights sleeping on the floor, I ought to book in to recuperate, undress and sleep in a real bed. The suggestion is tempting although I am worried that my group will leave without me. We go to the hotel. It is an old, tall building, the corridors wide and long, doors leading off on either side to rooms where beds are arranged closely in rows, side by side. There must be forty to fifty people of both sexes sleeping in each room. Each bed has a palliasse, a sheet and a blanket. I occupy one bed and look around. There are dirty, ragged people sitting on the beds and, to my horror, I see that most of them are grimly scratching, whilst others search their clothing, stitch by stitch, frequently squashing 'something' between their finger nails. Lice! — they are all lousy!

It soon gets dark but there is no lighting anywhere, either in the rooms or in the corridors. I set off to look for the toilets. Various shadowy shapes pass me on the corridors, so I ask one of them the way. At length I find the toilets but washing is out of the question because there is no water. Returning to my room, I see a distant glow at the far end of the corridor, which is moving towards me — eventually I can tell that it is three old women, one of whom is carrying a candle. They look like witches: tattered, dirty, edentulous, white hair wisping in strands over their faces — they are a frightening sight. Apparently they are in high humour because their laughter issues forth from their gummy mouths like the croaking of toads. I had once seen a similar scene in the Grand Guignole Theatre of Horrors in Paris. In one act of the particular play, there had been three old, mad women in a mental hospital who had just gouged out the eyes of a normal, young woman with knitting needles. The young woman had been placed in the institution by her family who were after her money. The actresses playing the roles of the three mad women had looked just like the three women now before me in the corridor. In the morning, I am quite determined to return to the station and squat on the floor.

This nocturnal episode does not herald the end of the nightmare in this hotel which is a shelter for the homeless. In the morning, seeing people cleansing themselves of lice and killing the vermin, makes no impression on me now but what does horrify me is the neighbouring bed which has been slept in by some man. When he leaves, I see that his bed is covered by a grey, moving 'carpet'. It is incredible that such a number of lice should be able to live off one human being — his bed is literally astir! I escape back to the station where it is incomparably cleaner.

On the station, lice also abide. In every free moment, when I am not sleeping, on duty at the canteen table, talking and smoking our circulating cigarette, I rush to the toilet to de-louse myself. More often than not I find a louse or two — I hope to goodness I am eradicating them before they have had a chance to breed on me. I keep catching the lice from the people who pass in the crowd — there is nowhere to get away from contact with humans and even on the benches, people sit tightly together. In spite of frequent trips to the toilets and in spite of searching my clothing regularly, I can still feel something biting me round the breast-bone though I cannot find any lice on me. It suddenly strikes me that I never undo the bundle of money which I wear on a string round my neck next to the skin. I unravel the hanky containing the money and — *voila!* The king of all lice — huge, fluffy and because it is clean, white in colour!

I am very frightened of getting head lice because it would be impossible for me to de-louse myself there. I have my fine-toothed comb fortunately, and comb my hair with it several times a day. I am also careful never to touch anybody's head. My efforts pay off and I never get head lice. The Russian women refugees are in worse position because many of them did not have the time to even bring a comb, not to mention a fine-toothed one. They are louse infested — they scratch, they know they have head lice but have no means of eliminating them. I have seen one young woman crying for this reason. I cannot lend her my comb because needless to say, I should never again see it. She is one of the multitude of women on the station who have no combs.

In my suitcase I have a change of outer clothing and underclothes but I do not want to 'louse up' the clean things although I have been wearing the same clothes for almost a month — I shall wait until I have a chance to have a bath.

I sometimes feel sorry for the refugee Russian women because many of them had lost their heads in fleeing from the Germans and have not even brought the most essential items with them. I had also forgotten to take eating utensils when they had come to deport me. One of the refugees had sealed up clarified butter in jars 'for the war' and had brought it with her but she cannot now eat the butter by itself and it is impossible to get any bread here. I render her a kindness and exchange some bread from my military friends' bread ration, for a jar of butter. The deal is satisfactory to both parties who consume the bread and butter.

The station is swarming with 'Krasnoarmiec' — that is people wearing the Red Army uniform, both men and women. One of these women who is carrying a baby in arms, comes over to ask me to hold her baby for half an hour whilst she goes to sort out her affairs in some office. She must have thought I looked as though I could be trusted so I feel, in my vanity, honoured and take the baby on my knees. Now I have already been holding it for almost two hours and feel less and less honoured by the mother's trust in me and more and more worried that she will not return, leaving me literally holding the baby. And what shall I do with it — I do not even know if it is a boy or girl? What shall I feed it on? The mother does return at last and thanks me for my kindness whilst I breathe a sigh of relief.

Our life on the station settles down into a routine. We have organized an excellent timetable for what to do when, when to keep an eye on the canteen, when to de-louse, when to talk. One problem has not been regularized — the problem of how to straighten our legs, stretch out and sleep. My 'guardian angels' try to fix me up as well as they can, the problem being that the crowds are all louse-infested, and there is no room to lie down without touching somebody. I am found a space on the floor by the exit and covered with their coats. People are constantly coming in and going out and since there is a severe frost outside, I get so cold that I am forced to move in the middle of the night. Small wonder that this space by the door is vacant at night! The canteen next springs to mind as a possible alternative to getting a good night's sleep — only the tables there are round. I make futile attempts to curl up into a small ball — dog-fashion — on a table but either my head or my legs keep falling off. The whole of the canteen floor is always occupied — some people keep permanent sleeping-places here and guard them well because there is never a free area on the floor, for me to grab. When I eventually resign from attempting to sleep on the table and climb down, I have to be very careful indeed not to tread on people. In the end I become reconciled to sleeping sitting upright on my suitcase.

There is no sight or sign of our train. Somebody gets the bright idea of going to the town market where it may be possible to buy something to eat.

Five of us depart for the market, having first ascertained that there would be no train to Saratov, that day. We find the market but find nothing to eat except carrots. There is a queue for the carrots at the stall but luckily, one of our young men, helped by a combination of his strong build and uniform, manages to push his way to the front of the queue and buys a large quantity of carrots. We are delighted because none of us has eaten anything raw for months and we are in danger of getting scurvy. We eat the carrots with great pleasure — they are juicy, sweet and crunchy.

On the station, I meet a young Polish woman who has also 'escaped' from the army in Tatischevo. The Miss is attractive, cheerful and worries about nothing. She does not yet know what she is going to do with herself but is confident that she will manage. For the present, she wants to explore Saratov. She departs and does not return. She must have met with success in finding a Russian protector. I have no idea if her name was mentioned in the edict as a deserter — anyway, both she and I are now traitors to the Polish Cause.

Unfortunately in the years to come I shall forget many of the names of the young men in my group and will regret not being able to thank them for looking after me. However, I shall always remember Officer Cadet K. because I cannot figure him out. I do not know who or what he is. He is a most interesting young man who particularly boasts of having friends in high places as well as in the Church. He is well-read, widely travelled, mentions names of people I also know. He tells us credible stories about people, just before the outbreak of war. Is he a spy or just a humbug? Is he telling the truth? I knew many people in Lvov, I also knew local relationships and certain facts which Officer Cadet K. mentions — so I know them to be correct. Whoever he is, he will help me enormously in Buzuluk. I am to see him again in Jerusalem in 1944, looking very elegant in civilian clothes, carrying a brief-case with the air of a confident and important person. Why should a young and healthy man be in Jerusalem in the middle of the war and not at the front with General Anders's Army? He does not see me and I do not stop him.

Early in December, we at last hear that there is going to be a train to Buzuluk, so we stay awake all night, fearing to miss it. At about five o'clock in the morning there is a bustle and we learn that a train has arrived and is on a siding. It is still night and the station is very dark — the train is unlit because of the blackout. *En mass* we board the train and the first thing which hits me is the heat! The Russian trains are either totally unheated or if they are heated, then unbearably so. Nobody bothers about tickets because everybody just has to get somewhere.

The conductor walks through the train just once during our journey, and shows no intention of checking any tickets, he must know that nobody has them. My 'guardians' find me a bench-seat and with an excess of solicitude, cover me up so well with their coats that in a very short while I am wet with perspiration. In addition to this they keep feeding me all the time — we have plenty to eat because, as the military who are travelling to fight against Hitler, they get bread and something hot to eat at every sizeable station. I am very underfed and thin, so I eat up everything they give me. After a few days' travelling in the stifling heat of the train, we lose a group of young men who have to change trains to get to Koltubanka. I and a few young people, including Officer Cadet K., continue on to Buzuluk to the Polish Army Headquarters, I to look for General Szarecki. We get to Buzuluk at about five o'clock in the morning.

BUZULUK

Buzuluk station is small and lies some way beyond the town. It is still dark — and in the dark we find the receiving point for the Poles, for civilians as well as the military. The Polish Army has no uniforms, so the several Polish military who are officiating here, wear British Army uniform but have attached the Polish Eagle to their caps. The emblems have been hastily fashioned from tin-can lids. The room is small but warm because the stove is burning full blast, and all the incoming Poles are given hot soup: English pea soup. The receiving point is open round the clock — necessary information is imparted, soup is distributed and the Poles are welcomed initially by the warm room and a dry roof over their heads. My companions decide to walk into the town but I sit down on my suitcase and wait for day-break. I am very tired — I want to rest a little and enjoy the feeling of being amongst my fellow countrymen. I feel quite secure.

Since the town is several kilometres away, I hit the road as soon as it gets light at eight o'clock, leaving my suitcase behind. Outside there is snow and frost. There are no buildings along the roadside, only snow-covered fields. I find it becomes increasingly more burdensome to march along the road, through the snow. I feel peculiar, I think I must be not only tired but also ill. The road is empty of human beings, so I must continue walking, were I to sit down, I should freeze to death. Somehow I reach Buzuluk at last and find the headquarters. To secure myself some place to sleep, I report first of all to the women's barracks where I am faced with a disappointing snag because there is an epidemic of typhus in the barracks, they are in quarantine and will permit nobody from the outside to enter. I decide to go straight to General Szarecki for help — and here a second snag crops up: the General is away and will not be back until tomorrow. By a happy coincidence, the General's aide-de-camp is Dr M., a friend of my husband's — they were together as prisoners in the Russian prisoner of war camp. Dr M. is very pleased when he sees me and learns who I am, proceeding to take a great interest in my affairs. Recounting my adventures takes up a lot of time and it is already late in the afternoon by the time I start walking back to the station, to my suitcase and my soup. I feel even worse the next day but somehow manage to get back to headquarters with my suitcase. General Szarecki welcomes me with open arms and assures me that he will find me work.

131

In the afternoon, I start looking for some lodgings. I ask around everywhere I can and eventually learn from a Russian woman that in a certain house there are some Poles alone, so they would probably give me shelter. When I get to this house, the first person I meet is dear, kind Professor L. who had been in my wagon when we had been brought to Kazakhstan. Professor L. is here with his family and they rent one room from 'The Colonel's Wife', who in turn has rented the whole house from a Russian woman, and is subletting rooms to the Poles. Mrs Colonel has a good head for business: she passed herself off as a doctor in Gieorgievka and here she sub-lets rooms. Just my luck to come across her again! Professor L. says he will gladly share their room with me but cannot do so without prior permission from Mrs Colonel, who is not at home at present since she works at headquarters and will not be back until the evening. In the meantime he proffers me bread and a glass of milk — I expect is is his supper I am consuming but I am very hungry and do not know when I shall next get a meal. In the late evening, Mrs Colonel returns, heads straight for the cupboard, takes out a can of tinned peaches and eats it by herself — because in her own words — "she must refresh herself" after a hard day at headquarters. Next, she categorically informs me that there is no room for me in the house, not even to sleep on the floor. Neither will she agree to my sleeping in the room rented by the L.s, though I beg her to. It is already nine o'clock in the evening, deep night outside, I am running a temperature and have nowhere to go. I have no strength to go back to the station.

Professor L. understands and appreciates my sad position and desperately seeks a solution. He personally goes to a neighbouring Russian woman to ask if she will have me. The neighbour has no room for me herself but gives Professor L. the address of another Russian woman who may be able to give me lodgings. I remain behind to await the outcome of his efforts, whilst it is getting later and later. The neighbour then herself goes to this other Russian woman on my behalf but time passes quickly and I lose hope that I shall be able to lie down to sleep this night, even if only on a floor. At last the neighbour returns with the other Russian woman who takes me to her house. How bizarre: in Kazakhstan, the Kazakh woman had come to me to offer us shelter for the winter, here there are many people, Poles, and I am almost expected to stay in the open and freeze to death.

We walk down various paths, in the total darkness, for some distance and at length reach the woman's home. The hut is tiny — there are only two rooms. In the fairly large kitchen, sleep the woman and her son — and a rooster. From the kitchen a door leads to the other room — my cubicle which is small, narrow, with one of the two windows boarded over with cardboard because it has no glass panes. There is no stove — it is ice-cold in the cubicle but there is a bed with a palliasse and a ragged coverlet. The Russian woman and her twelve-year-old son, sleep in the kitchen on the stove, as is usual in Russian huts — on a special wide platform built into the side of the stove. The rooster sleeps with them and does not move from his spot day or night. The kitchen is also cold because the woman works in the evenings in the theatre as a cleaner and does not return home until late at night when she then lights the stove. She is satisfied with her job because since she cleans the auditorium after performances she can pick up the many cigarette-ends which people drop. These she collects and after emptying the tobacco from the stubs, rolls her own cigarettes for free. She is a heavy smoker. I also have a smoke of home-made cigarettes, rolled from the stubs when she magnanimously gives me a handful of the stubs collected from the floor. I hardly ever see the son, as far as I know he hangs out on the streets and comes home but infrequently, at all times of the day, and then stays only for a very short while.

It is dark, cold and dirty in the hut. In my room the remaining window panes are so thickly frozen over that it is impossible to see out through the window. There is no furniture except for the bed, a chair and a small table. I feel so ill that it is a relief to go to bed and lie down flat. I cover myself up with everything I can lay my hands upon. Not only do I have a temperature but also to make matters worse I have developed diarrhoea. There is no toilet in the hut and one has to go outside, out into the garden, in the thirty degree frost. In my urgent need I worry that I shall not have time to don my shoes and coat before having to dash outside. One way or another, I have so far managed but often with the coat only thrown over my shoulders. I am each time afraid that I shall have an 'accident', which would be a catastrophe because I have no facilities for washing, either myself or my clothes. They keep only one bucket of cold water in the kitchen. I return to bed each time with great relief, from my enforced sortie outside but even the relief is spoilt by the expectation of the next expedition to the garden. During my first few days here, I am glad that the landlady's son is not around to witness my humiliating and ridiculous condition.

On top of everything else there is now something wrong with my heart. I am short of breath and my pulse is irregular, not to mention the temperature and my other ailment. What is going to happen to me? How, if at all, will Dr M. find me to bring me some food? The next day, who should appear like an angel but Officer Cadet K. with a billy-can of hot pea soup from the station, held under his coat. He continues to bring me soup twice a day for the next three days, walking more than ten kilometres a day in temperatures of over 20°C of frost. I am too ill to bother asking how he discovered my whereabouts. Officer Cadet K. has to leave Buzuluk soon, so I ask him to tell Dr M. where I am. Dr M. comes to see me as soon as he is told my location and takes me under his care — and from this moment he is no longer Dr M. to me but becomes Kazik. Kazik feeds me on warm milk, soup and bread, bringing the food under his coat, twice a day. He also takes over my medical care but in spite of treatment my condition continues to deteriorate and he therefore asks Major Doctor R. to come for a consultation. Later, in Teheran, Major R. is to be my daughter's god-father. They both treat me to the best of their ability but nothing seems to help and my heart in particular gets worse, my irregular pulse and shortness of breath, will not go away.

It is two weeks before I begin to improve and my temperature returns to normal but the irregular pulse and shortness of breath remain and will continue to remain for a year! For a whole year I shall be unable to move about quickly and will walk as slowly as a snail. Time alone will cure me. In Buzuluk, nobody can afford to pamper themselves over their health. As soon as I can, I get out of bed to go to the public bath-house, the so called 'bania', to make sure I am a hundred per cent de-loused.

Those who have never been to a Russian bania, cannot know what a delightful experience they have missed! Having queued for a fair length of time, during which I was intrigued by the sight of the Russian women holding birches in their hands, I obtain my ticket and walk into a warm room where there are many lockers. Placing my bundle of clean clothes, which I had had all the while in my suitcase, in my locker, I undress, tightly roll up the dirty clothes and put them together with my shoes into the bottom of the locker. Steam and heat is gushing out from an adjoining room and I can hear the splashing of water, laughter and voices — it feels somewhat strange to go into there in my birthday suit but as soon as I walk in and see the crowd of naked women, I feel better and realize that to be fully dressed in this environment would be to stick out like a sore thumb. There are wooden benches along two walls, many taps with hot and cold water along the third wall and plenty of basins which are not for washing in but for sluicing oneself down, so that they are clean. The concrete floor is covered by wooden slats on which one stands, which is hygienic because the dirty water runs off immediately. The technique is to fill a basin with hot water from the tap and then to pour the water over oneself. Then at leisure one can soap all over, sitting on the benches and again repeat the process of sluicing down with hot water. It is quite the done thing to repeat the ritual as many times as desired, not for cleanliness but for the sheer pleasure of it. Hair can be washed in a similar manner and the pouring of hot water over the head gives a childlike pleasure. One can splash, pour more water and I am not surprised that the women are all laughing and frolicking like children when there is no one to chastise them.

Many of the Russian women are beating themselves with their home-made birches — the 'vieniks' — which they have brought with them. They do not beat themselves very hard but only enough to slightly redden the skin — it is an excellent form of 'home' massage-hydrotherapy which the Russians have been putting into practice for centuries. I spend two hours in the bania and am loath to leave. I am so hot that it is a pleasure to go out into the other cold room to dress. Wearing my clean clothes I walk out into the frost outside. I still feel hot and even my wet hair which I have wrapped in a towel seems to be heating my head. The experience of the bania convinces me what an old wives' tale it is that one should not go to bed with wet hair and from this time onwards I shall wash my hair at whatever time of day it suits me and shall not hesitate to go outside with my wet hair in all sorts of weather conditions. If the Russians do so without catching colds, I can do so also.

On reaching home, I get down to further de-lousing. Having thoroughly searched my dirty clothes I wash them, dry them outside and finally iron them with a hot iron. My landlady who realizes and appreciates my attempts at prevention, lights her stove, heats me some water for the washing and lends me an old-fashioned iron which works by having a red hot piece of metal placed inside it, the metal having been heated beforehand in the fire.

Clean after my visit to the bania, dressed in clean clothes, I feel better and the very next day I go to see General Szarecki who must have had time during my illness, to decide in what capacity to employ me. I explain to him why and how I had escaped from Tatischevo and tell him that I have been expelled from the army for desertion but the General dismisses it all with a wave of the hand and directs me to the Stores with a personally signed form which instructs them to issue me with a uniform! I find myself in the army for the second time, involuntarily! This is only the beginning of the surprise which the General springs on me because he next tells me that I shall be sent to Semipalatynsk where an orphanage for Polish children will be formed. They want me to travel back the five thousand kilometres again, almost back to the same place to which I had been deported and from which I had thought I had freed myself for ever. I am scared but try not to show it and on the contrary, I express enthusiasm and thank the General.

The women volunteers' barracks are still in quarantine from typhus, so I remain with my Russian woman and her rooster. I have no contact with the Women's Voluntary Service, the SPK, my position is ambiguous and I feel very uneasy. It will become apparent later that my feeling of insecurity and sense of false pretences is justified. I belong neither to the SPK nor have I been officially designated to the army as a civilian doctor, but I am in uniform. There is nothing like being a female doctor during wartime, my position is an embarrassment to everybody and to myself most of all.

The uniform also worries me because it had been designed for the British climate whilst I have to go to Semipalatynsk, to Siberia, wearing it. The small cap perched on the crown of my head worries me most of all. My ears will be frost-bitten in the first half-hour and within the hour the whole of my face including my nose. Feverishly, I start to look for a fur cap which will have ear-flaps, such as the ladies who work at the headquarters wear — they have fox-fur caps! And their caps are correctly designed, made of thick fur, with ear-flaps and coming down the face as far as the eyebrows. I am told in the stores that they have run out of similar headgear — they are finished. The priest, Father Cienski, feels sorry for me and gives me his own astrakhan fur cap which though of a style differing from the Kazakh one is at least made of fur and can be pulled down over my forehead and ears. If I wear a woollen Balaclava helmet beneath it, my cheeks and chin will also have some protection from the frost. I shall wear the 'set' in Semipalatynsk but always with bated breath in case somebody should catch me and reprimand me for my irregular head covering. What a great pity that our trunk and the fox-fur cap my mother made me got lost in transit! I had wanted to meet my husband elegantly dressed and for punishment have now been left without a proper cap.

New Year 1942 finds me still in Buzuluk and Dr M., Kazik, invites me to a New Year's Eve Buffet at the headquarters, with the promise that there will be plenty of good food for us both. There is an amplitude of sumptuous food on the buffet table but we have not bargained for the change which the war has wrought in human psychology, with the result that we manage to profit but little from the buffet. We take normal helpings of hors d'oeuvres and then later return to the table for the main course. An empty table is before us — whereas I see the gentlemen carrying away plates piled high with everything: fish, salads, meat and gateau — in one heap. Civilization has flown out of the window — people have changed, have become bestial.

Shortly after the New Year, we start to pack the train wagon for the Orphanage — we load food, bedding and clothes for the children. During this occasion, I meet an old colleague, K., at the stores, who had abandoned medicine and who had later finished at the Institute of Physical Education in Warsaw. Colleague K. works in the commissariat and is supervising the supply of provisions for the wagon. He is surprised and pleased to see me again after so many years and without my asking him, promises to pack me a private supply of provisions. He packs me a large parcel containing corned-beef, sardines, and chocolate, etc. This parcel will later prove to be most useful to my friends in Semipalatynsk who literally have nothing to eat. Colleague K., will have given me great pleasure and service because thanks to him, I shall be able to play the fairy godmother, handing out tasty tit-bits to hungry people.

The whole wagon is loaded up to the roof with boxes of tinned meats, condensed milk, rice, chocolate, etc. As well as food we are taking large quantities of blankets, bedding and clothes for the children. We have also been given three large sacks of fresh coffee beans to take with us.

I meet my fellow travelling companions: Major M., a sergeant and a private. The Major is travelling to organize the orphanage on the spot, the sergeant and private are to act as crew on our wagon. All three are to return to Buzuluk later whilst I remain at the orphanage at Semipalatynsk.

There is very little room in the wagon and there is the immediate problem of arranging a place to sleep. Major M. takes control and orders the soldiers to push aside the stacks of blankets so a 'den' can be made for sleeping on, evidently for himself and for me, together. A make-shift wall of blankets is to separate us from the rest of the wagon. The Major is not concerned about the soldiers, they are expected to doze anyhow, by the stove which is placed in the centre of the wagon. Our journey will take about ten days and before the train has even started rolling, I have already been placed in a very awkward situation — I am nervous about the journey. I am completely at Major M.'s mercy. I decide the best way will be to act stupid. The soldiers smirk knowingly. Major M. is about fifty years old with a dignified paunch and whiskers, whilst his bearing and movements are 'rakish'. He is very garrulous and full of self-importance and mentions that he has managed to get in touch with his wife and sons, who like me, had been deported, that he believes in keeping 'his women' on a tight rein and that as soon as he gets them to join him, they will learn how much man and 'master of the house' he really is. Later when I sail from Egypt to England, I see Major M. with his family on the ship — his wife is big and bonny and energetic and beside her the Major is of no significance, he jumps when she speaks. I manage to avoid meeting him and he remains unaware that I am on board.

For the present, Major M. is very gallant in his behaviour towards me, serving out the bread and sardines to me first of all, entertaining me with conversation and remains altogether charming until night falls. I have no alternative but to go to bed in the double-den of blankets because there is no room to lie down elsewhere. When it becomes obvious that the Major does not comprehend what my 'stupidity' implies, I get up and sit down by the stove, next to the soldiers and there spend the rest of the night.

The private is eighteen years old — a good-looking and pleasant lad. The sergeant, who is about thirty, with more experience of life, now understands my position and no longer smiles. From this moment they both start to look after me and never leave me to the awkwardness of a private tête-à-tête with the Major. I sleep in their 'den' whilst they are up talking late, into the nights, by the stove and when they want to go to bed, we change places and I sleep in a semi-upright position by the stove. When I need to wash, they put up a blanket screen and turn away from me — they are very good to me.

Major M.'s mood changes after the first night in the wagon. He has stopped talking to me altogether and I am the last to be given the food which is left after the Major has taken a generous helping, after he has given the soldiers their portions. And this is how things remain to the end of the journey.

The worst problem I have is with a 'convenience' because there is no arrangement whatsoever in the wagon and my stomach has not fully returned to normal so I constantly worry that I will not have time to 'dash behind the hut'. Happily, after two days I do get back to normal but in the meanwhile my life is very miserable. Diarrhoea and the Major . . . . During our ten days travel, I never once see a 'convenience'. We jump on to the track from the train whilst it is at a halt. The problem is that one never knows how long the train will be stopping before it moves off again without any warning. It will sometimes stop in the middle of nowhere for five minutes and sometimes for an hour. It is easier for the men regarding the question of 'the number ones' but difficult for me because I worry that I shall have no time to rearrange my clothes, and that I shall miss the train to be left standing on the track in the middle of desolation. There is also the additional difficulty: the goods wagons have no steps and in the wilds, with no station platform, they are so high above ground level that the only way to get on is to clamber up with the aid of both hands. The men who are taller and have stronger arms have no difficulty in boarding the wagon but for me it is an unsurmountable problem — somebody has to give me a hand from above. 'My' soldiers always do this and one of them will stand and wait by the sliding doors of the wagon until I am ready and will lift me up into the wagon.

The Major is arrogant towards me and misses no opportunity to humiliate or torment me — I am longing for the journey to end, not knowing that worse times, if different, are awaiting me in Semipalatynsk.

The soldiers try to make life as pleasant as possible for me during what is for me a macabre journey and in talking with them I can forget the presence of the Major. We particularly enjoy talking late at night, when the Major is asleep and snoring, alone in the double bed. On one occasion they enable me to take a bath: several buckets of water are heated on the stove, a screen of blankets is held up by them for over half an hour whilst I wash all over. What would have happened to me had these soldiers been of the Major's ilk? Closeted with three men for ten days — I shudder at the thought.

SEMIPALATYNSK

At last we reach Semipalatynsk where a flock of starving and ragged Poles immediately appears at the station with Lieutenant R., to help us unload the wagon. Lieutenant R. has brought them because he expects that we will pay them in kind for their trouble. Major M. is displeased and disillusioned because he expected Lieutenant R. to have already found and furnished a premises for the Orphanage but Lieutenant R. had been under the impression that Major M. would take charge of the work because that is why he has been sent here. Lieutenant R. has orders from headquarters to recruit the Poles in Semipalatynsk into the Polish Army and runs the recruiting office very efficiently — and is also very helpful to the civilians. The Lieutenant is a charming man — cheerful, shrewd and resourceful, who knows how to deal with the Russians, the more so as he speaks fluent Russian. He quickly sizes up the awkward situation and to appease the Major, immediately invites him home with him.

In the meantime the Lieutenant's 'starveling army' commences to unload our wagon, stealing from it whatever it can. If their appearance is anything to judge by, then one cannot be surprised by the behaviour of these people but neither can one ignore it because they will loot all the food allocated for the Orphanage. But how can one shout at an old man, who casting furtive glances to left and right, to check if he is being watched, attempts to cram a tin of meat into his pocket with trembling hands when the pocket is too small to accommodate the tin? The Poles have a beano on the coffee: the sacks have split during the journey, spilling a lot of coffee on to the wagon floor — and because coffee has no nutritional value, we let them take it. The person who had been in charge of organizing supplies for the Orphanage must have had no idea what it really means to be hungry but had wanted to indulge the Orphanage in allocating the coffee. The Poles glean the wagon floor clear of coffee to the last bean. I shall never forget the sight of old men, crawling on all fours, collecting the beans from the floor and quickly pocketing their trophies. I feel both sorry for them and irritated by them because they have fallen so low, literally to the floor. Let them have their genteel cup of coffee later, but I fear it will be minus the sugar and the customary slice of cake . . . .

At last, the wagon is unloaded and everything has been stacked in

Lieutenant R.'s office, which consists of two rooms. I am rather surprised that Lieutenant R. does not invite me to his house but delegates me to remain in the office, together with all the supplies. He and Major M. drive off, leaving me behind in the stacked room, without a stove, without any washing facilities and without anything to eat. I am obliged to pull down some blankets to make myself a bed and all I have to eat is a tin of something. During the night I am very cold because although there is a stove in the adjoining room, it is only kept burning during the day. I bivouac in the office for two nights, sleeping fully-dressed in a cold room.

Major M. had imagined that his only function would be to formally open the Orphanage which would have been made ready by the Lieutenant and does not attempt to conceal his annoyance that this will now be an impossible target to meet in the time he had planned to remain in Semipalatynsk. I do not know if Lieutenant R. had been warned in advance of the date of our arrival or if he dissimulated the information, but the fact remains that nothing is ready, not even a premises, nor furniture, whereas the Major wants to leave for Buzuluk the very moment he has completed his mission of the ceremonial opening of the Orphanage.

Lieutenant R., who is an energetic man and well experienced in the ways of the world, gets down to the task in hand immediately and assures the Major that the Orphanage will be 'created' within a couple of days and the Major will be able to return to Buzuluk immediately after its opening. A few months later, when by then Lieutenant R. has gained confidence in me, he tells me that he wanted to get rid of the Major as soon as possible because all the Major did was to hamper him in his work. The Lieutenant knew his way around with the Russians and knew that he would manage best if left to organize the Orphanage by himself.

Suddenly on a certain day, Major M. informs me that the formal opening of the Orphanage will take place in a few days' time — I must be in a mad-house — we have no premises, no beds or tables or chairs, no staff and the supplies which we have brought are still stacked in the office: it is completely impossible to 'open' an Orphanage in a few days' time!

In between times, the Major lives comfortably with Lieutenant R. and his wife and I have been quartered with Officer Cadet J.'s family. Officer Cadet J., who is the Lieutenant's right hand man, lives with his mother, his sister and her small daughter, in one small room with a kitchen. The ladies are most friendly and hospitable, and since I am classed as a guest, I have a bed made up for me in the kitchen which suits me because alone, I shall have more freedom. I am petrified when during the first night somebody walks into the kitchen and comes to stand by my bed — I realize it is the Officer Cadet — in his nightclothes. It would be hard to misinterpret his intentions but because he is very young, I manage to get rid of him fairly easily. The very next morning, I ask his mother whether I can sleep with them in their room. And from now on I sleep in one bed — a grimy lair, with the

Officer Cadet's sister and her three-year-old daughter. I never mention my experience in the kitchen to the ladies J., I do not know if they can guess why I am disinclined to sleep alone.

Undoubtedly, Major M. must have put Officer Cadet J. wise to my second 'profession' as soon as we had arrived in Semipalatynsk because I cannot think that a nineteen-year-old boy would have the nerve and effrontery to visit me during the night unless he had been 'directed' by the Major. Major M. must have similarly warned the Lieutenant and his wife because why else should they be so reserved and cool towards me? For a long time I cannot understand their attitude until later, when after a few months, I establish a friendship with Mrs R. and gain her confidence. Mrs R. tells me that Major M. had in fact warned them against me and would not allow them to invite me to their house because "such a person cannot be permitted to live with a decent family." Now I know why I had had to bivouac in the office for several days and why I had been sent to live with the family of a man of lower rank and why that man had appeared in the kitchen, certain that he would receive a warm reception.

Though afterwards, Lieutenant R. changes his opinion of me, I feel, and this feeling is later confirmed, that on his part certain doubts yet remain. Either Officer Cadet J. continues to believe Major M., to the end of my friendship with the R.s, or he is himself as vile a man as the Major. He gives certain proof that he is the latter, during the journey of the Orphanage to the south of Russia. Major M. has wreaked his revenge on me for refusing to make the journey more pleasant. Fortunately, after leaving Russia, I never have the displeasure of meeting either of the two men again.

Though I live with Officer Cadet J.'s mother, apart from breakfast, I never eat with them but go to a canteen in town, where I get good service because I am in uniform. I eat like a horse because I am skeleton thin after my illness in Buzuluk and am constantly hungry. I will eat anything and everything I can get in the canteen except for kidneys, whose aroma nauseates me. It surprises the waitresses when I refuse the delicacy and make do with only the soup. It angers me to be depriving myself of my helping of meat but I cannot bring myself to swallow a mouthful. I also go to the bania several times where they always let me in out of turn because I am the military, and each time it is such a pleasure because apart from feeling so clean, the bania satisfies a basic primordial feeling of freedom when man roamed the earth as naked as the day he was born and nobody was surprised or ashamed.

At last — tomorrow we are opening the Orphanage! I rack my brains to imagine where the Orphanage can be and what it can look like. The Major, the Lieutenant, the Officer Cadet and some strangers set off in a group to the 'opening' and I go with them. We make our way to a certain large building and we are directed to a room where there is a table laden with tinned meat and sardine sandwiches. Adjacent, there is another room, empty of all furniture but crowded with a multitude of Poles and children. Even before Major M. starts his opening speech, I spy some elderly men creeping round the back of the table and proceeding to filch the sandwiches, meant for the children only. And again I am overwhelmed by anger and shame for them. I usher them away but at the same time, feel I am being cruel — after all they are hungry aren't they? After the speeches which are suitably uplifting and stirring, come the usual patriotic songs, the children are given their sandwiches and finally the Major bids us goodbye and leaves Semipalatynsk, whilst the rest of us return to our respective homes. Orders have been ditifully carried out. Major M.'s mission has been accomplished. The Orphanage has been opened, but is closed immediately upon the conclusion of the opening ceremony. I think we have acted cruelly: we show poor people plenty of good food and then we close the doors.

After Major M.'s departure, Lieutenant R.'s mood changes to very high spirits and he assures me that the Orphanage can and will now be properly organized. I find this hard to believe and comment that I cannot imagine how the Orphanage can function in only the two rooms. The Lieutenant laughingly says that now he has been left in peace, without Major M., he will try to find suitable premises, will furnish them, will hire personnel and when everything is ready we can start taking in children. And this time into a real Orphanage — the one today was only for show so that the Major could complete his mission and would leave as soon as possible. I do not know how much this stunt must have cost Lieutenant R. in terms of cash or bribes of tinned meat but he had hired the two rooms for the day only! He is an expert in such affairs but he lives well and lets live.

Having bidden the Major good riddance, the Lieutenant seriously gets down to work. He searches out and secures a house which has two rooms, almost the size of halls, and a large vestibule where there is a stove to heat the water and the building. The kitchen is housed in a separate hut, near by, in the yard. The building must have been a school or a Russian orphanage and Lieutenant R. has secured it for us by the usual and well-known method from the authorities — by bribery, probably using goods from our wagon. We also have a large shed, a wood-store and a well in the spacious courtyard: the whole compound is surrounded by a fence. From the authorities, the Lieutenant has also obtained metal beds and palliasses, benches, chairs, kitchen utensils and table-ware! In the circumstances, we have ideal conditions for an Orphanage. Orphanage Staff have also been engaged and of course, Lieutenant R. has given posts to his friends but because he is such a good organizer, particular positions have been filled by those people who are suited just for that work and no other.

Mrs D., by profession a teacher, has been appointed head of the Orphanage, having had experience of running a club-room. She is a young and energetic woman who had been deported with her mother and her son. She takes charge of the children's education, no mean achievement under these conditions because there is only the one room to her disposition, the room which also serves as dining-room and play-room. The children, of both sexes, vary in age from five to fifteen years. Neither does she have anybody to help her in the teaching.

The quartermaster is a young, resourceful and quick-witted woman, whose good point is that she has a younger brother who helps her, unofficially and proves as useful as his sister.

The lady nominated to be cook had been deported with her mother and two sons. She is allowed to take home meals for her family and so accordingly cooks as though for a family, her own family! If cooking pancakes — two per person — for over fifty children, in these circumstances is not a culinary achievement, then I do not know what is! She does not begrudge effort or time and works miracles from the provisions to hand.

The kitchen assistant is a gentle and hard-working lass and she does all those chores in the kitchen which do not require a knowledge of cooking.

A man has also been engaged as a caretaker, with the added duties of chopping wood, clearing snow, etc. Our caretaker is an epileptic; one of the Lieutenant's sons also suffers from epilepsy so it is not surprising that the Lieutenant wants to help another epileptic.

I am the only one to sleep in the Orphanage buildings with the children; the scullery maid sleeps in the kitchen and the rest of the personnel go home between five and six o'clock in the afternoon. About two months later, when the number of children in the Orphanage has increased, the Lieutenant engages my friend Irena S. to help with them. Irena sleeps in the dormitory with the children.

The Orphanage staff settle down to work with enthusiasm. One of the first jobs is to screen off an area in one of the large rooms to provide a stores and a clinic. Half of the width of the room is taken up by the stores, where we stack everything we had brought from Buzuluk, beginning with tins of provisions and ending with blankets, bedding and clothing for the children. I have to admit the Orphanage is well equipped except that we are short of coats and shoes for the children. Someone must have omitted to remember that children do need to go out into fresh air. On the other hand, we have more than enough bedroom slippers for them. The other section of the screened-off area is the 'doctor's room' which serves as a clinic, pharmacy and my bedroom. I have been supplied with such a large quantity of necessary drugs and medicines that I cannot envisage ever feeling helpless. When I request further supplies later, they are delivered to the Orphanage. Everything has to be transferred from the Lieutenant's office to the Orphanage and sorted out. The lack of various items constantly comes to light — particularly shortage of simple things such as for example a bread knife, so the Lieutenant has his hands full. He manages to supply everything we ask for. The staff do not quibble about the allocation of various tasks and regardless of position each of us works as hard as possible to get the Orphanage functioning as soon as possible. I may be painting a rosy picture but however this does not mean that there is no friction or upsets, sometimes quite undeservedly, but in comparison to the result of the happy home which the children find here, it is all insignificant. The Lieutenant has provided army uniforms for all the ladies working at the Orphanage and eventually even his wife is given a uniform because, although not a member of staff, she cares for the Orphanage and helps us, so the uniform adds to her standing and gives her greater authority. Mrs R., the Lieutenant's wife, is an intelligent and very tactful woman and although her position is a difficult one she never offends anybody but offers her services in the truest meaning of the word.

Now that everything is prepared, the Orphanage is ready to admit the first intake of children — orphans from Semipalatynsk. Some children, whose mothers had died whilst in exile, had been looked after by friends, some had landed in Russian Orphanages where they had rapidly forgotten Polish. Some mothers, finding themselves in tragic circumstances, consider it best to hand over their children to the Orphanage, into safe-keeping by the Polish Army. I remember one woman, who with tears in her eyes, asks us to save her son, five-year-old Antek. Is she right in so doing? Perhaps more experience of life will make me change my opinion? Is it right for a mother to part from her child? Antek later 'loses' his surname. We take him in as Antek Leparovski and then, when later we are sailing across the Caspian Sea to Pahlevi in Persia, all the lists of children and their details are lost and the supervisor has to make up fresh lists, from memory. She is unsure if Antek is called Leparovski or Kleparovski. If his family came from Lvov, then his surname is almost certain to be Kleparovski, because there is a district in Lvov called Kleparov. Antek is a sweet, composed little boy. In Uzbekistan he falls ill with malaria, follows me around like a dog after its mistress and looks very pitiable. I lose sight of him in Persia.

My position in the Orphanage is a conglomeration of mother, nanny, hygienist and doctor — in that order of descent. I wanted to treat the Poles in Semipalatynsk but Lieutenant R. is against the idea — I must limit my work to the Orphanage. Therefore apart from treating the children's trivial indispositions, I also cut their nails, inspect their hair, serve them breakfast and spend my evenings with them, when after supper we all sing popular songs, sometimes until ten o'clock at night. The children — and I — love these sing-song evenings and they are very loath to go to bed. At bedtime, I do a tour of all the beds in the dormitory, tucking them all in — some of the mites are so very little — and kiss each child good-night. As I am an only child and my daughter has not yet been born, I am unused to the company of children and am quite put out of countenance by the children's behaviour on certain occasions. Once, during my evening round of the dormitory, I know that Antek is walking behind me pulling faces. Initially when I am aware of him, I am uncertain how to react, but then instinct comes to my rescue. For a time I pretend not to see his antics and then suddenly turning round catch him red-handed in a grimace. Antek is very much put to shame whilst not one word passes my lips — we become firm friends from this moment.

The children quickly teach me how to deal with them. They play all sorts of pranks on me and often pull my leg as though I were their mother but they are also obedient because they want to please me. I never have to shout at them and only once do they put me out of patience when during breakfast one day they make a lot of noise and are very restless and I, with blisters on my hands from slicing bread from enormous loaves, for the fifty or more of them, cannot cope. At this juncture I hit the table with my fist — only the once and strongly — a deathly hush descends, until I actually feel sorry for them. From now on they behave themselves at breakfast. They give little trouble on the whole and I shall always remember the times when from six o'clock in the evening to nine o'clock the next morning I am alone with them, with great pleasure. With time, the numbers of children in the Orphanage increase to over seventy.

Our quartermaster supplies the Orphanage with bread, flour and sometimes potatoes. She once manages to obtain some raw onions, which the children are given for their elevenses as a tasty snack, with some bread. The cook prepares two hot meals a day from the provisions we have brought from Buzuluk. Breakfast consists of hot chocolate made with condensed milk and bread, lunch is usually hot Bovril with semolina or rice, often followed by cooked corned-beef and supper is again a hot meal but meatless. The children blossom and gain weight before our very eyes. I am only perturbed that we cannot take them outdoors to get some fresh air because they have no coats or shoes.

A few weeks later, when the Orphanage proves to be running smoothly and efficiently, Lieutenant R. decides to recover Polish children who have been deprived of maternal care because their mothers had died in exile and who have either been looked after by Poles in the kolkhozes or who have been taken into 'Diet-doms' (Orphanages) by the Russians. It will be necessary to look for them in distant villages to bring them back to our Orphanage. Lieutenant R. sends out Sergeant M. and another man to search for Polish orphans, lost in the deep provinces. Sergeant M. returns one night, having spend a week travelling, with about twenty children of both sexes and varying ages. He had had problems in extricating some of the children from Russian orphanages because the Russians already thought of them as theirs. Some have already managed to forget Polish.

The Orphanage is put on 'Red Alert': the fire in the stove is kindled into a roaring blaze for heating plenty of water, we prepare beds and make ready some fresh clothes for the new arrivals, whilst the cook whips up a hot meal. The entire Orphanage staff have been awaiting the children's coming and now they have arrived, in the middle of the night, cold and hungry. Mrs R.

too has come to help out and after feeding the children we tackle the task of scrubbing and de-lousing them. We stand the children on a sheet spread out on the floor, to undress them, and will later burn the sheet together with the dirty and louse-infested clothes. After bathing them in a tub in front of the stove, after rubbing their hair with vaseline and wrapping their heads in towels, we put them to bed in clean night-clothes.

Amongst the new arrivals are two sisters whose mother had died — the younger girl is not quite five years old and the elder girl of about eight looks after her sister like a mother, washes her, dresses her and will not leave her side even for a second. They had been ill with typhus and had only just come out of hospital where they had had all their hair shaved off. Their hair, which previously had been quite straight, begins to curl into beautiful ringlets as it regrows. I had seen several similar cases before, amongst friends. If typhus does not kill or cause invalidity, as in the instance of a school friend of mine whom I later meet in Teheran in a wheelchair with paralysis of both legs, it often leaves a 'souvenir' in the form of curly hair. Typhus attacks blood-vessels and the consequences can vary, depending on which blood-vessels are affected.

The Orphanage is full from the time of having admitted the large number of children from the environs of Semipalatynsk and we can now only accept the odd child who really is in a desperate situation.

The children get up at seven-thirty in the morning and after washing in basins of warm water by the stove, are given breakfast at eight o'clock. The 'head' arrives at nine o'clock and makes efforts to teach them if only a little, as far as possible because she is without any text-books or suitable accommodation: we have only one room for all other purposes apart from sleeping. The children are taught reading and writing, a little arithmetic, history and geography. After a break for elevenses comes the lighter side of their education such as singing and marching round the room — our main concern is to keep the children occupied. The children spend two more hours with their teacher after lunch and when she goes home at five o'clock in the afternoon, the children keep busy by setting the tables for supper. After supper, Irena S. and I are left alone with the children, who by this time are getting bored. Now comes the opportunity to exploit Irena's singing abilities and we organize group singing. The idea proves excellent! As soon as supper is over, the tables and benches are shifted so that we can all sit round in a big circle and the choral evening begins. The older children know various regional songs which are unknown in general, so that our repertoire increases with each day to such an extent that we sometimes have to stay up till ten o'clock to run through all the songs, and the younger children fall asleep; later we have to carry them to bed. The one particular song which enjoys great popularity is about a gentleman who 'breaks a lassie's water-jug', has about ten verses, and concludes with a wedding. This song always elicits general pleasure and applause at the end of the evening. The gentleman offers the lassie marriage as a reparation for breaking her water-jug. I have to admit that often I am very sorry to have to break up this homely, happy gathering to order the children to bed but I am afraid of the head's displeasure — I have no right to be keeping the children up so late. I think that the Orphanage administration people and Lieutenant R. never do learn of our singing sessions. I accustom myself so much to life at the Orphanage that one night returning home from visiting friends, I find myself hurrying to be back in time for our singing, and when from afar I see the lights and hear the children's voices, I almost break into a run, eager to find myself 'back at home'. We always end our evenings by singing the well-known and much loved Polish hymn 'All our daily deeds'.

One day, Lieutenant and Mrs R. invite the Orphanage staff to the theatre and afterwards dinner at a restaurant. There is a kind of theatre-cum-cabaret in Semipalatynsk which as throughout in Russia is of quite a good standard. One actress in particular sticks in my memory because, although getting on in years, her acting portrays such life, verve and talent that it is a pleasure to watch her. After the performance we go to the restaurant where we are served quickly and well because Lieutenant is a regular customer. At the same time we discover that Lieutenant R. not only speaks fluent Russian but can also sing well, particularly ribald Russian songs which sometimes sound very funny to the Polish ear in view of the cognation of certain words which in Polish would be vulgar but in Russian are comical and do not offend or jar. Lieutenant R.'s aide-de-camp, Officer Cadet J. is also interested in light Russian music and writes down the words to all the melodies. He has a whole note-book of these — in particular those songs which to us contain comical expressions.

We give all the children a bath once a week in the tub by the stove and change their underclothes, their clothes and bed-sheets. The younger children need to have their clothes changed more often, usually in the middle of the week, but the older ones wear their clothes for longer and change them as and when necessary. Bath time is at night and after getting dressed in clean night-clothes, the children go to bed, whilst we collect their dirties and place a small pile of clean clothes by each bed in readiness for the next day. As luck would have it, one day the clean clothes are not put out that evening but are to be distributed the next morning. And that night there is a fire at the Orphanage — not in the actual Orphanage building thank goodness, but in the kitchen which is in the courtyard but connected to the Orphanage by a high wooden fence. I hear somebody banging on the door in the middle of the night and shouting "fire!" The kitchen where the cook's assistant sleeps has caught fire, the smoke had woken her and she has raised the alarm. Running outside I see the kitchen in flames and the fire beginning to spread to the wooden fence along which it could travel to reach the Orphanage building itself: both buildings — that is the kitchen and the Orphanage are wooden. Irena S. and I wake the children but we have nothing to dress them in. It just had to be today that their clean clothes have not been put out. We tell them to wrap up in their blankets. Some of the bigger boys still have their clothes by their bedsides because being almost grown-up they wear them for longer and their clothes had not been removed for exchange. So getting dressed quickly, they grab axes to go and chop a fire-break in the wooden fence to prevent the fire from spreading to the Orphanage. In the meantime a crowd of people has gathered. Somebody has told Lieutenant R. and he immediately appears on the scene with his wife. The Lieutenant is angry — the children in their slippers and blankets are standing at the ready to evacuate the building, people have formed a human chain and buckets of water are being passed from the well to douse the fire. The break in the fence does stop the fire from spreading. The situation is under control but the Orphanage has been left without a kitchen whilst the children will have to be fed. The Lieutenant is very annoyed but things could have been worse: we can use the stove in the Orphanage to heat the water almost to boiling point, we have Bovril, cocoa and tins of food and can manage without a 'real' kitchen for several days. Within two days the stove in the kitchen is repaired and the cook, still smelling of smoke, cooks in a cold kitchen because part of one wall has been damaged by the fire. Eventually this is also repaired.

The Russians begin investigations into the possible cause of the fire — the building is State property, naturally, and the cost of repairs is high. The Lieutenant also makes enquiries privately and it comes to light that the fire was started by a Pole who was jealous of the Orphanage and wanted to take revenge.

The Russians never learn the outcome of Lieutenant R.'s investigations and continue to search for a possible cause of the fire, which suits us, because we are anxious to conceal the fact that a Pole was responsible.

I now witness how affairs may be hushed up in the USSR. I do not know with whom and about what matters Lieutenant R. has talked but two days later, Mrs R., his wife, wearing army uniform arrives at the Orphanage early in the morning, asks for the key to the stores and proceeds to closet herself in there with our quartermaster. After a long time they emerge and Mrs R. warns us all not to speak to the Russian who will be coming at any moment. At about eleven o'clock the Russian 'authority', wearing army uniform, arrives and he and Mrs R. lock themselves away in the stores. Half an hour later they emerge, Mrs R. with a charming smile hovering round her lips and the Russian also beaming, and with his pockets bulging with thick socks, tins of meat, chocolate and sugar. And that is the end of the affair of the fire! I am most impressed by Mrs R.'s action. Never in my wildest dreams could I have so tackled the problem.

In any case, I like Mrs R. because she has common sense, helps a great deal at the Orphanage and is very tactful woman. I am also very sorry for her because on of her sons is a severe epileptic who suffers several attacks each day whilst all his mother can do is to stand helplessly beside him, waiting for the fit to pass and never knowing if her son might not die during the convulsions. She blanches each time she hears the cries which herald his epileptic attacks and runs to him. Her son has been an epileptic from birth and is now eight years old — eight years of a mother's suffering! We have no anti-epilepsy drugs here and in any case as yet there are no effective drugs for preventing epileptic convulsions. The boy is physically well developed but mentally retarded — he cannot walk properly but staggers and can barely talk. Mrs R. dreams of going to India to find a fakir who could cure her child. The poor tormented woman — her son is most certainly an incurable epileptic.

It grieves us very much that our children have no outdoor footwear and only indoor slippers but we have had to buy several pairs of valonki for the few boys who help with the chores in the Orphanage. These boys, ranging in age from twelve to fifteen years, fetch meals from the kitchen and return dirty plates several times each day and to do this have to go outside across the courtyard. The Orphanage could not cope without their help. The four or five of them carry the heavy containers of food, serve it out at the tables and return all the dirty and used utensils to the kitchen. Always smiling and willing to work, they are often harassed and out of breath but thanks to them the meals are served up efficiently, punctually and without delays. The 'crew' eat when everybody else has finished, as much and what they like.

Initially we have no pillows for our beds, so we had put blankets inside pillow-cases as subsititutes. This state of affairs changes when two brothers, who had set off to find us of their own accord, arrive at the Orphanage! The elder brother Kazik, is fifteen years old and the younger, Staszek, thirteen years old — their mother had died, and since they had got to know of the existence of a Polish Orphanage, they had packed all their possessions and have come to us bringing all their inheritance. Kazik donates several large pillows and douvets and from them our ladies make over thirty pillows for the children. I also get one since I live at the Orphanage. I shall place my new-born daughter on this pillow in Teheran and my daugher will use it into adult life and will refuse to part with it. Both boys speak Kazakh and Russian fluently and without an accent. They join our work force at the Orphanage and are strong,willing and industrious. They will later leave Russia with the Polish Army as 'Junacy' (young Army conscripts) and will go to Persia.

We have too, our share of comic moments. Amongst the Poles in Semipalatynsk there is to be found a Ukrainian who is desperate to place his four-year-old son in the Orphanage for feeding-up — though the child looks healthy and well, the father is so insistent that it is hard to refuse his request. The child seems very shy, does not want to speak and cries during the night. I get up to him and try to discover why he is crying, but to no avail, the little boy refuses to speak a single word. After two more days or rather two nights, we call the father who explains that the boy understands not a word of Polish because they speak Ukrainian at home, and had cried because he wanted "wee-wees"! The poor little soul had suffered, had not understood a word of what I had been saying to him and somehow had not been able to indicate what he had needed! Father takes him back home.

Lieutenant R. decides that we should admit a Jewish boy to the Orphanage, to show, I suspect, that there is no anti-Semitic prejudice amongst the Poles. A boy of about eleven, a tall, thin, shy orphan arrives. The head feels uneasy because what are we to do with him during the morning and evening prayers? She confers with Lieutenant R. and they decide that he cannot be treated like a black sheep and asked to leave the room during prayers, therefore if he so wishes he can remain and pray according to his own beliefs or pray not at all. At first the boy stands silent and embarrassed during our prayers but after a very short time he picks out certain of our prayers, such as "Our Father", which do not touch any dogmas which might conflict with any of his beliefs and repeats them with us. He seems to enjoy singing hymns too, and gradually becomes so drawn to us that he asks to be baptized into Christianity. It does not surprise me that he has developed leanings towards our religion because the atmosphere which he finds at the Orphanage is so cordial and secure that he wants to 'belong' to us entirely. Nobody had discussed his resolution with him and in any case he is of the age when according to Polish law the religion cannot be changed because children of his age are considered to be too grown-up to have their religion changed without their consent and yet are not grown-up enough to decide for themselves. He will leave the Orphanage when we are in Uzbekistan to join the army as a Junak, thrilled to think that he will be fighting for Poland, for his fatherland. I never do find out if he does eventually become a Christian.

The children in the Orphanage are excellent patients, like most children in a tête-à-tête situation with the doctor, without the presence of the parents. When I dress their boils or give them injections they do not cry. I never take them by surprise with anything, I never tell them it will not hurt when I know that something must hurt a little and I always tell them what I shall need to do. Thank God that we are minus any parents, whose fear and tension would communicate to the children, throwing them into a panic.

In February, 1942, we all get the mumps! Ninety per cent of the children, the head, the quartermaster — and I. There is no question of staying in bed — we, the staff, have to continue working whilst the children refuse to be left alone, in bed, in the dormitory. So we put on our Balaclavas to keep our faces warm because then it hurts less and also, because then it does not show, and we do all look horrible. We all weather this illness on the go, without any complications. The worst thing is the pain which accompanies the start of any meal when our mouths begin to water at the sight of the food but nobody complains and it suffices to glance round at one's companions with their swollen jowls and double chins to start laughing.

The mumps is barely over when one of the little girls falls ill with infectious meningitis. With this there is now the threat of an epidemic of a serious illness. I am lucky to succeed in getting her sent to hospital on the same day the first symptoms appear. Nobody else becomes infected. The little girl never returns to the Orphanage. During the quarantine period we wait with trepidation to see who will fall ill next, but happily there are no further cases.

There is still a frost of -35°C and sometimes it may be warmer — -30°C! In spite of wearing Father C.'s cap over my Balaclava, my cheeks become frost bitten — nothing can replace the Kazakh fur caps. I have two large purple blotches on my face and must not venture outside into the cold, for two weeks — my cheeks heal without a trace! It is far worse when my nose becomes frost-bitten — and now I am tormented by fear. One day whilst walking along the street I notice a Russian woman shouting and gesticulating to me from the far side of the street, who seeing that her antics elicit no reaction from me, comes running over and pointing to my nose says " your nose is white." Instantly, I realize the threat: my nose must be a solid lump of frozen flesh and could fall away from my face at the merest touch. If I am to have the slimmest chance of saving it, I must immediately risk rubbing it vigorously with snow. I grab a handful of snow and start rubbing my nose — I can feel nothing, my nose might as well not be there and I am scared to look in case I see it in my hand. As soon as I can see that as yet my nose has not come away, I begin to rub it more energetically until at last, to my relief, I can feel pain because I have rubbed it raw. Now I know that my nose still exists. I had been fooled because I had been able to feel my nose dripping and had constantly been wiping it with my handkerchief and had thought that I still had feeling in it, that there was no danger of frost-bite, whereas, had it not been for the Russian woman, I should probably now be without a nose. Again I have to confine myself to the indoor warmth of the Orphanage, my nose swollen and of a bluish-red hue. Now I shall know, one cannot be guided by the sensation of touch alone — I had 'felt' my nose and had almost lost it. The only reliable indicator is pain. If the nose hurts when being wiped it means it is alive, that it is not frost-bitten. I think the Russian woman has saved my nose, literally in the nick of time.

I visit Mrs S. and her son fairly frequently. Even though her daughter, Irena works at the Orphanage, they are badly off for food. Irena eats at the Orphanage but is not allowed to take food home. So I always take them something from my private supply of tins which colleague K. had given me in Buzuluk. Amongst others, I had a ten-kilo tin of corned-beef which I had opened. I had put the beef in an out-house — it has frozen solid and now when I want to take them a piece, I have to use an axe to chop it and even with an axe it is difficult to split the meat which is frozen to -30°C.

I do not want to keep any hoards because I have already learnt that giving away to people in need is always repaid! Personally, I eat very well at the Orphanage and am gaining weight rapidly. I now carry my own reserves of fat on me which can only be taken away by hunger. My uniform is too tight and Mrs S. has moved the buttons twice already and again I can barely fasten them. On my way to see them I am pleased because I have an even better suprise for them: two sacks of flour! Lieutenant R., that master at obtaining food, has wheedled a ration of flour for the Orphanage staff from the Russians. And I had automatically been allocated my share though I have not the slightest need of it. I tell my friend about receiving the flour and ask her son Eddie to transport the sacks by sledge. I have in mind for him to bring the flour to their house but Eddie at first thinks I want him to take the sacks to the Orphanage for myself. When he realizes that the flour is for them, his face lights up in disbelief, then astonishment and finally with joy. I reap great joy from watching the emotions flit across his face because it is sweet indeed to be the 'fairy Godmother'.

The basic supplies of drugs and medicines which we had brought with us from Buzuluk have proved insufficient and are almost finished. So I write to put in an order for fresh stocks, at the same time asking to be supplied with larger quantities than previously. In due course I receive a huge consignment, not only of those drugs for which I had asked but also others, strange ones to me. We are now in the year 1942 and I have been out of touch with the pharmacy world since the outbreak of war. The drugs are packed in bulk, not in measured doses, and there are no instructions for their appropriate dosages. Likewise, I have no reference or hand-books to look up what some of the drugs are for. I know there are some friends of mine from Lvov in Semipalatynsk, with their two daughters who used to be my school friends and their father Mr S. is a pharmacist : he used to have a pharmacy in the centre of Lvov and was very well off — he used to live in a magnificent villa and — had a car and a chauffeur. With Lieutenant R.'s permission, I hire Mr S. to act as pharmacist at the Orphanage for two weeks to sort out the drugs for me, to weigh them out into doses and to explain — in the case of the new to me drugs — what they are to be used for. He will be paid and will receive board and keep at the Orphanage for the duration of the work involved. 'Sir Pharmacist' slaves from dawn to dusk but I notice that he is making very slow progress indeed and suspect the work will be made to take longer than two weeks and is more likely to take two months. Also, the head draws my attention to the fact that we cannot possibly afford to feed him for so long. His keep is generous and good, but he secretively sips the tasty vitamin syrup meant for the children and also takes some away for home. I do not inform the head of this but am disgusted with him. He would have polished off all the children's tasty tonics and medicines, if he could have. The head is right: he is dragging out the work intentionally. It is designated to me unfortunately, to give him a 'gentle prod' and the job is completed within three weeks. I am sorry and also embarrassed on his behalf because all his family look exceedingly fit, are well dressed — his ladies in furs — and yet he has succumbed to theft.

It is now March 1942 and in spite of continuing severe frost and a lot of snow, one can tell the sun is already shining differently. It would indeed even be possible to sunbathe at midday in a sheltered spot. We decide to let the children outside into the sunshine but they cannot all go out at once because we do not have enough shoes and coats to go round. They must go out in groups, a few at a time, suitably dressed against the frost. We let out the first group of children to go and sunbathe on the roof of the shed from which the snow has been cleared. The children who have not breathed any fresh air for several months go simply berserk in the snow and we have to watch that in their enthusiasm they do not take off their coats and catch colds. They get a golden tan whilst a weight drops from my shoulders — all winter they had been cooped-up indoors, even worse than in a prison and at last it has been possible to release them outdoors.

Spring, and a general excitement stirs in the air, more especially so since Easter is approaching. I manage to obtain a handful of oats from the wagon driver, which I sow in a box on the window-sill. The oats come up a beautiful green. At Easter time it is traditional in Poland to make a centre piece for the Easter table of cold food, of the Pascal Lamb standing in a field of oats together with a small red flag. I also manage to fashion the lamb out of kneaded bread and now only have the problem of making the red flag because there is no coloured paper of any sort to be had here. I hit upon the idea of making the little flag from the red wrapping paper of Cadburys chocolate which we have in the stores. Everybody in the Orphanage participates in preparing for Easter: the staff as well as the children. Eggs too are found, one for every child and the final result is that we at the Orphanage achieve a proper Easter table, with real green oats, a lamb, eggs in a bowl, and the best food which the cook is able to prepare. The table is spread with a white sheet. Easter at the Orphanage proves a noisy event. The head has been practising various songs with the children and when Lieutenant R. and his wife arrive, all the staff and the children await them around the festive table and greet them with a song. All of us sing gladly and enthusiastically various religious, patriotic and folk-songs. It is all very happy and appropriate. In the afternoon, we pay calls at the homes of the Orphanage staff and everywhere we go we are welcomed with vodka and sauerkraut in various guises. On Easter Monday which in Poland is called 'Dousing Monday' everybody gets a proper dousing because instead of symbolically sprinkling each other with water, we use buckets of the stuff from the well! In Poland this custom is called 'smigus', here we really go to town and have ourselves a fine old smigus. And the soul of the party is Lieutenant R! Smigus is part of Polish tradition and dates from pagan times, before Christianity came to Poland in the tenth century, when it became incorporated into the celebration of Easter. It is probably a symbol of the coming of spring when the snow melts to water. With the passage of time, it became generally accepted as a social custom when at gatherings and parties people would unexpectedly sprinkle each other with perfume from special small containers tucked away in pockets or handbags. On Easter Monday no social event would pass without the time-honoured 'dousing', leading to much merriment, shouting, chasing and apprehension on the part of the hostess in fear for her furnishings! It would be mainly the young people who would participate but the older generation, after a good supper and its accompaniments would also join in like children.

After Easter it is decided that some of us should go to see the museum with Lieutenant R. and his wife, in Semipalatynsk. The museum houses hardly any exhibits, save for a few items from churches with suitable explanations. We find some chasubles on show, some vestments and ecclesiastical articles and epaulettes, in Russian called 'pagony', which had been worn by officers in the Tsar's Army. They are descibed as being the very height of gentility and decadence. Not a year later similar epaulettes are introduced as part of the Red Army uniform.

Shortly after Easter we are sent a Lieutenant from headquarters for an official check on how the Orphanage is being run. He begins with me and request to be shown lists of how many calories per day each child receives in the diet. I know my job but unfortunately not the 'ways of bureaucracy'. I should have written him out some random figures to satisfy the statistical requirements. Instead of which I conscienciously sit down to calculate how many calories there are in each meal which each child receives, with the help of some approximate calorific values of foods given in a pocket diary. This naturally takes a little time, the Lieutenant becomes impatient and is very rude to me — but what can I do? The world has to be large enough to allow even people like him to live. The visiting Lieutenant had arrived with an onion, which he must have bought on his way to us — a raw onion is a tasty morsel here and what is more is a source of vitamins. During the meal with us he had eaten the whole, big, juicy onion all by himself — perhaps that had disagreed with him.

After arranging matters with the Russians, Lieutenant R. begins to recruit Poles into the Polish Army. I am appointed the recruitment doctor which does not jar on the Russians since in their army women doctors bear the rank of captain and are mainly employed behind the lines where there is still plenty of work for them without it being too exhausting — very suitable work for women doctors. The recruiting takes place in a large hall. The recruiting board consisting of Lieutenant R., and the Russians sits behind tables, whilst I sit at my table, to the side of them where I am supposed to 'inspect' the men to see if they are fit for army service before they present themselves before the board. When I judge a man unfit for service due to some defect, the board eliminates his name from the list and takes no further interest in him. My instructions from Lieutenant R. are to pass as many men fit as possible, within reason, because the aim is to get as many men out of the USSR as possible with the Polish Army.

The naked men stand in a line and walk up to me — I shall never forget the sight of them, I feel so sorry for them! Poles are not accustomed to army parades in birthday suits before a woman doctor — they are very embarrassed and modestly try to cover up as much as possible, whereas my instructions are to examine them all over! I try not to look at the whole line of men awaiting medical inspection but limit myself to looking only at the man standing directly before me in an attempt to embarrass them only as much as I must. And it is because of this that I make a terrible gaffe. The man standing before me is a young, strong lad so I pass him fit for army service — whereas in fact he is lame! Since I did not observe him as he walked towards me from the line, I miss this fact and have made an idiot of myself — all because of misplaced sensibility. The whole board including the prospective candidate for the army roar with laughter and I have no choice but to join in the general amusement at my cost.

I feel most embarrassed of all when I have to examine friends — I try to put on an impersonal official expression, hoping this will alleviate their discomfort. As a doctor, I have seen as many naked people as one could wish to see but because they were ill and in need of my help, there was no question of any embarrassment but this recruiting is quite a different matter. Here they are, a line of young, naked, embarrassed men, standing before me, and I can do nothing to help in the situation — there is no drug for embarrassment. I do not ever again wish to be a 'recruiting doctor' — I suffer for them too much.

Spring arrives suddenly with the end of April. The snow starts to melt rapidly but the sun quickly dries out the resulting puddles. The children can now be allowed into the courtyard in their slippers, so as soon as it becomes drier still underfoot we take some of them for an outing to the market. Amongst other articles for sale on the market there are some imitation embroidered Kazakh skull-caps. These caps are made from the brocades and velvets of clergys' vestments, which have been cut up! Some of the materials are embroidered with gold thread and the church designs can be distinguished in some of the cut up pieces: they are all hand-embroidered but obviously not by Kazakhs. They have found a use for the clerical vestments be it for a purpose differing from the intended.

In May we are stunned by the news that the Orphanage is to move to the south of Russia to join the Polish Army which has already reached Uzbekistan from the north of Russia. Now there is agitation in the air, the children are excited, whilst the Orphanage staff worry that they may not be allowed to take their families with them — it will all depend on Lieutenant R. The Lieutenant accommodates everybody but cannot help teasing people in the meanwhile — in some instances causing not a little anxiety. Neither do I escape his joking: sometimes he will say that as I am in the army, certainly I shall go with the Orphanage, the next time, that since he has none of my papers (which is true and my position with regards to the army has never been made clear), he cannot say if I have the right to travel as army personnel. I had been engaged personally by General Szarecki who had bypassed all the paths of bureacracy. In Semipalatynsk, I receive my salary from Lieutenant R., as a civilian doctor attached to the army. The remuneration is very reasonable and having accommodation and my keep at the Orphanage, I have been able to save some money.

Lieutenant R.'s wife thinks that we ought to use up our money here because in the south the Polish Army will take care of us and we shall not need any money. Time will tell that sadly, in my case, she is mistaken. A whole group of us goes to a State-owned goldsmith's shop (private shops do not exist here) to spend our money on jewellery because 'jewellery is always an investment of capital and also a pleasure in the meanwhile'. I want to buy as much gold as possible, so I choose a heavy though ugly ring and a matching brooch. For 'pleasure' I buy a lovely topaz bracelet, six small silver vodka tumblers which are beautifully engraved, and a larger one which is typical of the ware made in Tula — a town in Russia famous for its silver-craft. I also buy a string of coral beads which my daughter wears to this day. Later I give away most of the jewellery: in Persia I exchange the ring and brooch for some ham, the topaz bracelet becomes a christening present for a boy whose mother exchanges it immediately in Persia, also for ham and I give two of the silver tumblers to some friends as keepsakes. However this state of affairs does not last for long and once I have given away various valuables, I am again poor.

At last, a list of people who will be going south with the Orphanage is produced: all the Orphanage staff and their families are included. Several families who are in no way connected with the Orphanage have also been smuggled on to the list as staff. We are all thrilled. Our transport is two train wagons: one for the personnel and the other for the children and thanks to this there is enough room to enable us to make up beds for the children, for the nights, on the benches and aisles because the journey will take several days. We arrange duties for the children's wagon, so that they will never be left unattended. Whilst everything is being loaded on to the train, I have the opportunity to observe the happenings on the station. There are masses of Poles from Semipalatynsk here and they all want to board the train. I see Officer Cadet J. who is here in his 'official' capacity and watch as he accepts bribes — in the form of gold coins — from the Poles for getting them into the train — and not only from one family. I can see Mrs R., the wife of one of my University Professors, with her family, in despair because she seems to have no hope of getting on board the train in this crowd. With Officer Cadet J.'s help — but this time without bribery — I manage to get them on to the train. Mrs R. and her sons will never know how they got out of Semipalatynsk because of course they do not know me.

We are all in a festive mood: we are going south, to where it is warm and sunny, under the wing of the Polish Army.

Shortly before leaving Semipalatynsk, I had received a letter from my husband with the marvellous news that he has managed to find my mother! A load is taken off my mind! It appears that the train in which my mother had left Tatischevo had had no directions where to go. The train had been supposed to convey the civilians, chiefly women and children to civilian camps in the south of Russia. These camps had been planned and were to be eventually established (as the one, for example, in Guzar) but only six months hence. The train from Tatischevo had set off towards, as yet, a non-existent camp. How could it possibly have been allowed to happen and why did nobody check beforehand, if and where these camps existed in the south before despatching a train full of women and children into the unknown?

Later in Teheran my mother will relate the events of her journey to the south. The train had just travelled aimlessly across the country. The crew had no idea where the train was supposed to be going and spent the time enjoying themselves in their wagon, eating, drinking and entertaining young ladies — the passengers were left to fend for themselves. What little food they had had at the start of the journey was soon finished and people had nothing to eat. At some station, through the wagon window, my mother had exchanged a gold bracelet for a loaf of bread. She had kept it because the bracelet had not been a heavy gold one but only beautifully made and had been of no value at the gold mart in Altaj. The train had almost reached the Chinese border and when it came near to the river Amurdaria, the women passengers had jumped down and had lain across the track! The train could not move because the women said it would only move further east 'over their dead bodies'. Faced with such opposition, the train was directed to travel towards the west, and then towards the south. Came the time when my mother, realizing the train was in fact without any genuine destination and she a completely helpless, though reluctant passenger, decided to get off at the next station. Together she and Mrs Z. had then walked to the nearest village and had asked for shelter. My mother had then written letters and sent telegrams to my husband in Tatischevo — sending in all more than ten letters and five telegrams. None of the letters had reached my husband and only the last telegram had caught him whilst he was already on board a train with his unit, waiting to leave Tatischevo.

When my husband's unit had arrived at its allocated destination, he had started to search for my mother and much to his astonishment had learnt that the spot where she had alighted from the train was quite near to where his unit was stationed! He had therefore taken a wagon to fetch her, had found her lodgings near to the unit, with a Russian woman, had fed her and had put her on the first transport to Teheran in Persia. Miracles do indeed happen!

JOURNEY TO UZBEKISTAN

Our spirits are soaring as we leave Semipalatynsk. We feel very safe, we are on our way to join the Polish Army and have high hopes of getting out of the USSR under the auspices of the army. There is chaos and panic on the stations through which we pass and the military are in evidence everywhere. We reach a station where the train will halt for a longer time, so a few of us take this opportunity to go and see if we can get something hot to eat. I happen across a group of people who are in Red Army uniform but whom I hear talking in Polish! Having seen several women amongst them, I approach one and ask her what they are doing here. The woman is a doctor. The doctor is very agitated. They are all Polish Jews who, wanting to get out of the USSR as quickly as possible had joined the Red Army as volunteers, mistakenly hoping that this way they would get back to Poland sooner. Instead of which they are being sent to the front! I get the impression they are surprised by our British uniforms and by the fact that we are travelling to join the Polish Army. They now reproach themselves for hitting upon the idea of joining the Red Army. They have outsmarted themselves and now there is no turning back — the front is where they must go. I cannot decide whether they were ignorant that a Polish Army was being formed or whether they had expected to win special treatment and privileges amongst the Russians but I am certain they cannot have expected to be sent to the front so soon. There are several doctors amongst them.

In our wagon there is a festive atmosphere — we are all happy and making plans for the future. The Lieutenant's wife, Mrs R., would like to get to India to find somebody to cure her son: it is all she can think about. The wagon is humming with laughter and voices. They laugh at me because I had sat down on the wagon steps whilst the train was in motion and my skirt had caught fire — the wind had blown a spark under my skirt and it is a good thing I managed to put it out quickly.

We are still travelling south and it is getting warmer all the time. Instead of the dull steppe along the lines, there are now fields of wild tulips, which shimmer with all possible colours of flames — from yellow to bright scarlet. When the train stops at small stations, groups of children carrying armfuls of tulips come running up and we 'buy' the flowers in exchange for bread. Soon, our wagon is full of the scented, colourful blooms. God knows why we buy so many tulips — we are in transit and the flowers will soon wilt without water. But we long for the colour, the scent and the freshness of the flowers having been deprived of their pleasure for so long, indeed we are greedy to have some and cannot resist the temptation to touch them and bury our faces amongst their petals. Nobody amongst us has held a live, scented flower in their hands for over two years. After the drabness of the north, the mere sight of our flower-bedecked wagon is enough to uplift our hearts, whilst their strong scent intoxicates us.

We have arrived in Alma-Ata, the capital of Kazakhstan (Alma-Ata means 'Father of Apples') which as the name suggests, lies in a valley amidst orchards. The wide valley has a river flowing along it, with many streams joining the river from the surrounding hills. The orchards are in full bloom now so that the whole valley and its slopes appear to be veiled in a pink haze. Snow-covered peaks can be discerned on the horizon, glittering in the sunshine. The scenery is beautiful, the air clean and so clear that one can easily see distant features and details. There is no wind, it is still and warm and we make most of the opportunity to wash in a stream, everything seems unreal — as in a fairy-tale. We are at Alma-Ata station for two days because we have to reload on to another train. This time unfortunately, we are not allocated two adjacent wagons and to reach the children we have to walk through two other wagons, full of local people — it will now be more awkward being on duty with the children. The nights are the worst problem because we constantly worry that the part of the train carrying the children may be detached and we shall lose them. We try to have two people on night-duty at any one time in the eventuality that should the worst happen, one person alone will not be left with the wagon full of children, at the mercy of the Russians. The separated wagons give Officer Cadet J. a marvellous opportunity to wreak vengeance on me for having rejected his 'offer' in his mother's house in Semipalatynsk.

Presently my turn for the night duty arrives and as it happens I am alone, sitting in the semi-darkness, since the wagon is darkened for the night, and the children are asleep on the benches and on the floor in the aisles. I sit and am bored — I can feel my eyes closing and fight against the overwhelming desire to sleep until about ten o'clock at night when Sergeant M. arrives to keep me company. I am so glad because we start talking and I can stop worrying about falling asleep accidentally and perhaps finding myself alone with the children at some station.

Some time during the night we hear a noise as though the door of the wagon was being opened or closed but because nobody comes in we pay no particular attention to the event and attach no importance to possible consequences. Roughly fifteen minutes later we hear people talking and banging on the door which connects between the wagons. The din gets louder and louder until we hear the door crashing open and in walk Lieutenant R., Officer Cadet J. and the conductor of the train. Totally unambiguously Lieutenant R. accuses me of secluding myself with Sergeant M. I find myself in a situation straight out of a comic opera. I would never have believed that something like this could happen to me, especially when I learn that the door had been locked and not only locked but locked with the special key which only the conductor carries. There is no time for me to question what has happened because Lieutenant R. will not let me say a word. In any case, I have no intention of degrading myself — I manage only to bring myself to tell him not to threaten me with exposure, to say what he likes and to whom he likes because nobody will believe him. During the course of this scene, Officer Cadet J. stands by smiling ironically, while the conductor is bewildered and looks sheepish. The situation is completely unreal because even leaving out of account my 'honour' as a woman, how can anybody imagine that I was capable of locking myself up with Sergeant M. in a wagon full of children, children who are lying on the benches and on the floor so close together that it is difficult to get by? The Sergeant and I had been sitting on the edge of a bench, unable to move.

In spite of indignation and anger I want to laugh because the whole scene, though such a very unpleasant experience for me, is yet comical. In the morning Sergeant M. instigates an enquiry. And I realize only after the incident that the crash which we had heard minutes after the sergeant had joined me had been the sound of the door being locked. When the sergeant asks the conductor why he had locked the door of the wagon, he replies that he had done so at the orders of Officer Cadet J., who had told him it was for the safety of the children. The case is clear: Officer Cadet J. had ordered the conductor to lock the door and a little later had fetched Lieutenant R. to show him the evidence of my conduct. Remembering the slander against me by Major M., the Lieutenant had thus, bona fide, believed Officer Cadet J., while the Officer Cadet had the satisfaction of watching me caught 'red-handed' in front of Lieutenant R. Years later I come to understand better the motives governing Officer Cadet J.'s behaviour: he had also believed Major M. and his male pride had been hurt because if others 'could', then why could not he? And he had arranged this vile revenge.

Sergeant M. wants to salvage my honour but it is really impossible to effect any action. We are on the move, the conductors change and it is not feasible to consider investigations, witnesses, confrontations, etc. Besides, an officer's word, in this instance the Officer Cadet's word, carries more weight than a sergeant's, on top of which the Officer Cadet is the apple of Lieutenant R.'s eye, so any investigations or explanations are doomed even before they are begun and would only jeopardize the military career of Sergeant M. who has a wife and children. I feel very unhappy about the whole affair for these reasons. I never broach the topic with Lieutenant R., although for a long time we remain in contact and get on amicably enough.

I believe that women doctors are particularly exposed to such adventures because of the odd attitude of men towards them, who generally feel that a female doctor need not come into account as a woman. Or, if she does count at all, it is as a creature of equal footing. I have already had a foretaste of this attitude during my studies: a colleague had shown an interest in acquainting himself better with me and to encourage me had promised to take me out for a beer — liking beer himself he had thought it would be just as enticing to me. There had also been misunderstandings of a different sort in social life: once at a ball, I had been asked to dance by an elegant and handsome young man with whom I enjoyed dancing until — he asked — what methods of contraception were in existence! And all the while I had thought he found me attractive.

The rest of the journey has been spoilt by the incident and I am glad when we reach Shakhrisabz in Uzbekistan.

UZBEKISTAN

At Shakhrisabz we unload the Orphanage at the station, after which army lorries take us to the Molotov Kolkhoz where accommodation has been prepared for the children. The accommodation very soon proves to be inadequate and consists of a small house, which we turn into a sick-bay, and two other huts with bunks. For a while then the Orphanage has a roof over its head but as the number of children joining us increases rapidly, we soon have to put up some tents for further accommodation. The surroundings are beautiful: small houses amidst trees and shrubs stand on the river banks — apricots, mulberries and wild vines, which climb up trees and hang over the water, grow here. It is warm and the air is sweet with the scent of wild flowers. The children immediately fall on the fruit and discovering that the red and white mulberries are delicious gorge themselves, as do we, the personnel.

There are two rooms in the house and one room is divided by a screen. One area is organized as a sick-bay and the other area serves as a clinic and also my bedroom. The other room in this house is allocated to the Supervisor of the Orphanage, her mother and her little son. The rest of the staff find accommmodation in Uzbek homes. Early in the morning on the very first day after our arrival, Lieutenant R. and I go to see the regiment doctor in Shakhrisabz. I recognize several colleague doctors and we start to talk avout the Orphanage, the pharmacy and collaboration with the regiment doctor, Doctor G. We had set off for Shakhrisabz wearing the regulation uniforms, which are woollen and heavy and include full length capes: on arrival we were completely soaked with dew from below and with perspiration from above. We should not have walked cross-country through the meadows and shrubs. From the first day in Uzbekistan the British uniforms prove to be a nuisance — this time not because of the cold but because of the heat: in this climate the shirt and woollen tie are suffocating and within half an hour both are wet enough for the sweat to soak through to the jacket, which develops a dark patch on one's back which then trickles with rivulets of perspiration.

The families of the Orphanage staff who live in the Uzbek huts delight in the sun, in the warmth and in the plenitude of food: amongst other tasty morsels they cook a type of ravioli stuffed with mulberries which when

162

cooked taste similar to bilberries, and generally make the most of this holiday in the sun. I explore the surroundings and am constantly discovering wonders anew: by the river, apart from the trees covered with the climbing wild vines, I find whole meadows of wild pink and white hollyhocks, also scented roses, their huge bushes covered with pink and white flowers. I must be in a Garden of Eden! A garden which however later proves to be full of dangers and becomes a hell.

A few days later some of the children start to behave rather oddly: they stagger about and keep lying down, yet physical examination reveals nothing. A 'detection' hastily organized brings to light the fact that the children had feasted on apricots and had also broken open the stones, eating the tasty nutty kernels. They have poisoned themselves with the apricot stones which contain prussic acid, that is cyanide, for which there is no antidote. They recover after we have spent several hours of intense anxiety. Fortunately, they have not eaten enough 'nuts' to poison themselves fatally. It is necessary after this experience to issue an order forbidding the children to eat anything at all without first asking an adult.

The water in the river is clear and rapidly flowing, so the children are allowed to splash and bathe under supervision in the shallow places. We are similarly happy in watching the children frolicking in the water, in the sun and fresh air after a winter of stagnating indoors in Semipalatynsk. All is well until we suddenly receive orders from the regiment doctor that not even a toe may be dangled in the river water for fear of becoming infected with a tropical disease whose parasites live in the water. The children must now be deprived of even this simple pleasure and much to the distress of the staff, we have to forbid the children to go anywhere near the river. The order is revoked a few weeks later when after tests the water is found to be free of any parasites.

We are admitting yet more children to the Orphanage, so presently there is room for only the youngest to sleep with a roof over their heads and the rest have to camp-out in tents, which as a matter of fact, is much to their liking. I sleep behind the partition in the sick-bay which is gradually filling up with children. The first to fall ill with pleurisy is one of the small boys who used to serve at the table in Semipalatynsk. We nurse him as best we can, the cook makes him special meals of dishes he particularly likes and I on my part treat him as best I can under the circumstances. Barely has he started to recover when the next child falls ill, a seven-year-old boy — still only a baby really — who requires more constant nursing. Since I am left alone with the children in the sick-bay at night I often have to get up to attend to them. I try to be a surrogate mother to them during their illnessess — changing sheets, washing them and encouraging them to eat. All is well until one day my seven-year-old patient tosses his head away from me as I tuck him up for the night and appears very annoyed with me. When I ask why he is behaving so, he looks at me with the eyes of an adult man and says

"I love you." Unwittingly I have done him harm in acting as mother — he has fallen in love with me and for a long time is so jealous that I may not be seen talking to any man in his presence because he sulks and remonstrates with me. Being unaware of awakening feelings of an unsuitable nature in a boy of his age, I have let myself in for a lot of trouble and now I have to take great pains to make him 'fall out of love' without leaving any traces of bitterness or scars which might remain with him for life. I think he eventually does stop loving me and accepts me as a person who wishes him well. I never discuss the matter with him but from now I never attempt to 'mother' my small patients.

I visit the market-place in Shakhrisabz in the company of several of our ladies. Here they sell hand-woven silk materials for dressmaking. The materials are woven in bands of beautiful pastel colours since the Uzbeks use the raw silk from the naturally coloured cocoons. A complete silk industry flourishes here: silk worms are bred on the mulberry trees which grow round the huts, the silk is hand-spun and woven. As well as the silk cloth they also sell whole baskets of the cocoons which have been segregated according to the various colours. There are blue, pink, green, and cream coloured cocoons. What a pity I cannot afford to buy some beautiful Uzbek silk for a dress. But, from being a civilian doctor attached to the army, here in Uzbekistan I have become a mere volunteer-private, on pay which is even insufficient to buy cigarettes. The money spent on gold in Semipalatynsk would have come in useful here.

One day I set off for Shakhrisabz with a group of the older children. It is very hot and after we have explored the village we are tired and very thirsty. We cannot find any bottled drinks and I am afraid to draw water from the stream, so we are very pleased when we see an Uzbek who is selling grape juice. We all quench our thirst and then the outcome is catastrophic! The grape juice turns out to be young wine, sparkling like lemonade, delicious but also alcoholic, something I had not realized. Initially we all feel very good and merry but then on the return journey to the Orphanage across the fields our feet begin to drag and it is an exertion to place one leg in front of the other. Ultimately we all make it safe and sound to the Orphanage and immediately flop down on the ground in the shade of the trees.

With each day the heat is becoming more intense, it is simply dangerous to venture out abroad alone at midday. I had personally experienced this hazard on a business trip to Shakhrisabz. I had set off in the early hours of the morning but was returning at noon. I had been very hot and had gradually stripped off various items of my uniform but all to no avail, becoming hotter and hotter and also faint. My skin had been completely dry because my body had no fluid to perspire with and there was no water to be found in the fields through which I was walking, not even the tiniest puddle. I realized I was suffering from heat-stroke, the treatment for which is lying down, shade and plenty to drink. Of these three remedies, only one was available to me, namely, lying down under some shrub, in relative shade. I had begun to worry that I might not make it back to the Orphanage. Lying down every few steps for a couple of minutes, I had somehow reached my destination but I must have presented a horrifying picture, half-undressed and half-conscious because the Supervisor was shocked by my appearence. From that time I have been more careful and do not trifle with the hidden menace of the sun and its rays, especially as my heart is not yet back to normal and I find it impossible to walk quickly.

I begin to look upon my army uniform as an instrument of torture in this hot climate: heavy leather lace-up shoes, thick stockings, knee-length elasticated bloomers and over the top of all this a thick woollen skirt and jacket — also a button-up to the neck blouse and the woollen tie. Just the very garb to precipitate sun-stroke which is postively invited by the small cap perched on the top of one's head, or heat-stroke which is invited by the Victorian underwear and woollen top clothes. Yet in Semipalatynsk one could be left minus a nose, ears, fingers and toes in the very same outfit! It is worst on Sundays when we are expected to attend a church service wearing the full uniform. Even before I have finished donning all the articles of the uniform I can feel the sweat running down my back. By the time the service has ended my jacket has a dark patch on the back and the shirt is fit only to be wrung dry. Only towards the end of our stay in Uzbekistan are we allowed to dispense with the jacket on formal occasions. Everything has to be in proper shape!

I rebel — as is often my want — because it is impossible to work under these conditions and ask a friend to sew me a dress from a sheet. She makes me a smart and plain dress which has the advantage of being cool and non-transparent, so I can dispense with the underwear. So I work in my 'white robe' but have to be careful that nobody in authority will spot me without my uniform. As soon as I see that somebody from the regiment has arrived I hurry to change into my uniform. This system works until one day I miss the arrival of the Colonel who, to make matters all the more awkward, happens to sit down for a rest under a tree where his presence cuts off my access to my clinic-bedroom. I have no choice but to gain entry through a window at the rear of the building. An action most unsuited to my position — but what else could I do? I cannot possibly let him see me in this improper outfit.

I come in contact with the Uzbeks but little — our stay in Uzbekistan is short and living in the Orphanage I have few opportunities to meet them. I do not know either their language or their customs. Physically they do not resemble the Kazakhs — though of course of Mongolian origin, with the high cheek-bones, slightly slanting eyes and the 'third' eyelid — yet much taller. They have longer faces, straight noses and narrow lips. I think they are rather sullen — but perhaps they are merely reticent and want to have nothing to do with the strangers who have 'invaded' their country? And besides, they are being destroyed by malaria — all of them either have or have had malaria, even the new-born infants.

Officer friends tell me that they had met an Uzbek who knew the history of the 'Hejnal', which is an hourly bugle-call sounded by a bugler from the tower of St. Mary's Church in Krakow. At one time this town used to be the ancient capital of Poland and is situated on the banks of the River Vistula, the main river of Poland. St. Mary's Church was built in 1223 and was later much enlarged and embellished by a tall tower in the next centuries. There would always be a watchman on duty in the tower looking-out for the approach of a possible enemy. In the case of such an event he would warn the townspeople of danger by sounding his bugle. In the Middle Ages, Poland was invaded several times by the Tartars and during one such raid, the watchman was killed by an arrow whilst sounding the bugle alarm. An arrow fired by the Tartars pierced the man's neck and the bugle-call was suddenly cut off. Even now the bugle-call is still sounded and stopped abruptly each day.

The Uzbek had been thrilled to see the Polish Army, much to the astonishment of the officers, who asked for an explanation of his great jubilation. The Uzbek then told them of an old Uzbek prophecy which was handed down from one generation to the next. The Uzbeks believe that as punishment for their having killed a man, who according to them had been praying in a tower, they must do penance and must accept the Russian oppression until such a time when there should arrive in Uzbekistan, an army from 'the land of the Vistula' which they had attacked many centuries ago and only then would Uzbekistan regain its freedom. The Uzbek owned that now the time for a revolution had arrived, now was the time for the prophecy to be fulfilled. Our officers had been horrified — did not the Uzbek realize the true position of the Polish Army? They were very loath to disenchant him but did their best to dampen his enthusiasm, nevertheless, news of 'the Army from the land of the Vistula' spread amongst the Uzbeks and gave our military authorities occasion for serious anxiety. The Uzbeks had to be told that this time their prophecy would not come true, to prevent an uprising.

It is interesting to speculate whether the bugler on the tower of St. Mary's Church in Krakow had been killed by a Tartar or an Uzbek arrow. Or perhaps we had inaccurately called all the Asiatics Tartars? For how else had the Uzbek known the history of the 'Hejnal'? Unfortunately the Uzbeks are doomed to yet suffering a long time for killing a man 'praying in a tower'.

The idyll of our stay in the Molotov Kolkhoz is soon spoilt by stark reality! On the Colonel's orders we have to forbid the children to eat any fresh fruit because he is worried they will get dysentery. How can children survive without vitamins? Even in Semipalatynsk we had the sauerkraut as a source of vitamin C. What an impossible undertaking to ensure that they will not eat the fruit, of which there is plenty growing everywhere, secretly! My argument that the fruit can be thoroughly washed in boiled water falls on stony ground — orders is orders! Yet there are clouds of flies everywhere — not only on the fruit but also crawling over our bread and in our tents. I am subordinate to the military authority and the Colonel firmly believes that dysentry is caused by eating fruit. Even my old grandmother knew this to be untrue.

Our drinking water which is kept in barrels, is tepid and afloat with dead mosquitoes and I have strict and detailed orders as to its disinfection. Twice a day finds me running from barrel to barrel pouring into each a measured amount of disinfectant fluid — and no one wants to drink it.

As the tinned meat soon goes off in this heat, although theoretically it should not be affected, to prevent an outbreak of food poisoning, I am made responsible for passing it fit for human consumption. Once again I must surely be consciencious or else very naive because I feel obliged to taste from each tin. Our camp kitchen is in the open, heat radiates from beneath from the fires and in spite of a small awning, the sun beats down from above. There are rows of opened cans of corned-beef which ooze with clear, melted fat. I sample a small mouthful from each tin but after a few days cannot stomach another morsel, so modifying my technique, and feeling guilty about so doing I begin to use my eyes and nose to test the meat by appearance and smell. I continue to feel dishonest but cannot force myself to taste the mess which is now so very repulsive to me. Corned-beef will never again pass through my lips!

The other unpleasant function which is delegated to me is the supervision of hygiene in the cooking. One of our military command has noticed that the cooks wear nothing to cover their hair, and bare heads in the kitchen are unhygienic. An order is issued that the cooks must have their hair covered. I have to tell the cooks, amongst them the mother of the Officer Cadet, Mrs J., who is an elderly lady, ill with malaria, that they must wear a kerchief. Mrs J. looks at me reproachfully and says,"Miss Danuta, I am barely alive as it is in this heat and now you want me to bind my head with a scarf!" The poor soul is red-faced and wet with perspiration and I can see that she is really struggling yet I have no alternative but to tell her that such are my orders. Mrs J. begins to wear a kerchief and I am left with the feeling that I have treated her cruelly. Is it really necessary to apply army discipline so strictly in these circumstances? Were this the only unhygienic thing in our Orphanage-camp all would be well, very well indeed.

The Orphanage gets an eight-year-old laddie who had previously latched on to the army whilst it was yet still in northern Russia and then found himself with it in the south. The soldiers had looked after him well, too well, calling him their mascot and thoroughly spoiling him. He has been sent to us, or rather delivered forcibly because he did not want to leave 'his' regiment. The rebellious boy cannot accept the fact that he is only a child and not a soldier and shortly after joining us disappears. He has run away. We find him eventually high up a tall tree. It takes the Supervisor a long time to persuade him to come down. Once safely on terra firma he announces that he will not listen to a load of females because he is a soldier. Poor child — he runs away again several times more. I do not know if the Supervisor ever manages to correct his distorted attitude or whether he will suffer for the rest of his life as a result of being the soldiers' mascot.

Several stops away from Shakhrisabz on the railway line lies Guzar where a camp for Polish civilians has been established. It is possible that the train carrying my mother had been sent there although at that time there was as yet no camp there. Hunger and disease is rife at the camp, people are dying like flies and the mere utterance of 'Guzar' is enough to sow seeds of fear. Under the wing of the regiment our Orphanage is well-off — we have enough to eat and our children are strong and healthy. A decision is passed to take in a large group of children from Guzar in order to save them from certain death. Several dozen little, diseased, skeletons arrive. The sick-bay holds only adequate beds for the children from Semipalatynsk and with the arrival of the group from Guzar there is a desperate shortage. We find it necessary to vacate all beds available under cover for the newcomers. The Supervisor and her mother move into a tent. I move out or rather give up my bed in the Clinic and take up residence in the open because we are also short of room in the tents now. We fix up the pharmacy in the porch of the sick-bay which also serves as the night nurse's duty-room and houses my bed on which I place all my belongings contained in a suitcase and rucksack. By these means we gain two vacant rooms where we can install several beds for those children from Guzar who are gravely ill. We also vacate two sheds for them, where up to now the small children from Semipalatynsk had slept. Because the Semipalatynsk children are well-fed and relatively healthy, they will sleep in the tents. However, since we are all suffering from malaria and there are not enough beds under a roof, the children who are in relatively good shape have to suffer their illnesses under canvas.

I sleep outside, lying on a table, on which the children eat their meals during the day. This is our dining-room — several long trestle-tables and benches beneath the trees. Sleeping on a table I can stretch out and not worry about the scorpions and poisonous spiders. Often other people beat me to the tables and when I come all the tables are occupied for the night. I have to seek alternative sleeping accommodation. I think the safest place would be on the hard-trodden earth alongside the wall of the sick-bay but heat still radiates from the walls and in the mornings I get up tired and heavy with sleep.

The nurse on duty suffers yet worse at nights in the porch of the sick-bay, where it is stuffy, airless and hot and where the biting mosquitoes swarm to the light of the lamp. In the mornings the nurse completes her duty with face and hands swollen with bites. The ill children too, in the sick-bay cannot sleep because of the heat and the mosquitoes which are attracted to the light. The children under canvas come off better on that score because of the dark and also because they can sleep outside the tents in the cooler air. The nurse's chores at night become a nightmare: she is confined to the porch, in the heat with the mosquitoes, has to attend to the sick children and concurrently has to prepare the appropriate quantities (hundreds) of doses of quinine in readiness for the next day because we receive the drug in bulk quantity. Initially the nurse makes an effort to weigh each dose of quinine but the procedure takes so long that the requirement is not ready in time for the next morning. I therefore permit her to wrap each dose after judging the weight by eye. I have now checked several of these doses a couple of times and have come to be convinced that they are almost a hundred per cent accurate in each case. The nurse has plenty of experience in judging the amount of quinine by eye and I abandon the weighing of the drug with a completely clear conscience. The Orphanage consumes an incredible amount of quinine which has become the main drug in use.

With the first appearance of the malaria, the Semipalatynsk children who had arrived here in excellent health begin to sink fast before our eyes. Additionally, the Guzar children have brought us dysentry, not to mention that most of them are suffering from avitaminosis of many kinds. Everybody is ill with malaria and dysentery. We did not know that malaria is endemic in Uzbekistan. All the Uzbeks have malaria from infancy with the result that they are anaemic and yellowish-green in colour. I realize now why the Uzbek children have such large tummies in spite of being reasonably well-fed. The malaria causes gross enlargement of the spleen to such an extent that it makes their stomachs bulge. Malaria is destroying the Uzbek nation. Their continuing existence may probably be explained by the development in due course of time to a certain degree of immunity to malaria. Had the Russians wanted to finish us off quickly they need only have deported us to Uzbekistan. I cannot imagine any of us surviving here beyond two years. Transported to a sub-tropical climate, the starved and malaria-ridden Poles would have no chances of survival. Though harsh, the climate in Kazakhstan was healthy.

All the Orphanage staff contract malaria but nobody can permit themselves the luxury of being ill. The ladies put themselves to bed for one or two days during the height of the attacks but as soon as these lessen — thanks to the quinine — they come back to work, in order that they might return to bed again for one day with the return of another attack. Our circumstances and work-conditions here are against any possible cure of malaria. The sick person can only be brought to semi-recovery because we need every vital pair of hands to look after the children. I get malaria too, obviously. I even enjoy the first onset because it is very hot and I suddenly get an attack of the shivers, as though I was taking a cold shower. It is less enjoyable when the fever ensues. I suppress the malaria with quinine and continue to work without a break but the attacks recur, albeit less frequently. It is only in 1947, after our arrival in Britain that the malaria attacks finally cease.

Dysentery is the other plague of the camp. Hygienic conditions are dreadful: millions of flies and no means of combating them; the toilets — those open trenches close to the Orphanage, which though sprayed with lime, still swarm with flies. We have no potties for the children and even if we had there would be nobody to empty them, so the poor children answer the call of nature around the tents. The stench around the camp intensifies. My shoulders droop in despair to see the sick children whom I can help but very little in fact — thin and weak, they barely have enough strength to drag themselves from the tents into the fresh air to lie down. The total medical aid which I am able to ofer has been reduced to the act of going from tent to tent to prescribe quinine and anti-dysentery drugs. We are no longer in any condition to enjoy either the swiftly flowing river or the trees with their grape-vine vegetation or the meadows of hollyhocks or the scented orchids — tragedy and disease displace all else from the mind.

Sleeping outside becomes more of a problem as there is almost never any room for me on the tables. Other people get there before me because I usually arrive in 'the dormitory' at a late hour. I experiment in spending the nights with my friends, Mrs S. and her daugher and son, who lodge with an Uzbek woman. The ladies have to share one bed and when the three of us try to sleep in it we are so cramped that we virtually stick together. It is no better sleeping outside beside the house because the hard earth and clay walls are as hot as a furnace. I try sleeping out in the fields — being desperate enough now not to care about the scorpions — but soon discover that other people have had the same idea. There are sleeping forms lying everywhere, the night is dark, there is no moon and it would be easy to tread on the inanimate shapes or be trodden upon. It is a nuisance to be without permanent digs — there is no corner I can call home, my things are crammed into the porch of the sick-bay and when I need to get into my suitcase I must carry it outside. It is impossible to be alone, even for a single minute, washing in the river is never private because somebody may happen along at any moment.

There is a great change in the meals in the Orphanage — we are on army rations and though there is sufficient food, it is not entirely suitable for children in respect of quality. For meat we have the corned-beef, running with liquid fat and even though the cooks try as they may to ring the changes in the diet, home-cooking, on a par with that in Semipalatynsk is out of the question in these circumstances and with the numbers of children involved.

I become conscious of the lack of vitamins in the diet personally but cannot afford to buy any fruit. As a private-volunteer, I receive what really only amounts to pocket-money but a cleaner at the Orphanage who holds a civilian post and consequently receives a good wage takes pity on me and buys me some fruit because: "You, doctor, are hard-up." I am embarrassed but accept the fruit which I eat with great relish. I am embarrassed that doctors in the Polish Army are so treated. In the Red Army each doctor begins with the rank and pay of a captain, regardless of gender and later gets promotion. The 'equality' which is accorded in the Polish Army, to a person of higher education, who as in the case of the doctors — actually work in their professional capacity for the army, is not even to be found in the USSR. I supplement my diet by cooking dried grapes called Kisch-misch in Uzbek and rice (rice which I had brought from Buzuluk) in a billy-can over a fire by the river bank.

By now all the children look very poorly. Poor Antek Leparowski or Kleparowski, who is ill with malaria, lies on the ground by the sick-bay wall with never as much as a prank on his mind — he reminds me of an unhappy puppy whose melancholy eyes follow me around, begging for help. There is nothing I can do for him except to give him quinine. I am far too busy to give him any special attention or even just to show him some love. The daughter of one of the ladies has cerebral malaria and though without a temperature is delirious and seriously ill and again I can only give her the quinine. It has all become very dreadful and we are more and more grief-stricken.

I arrange to go to Shakhrisabz to see the regimental doctor to ask for help, for drugs and to discuss the treatment of malaria. They send an open cart pulled by two horses and driven by a soldier to fetch me. The seating arrangement for the driver and myself is a narrow plank without any back-rest or hand-hold and the soldier drives like a bat out of hell. Seemingly he desires to impress me with a display of his driving skills and display them indeed he does. The horses plunge madly forwards at a spanking pace, the front wheels at one moment fall into a pot-hole in the road, the soldier whips them on, the horses jerk the cart out of the rut, and I catapult out of the cart on to the road in a high arc. I can remember nothing of my trajectory, all I can next recall is watching the wheels of the cart rolling past a few inches away from my face. By the time the horrified soldier has pulled up the horses and has come running over to me, I am already on my feet, having sustained no worse an injury than a grazed hand. I am helped to scramble back up on to the plank seating and feel most insecure, imagining that at any moment I shall be thrown off again but I try to put on a good face and somehow we finally reach the clinic at the regiment headquarters. I must look bad because I am in shock and trembling all over. My colleague doctors make me lie down and stand over me, obviously uneasy about my condition. It takes me an hour to recover. The whole incident had happened so fast that I had had no time to be frightened. Had the cart wheels passed a few inches closer to my head, my skull would have been crushed and I should have died quite happily without having time to realize what was happening.

My visit to Dr G. at Shakhrisabz results in my being sent help in the form of a doctor who is a private. I can breathe a sigh of relief! My new colleague is a Jew and as he had not done National Service, when the war had broken out he had been called-up as a private — he had not been at Military College. However, he had been an Assistant at the University Clinic in Krakow. He is an excellent doctor and a charming, good and cultured man. His knowledge and experience of medicine is greater than mine and yet he is now my subordinate. I find the situation rather embarrassing but from the very beginning our relationship works out very well. I call him my junior-senior colleague since I am his boss officially but his junior colleague when it comes to asking his advice on a patient's treatment.

My life has been easier since the arrival of another doctor and I can once again go and bathe in the river, far from the camp, where I can be private. And apart from anything else, I feel much happier being able to share the burden of medical responsibility with another doctor. There is now somebody with whom I can discuss certain cases and it is easier to make decisions after conferring with my junior-senior colleague.

And so, the summer of 1942 stretches out endlessly — beautiful weather, heat, beautiful surroundings and — diseases, diseases which demand great efforts — we have no free days, the work is continuous. We await the arrival of Bishop Gawlina, the Bishop of the Polish Army in the USSR, who is supposed to be coming to visit the Orphanage. Preparations for the Bishop's visit had already begun several weeks previously. The Orphanage Supervisor is busy rehearsing hymns and anthems with the children, to welcome Bishop Gawlina and the cook feverishly discusses with her how and with what to feast the Bishop. It is decided he will be greeted with a glass of wine served in our 'dining-room' under the shade of the trees. There is tension whilst we await his arrival because he is delayed and the children, who have been scrubbed clean and dressed in their very best, such as it is, are hot and tired. At last we hear the drumming of horse's hoofs and presently the Bishop's entourage materializes before us. The scene conforms to a picture which could have been plucked out of medieval Poland: before us is a chaise and sitting on it is the Bishop dressed in his fine, purple robes, surrounded by an escort of cavalry officers. The whole entourage had cantered up to the Orphanage swathed in clouds of dust. There are the usual greetings, hymn singing, speeches and the inevitable photographs, from which I opt out since my traumas in exile have left me without any ambition to have my likeness perpetuated in the company of a Bishop. Bishop Gawlina distributes holy pictures to the children and fortified with a glass of wine, departs. What a pity we had no cine-camera to film his visit and particularly his arrival which was indeed impressive and picturesque.

It is rumoured that the political situation has changed and the Polish Army's departure from the USSR is now under question. Initially, when

Hitler had invaded Russia in June, 1941, the Russians had permitted the Poles to form an army on Russian territory, with the promise that this army would act independently, would be allowed to leave Russia and would join the British Forces. The Polish Government in exile in London was instrumental in liaising with the British Government to form the Polish Army in Russia, which was built up from men who had been deported to Siberia and men who had been in prisons and labour camps in Russia. The rumours now suggest that the Russians have changed their plans for the Polish Army and intend to send our army, which is under the command of General Anders, to fight on Hitler's Eastern Front, to 'liberate' Poland from the Germans. The rumours gather in strength and exert a detrimental effect on the men whose gore rises at the thought of being used by the Russians in this manner.

Unexpectedly one day, a doctor friend from Shakhrisabz comes to see me and tells me, in confidence, that our regiment is preparing to make an armed break-through tonight with Afghanistan as its proposed destination. He asks for discretion on my part because should the resolution be made definite, the regiment will go alone, leaving the Orphanage behind in the USSR as under the circumstances, it cannot be encumbered with women and children. He advises me to go with the regiment, and promises to send a dispatch-rider for me should they be setting off tonight.

I am in a terrible dilemma! Common sense tells me that to remain with the Orphanage would be to contemplate a senseless sacrifice because the moment our Division leaves Russia, the Orphanage will be taken over by the Russian authorities, the children will be put into Russian Orphanages and the staff put in prison. Surely such a sacrifice would be madness? By remaining, I would in no way be able to help the children and would run the very real risk of only perishing myself! On the other hand in spite of cool and ruthless reasoning, I still feel like a traitor because how can I possibly desert the Orphanage and abandon the children? It would be tantamount to treason to so betray the children's trust and confidence. And yet finally, the instinct for survival takes the upper hand in my conflicting emotions — deciding I do not want to be left behind in the USSR, I resolve to pack my belongings and to wait for the dispatch-rider. Returning to the Orphanage, I begin to pack discreetly and cautiously in the porch of the sick-bay so that nobody will notice my activities. I avoid the ladies and the personnel of the Orphanage because I am unable to look them in the eye. I recall Nadvorna in 1939, when the Colonel had said: "Do as you wish, there are no longer any orders." I had then been faced with two options: to go to Hungary with the army or to remain in Poland and I had chosen Poland, but this time I do not want to remain behind. I wish to escape because here, I shall not be able to do as I wish, I shall be completely at the mercy of the Russians who will throw me into gaol. Having packed essentials into a rucksack, I wait and wait all night long for the dispatch-rider who never comes. In the morning my friend lets me know that the situation has suddenly changed for the better and the army and the Orphanage are to be evacuated to Persia! Never again should I like to live through another such night.

A few days later we are officially informed that the Orphanage is to leave for Persia. Not only are the children to go but also all the staff and their families and as many civilians as we can take.

To myself and my senior-junior doctor friend falls the very unpleasant task of segregating those children who are unfit for transport because the Russians do not wish us to take children who have no chances of surviving the very arduous journey or the children who are hopelessly ill. And we have very many of these children. Though indeed the Russians promise to look after the children who are left behind, promise to get them hospitalized, how can we leave them here? We both feel dreadful: we cannot abandon them, we cannot betray their trust and leave them in the USSR. We try to certify that they are all fit to travel but in several cases this proves impossible and we both feel like murderers even though it is through no fault of ours.

To add to our worries, my senior-junior colleague is having difficulties in obtaining permission to take his wife and children, whom he had brought out of Siberia, with us. His application has been refused. He feels it is impossible for him to depart with the army leaving the family to certain doom alone in the USSR and cannot desert the army and remain with his family because he is too decent a man to take such steps, and in any case probably no good would come out of it anyway. The Russians would arrest him after our army had left and the family would still be left alone. My colleague is in despair and I feel desperately sorry for him and ashamed of our Command. How can they so treat a man who had worked constantly and with great dedication doing everything possible as a doctor for our Polish children? Ultimately, the day before we leave, permission is granted for this doctor to take his family with him. Need he have been so tormented?

We work together in segregating the children and together we cheat as much as possible. But 'little fleas have bigger fleas upon their backs' and we have the regiment doctor on our back who in turn is accountable to the Russians. We do not succeed in smuggling through a handful of children who are so hopelessly ill that they cannot stand up. They will have to be left behind when the Orphanage leaves with the army.

Amongst these children there is a seventeen-year-old girl who is suffering from such an advanced stage of pellagra that irreversible changes have taken place in her body and in spite of treatment — she had come to us too late from Guzar — we cannot save her. She is condemned to die, a slow and cruel death. The poor creature lies in a tent, on the ground, in the heat and in her own filth — and she is no fool and is also fully conscious — her eyes beg for help . . . . My colleague, a Jew, returns at night to the abandoned camp and the children we have had to leave behind, from the station where the Orphanage is waiting to board the train for Perisa, in order to clean her up and wash her underclothes before she is finally deserted by us.

Will it ever again be possible to lead a normal life after having seen so much human misery, suffering and unhappiness? Many years later in England, a Polish doctor who had also been through Russia said that after such experiences all of us who survived can never again be normal — we are all weighed down with a burden which has to be shouldered for the rest of our lives. He was quite correct.

All Poles who have experienced Russia are beyond the pale of normal society. This is evident amongst the Polish emigrees who can instantly recognize a 'colleague' from Russia upon meeting a compatriot stranger. We have somehow become more human, we have shed the old standards and prejudices which decreed that breeding, education and social status have a bearing on a person's worth and qualities. For us now there exist only good or bad people of whom besides, there are happily, few. People may have strong or weak personalities, may be altruistic or egotistic, may have varying degrees of intelligence. All these factors will influence their behaviour and one must judge people with an understanding of these qualities. Factors, which before the Second World War were used to assess a person's worth, have proved immaterial. During deportation I had three friends upon whom I could rely: one was from a family of landed gentry, educated and cultured, another was a cook in a restaurant before the war and the third, a German married to a Pole, with a great flair for art was an exceptionally interesting person. Each of these women, in their own way would uplift my flagging spirits and the company of each one would give me great, if different, pleasure.

In the USSR I never did see any violent scenes, beatings, shooting, killed or wounded people. I was only a deportee, I was never held in a labour camp. Neither did I see any physical cruelty. I only saw and experienced cruelty of a psychological nature. Nor did I ever hear swearing or coarse language from the Russians, who in civilian life made an attempt to behave in a cultured and civilized fashion. However I left Russia shouldering a burden and I carry it to this day.

Towards the end of August our camp prepares to move out of Russia. The army intends to take all its equipment but there are insufficient rucksacks for the soldiers to take everything, so sheets and men's underclothes are given to the women to transport. In Pahlevi in Persia, the sheets become marvellous items to use in exchange for getting cooked ham from the Persians. Immediately upon our arrival in Pahlevi, naïve as ever, I return the sheets which I had carried, to the army stores where the storekeeper is not very keen to accept them because he is perplexed where to enter this surplus in his books.

Well in time before the Orphanage's departure, we had sent the older children to join the army as Junaks so that now only the younger children remain with us. On the day of departure from the Molotov Kolkhoz, army lorries transport the children in batches to the railway station at Shakhrisabz. I am to leave in the last lorry with a few of the ladies and Orphanage staff. The children who are unfit to travel and whom we are to leave behind remain with one of the nurses who will be the very last to go.

I am left with several hours before it is my turn to go, so I walk down to the river for the last time to wash. The day is already drawing to a close and in the evening light the river and the surrounding landscape looks sad and mournful. Autumn has already arrived, the grass has lost its colour, the hollyhocks are in seed and their leaves dry, there are bunches of tiny green grapes hanging from the vines growing on the trees by the river. There are no longer any flowers in bloom, everything is dull and cheerless — I am alone and as I bathe in the river for the last time, a pang of some strange emotion tightens in my chest. I bathe because I am wet and sticky with perspiration. Afterwards I feel better and return to our deserted Orphanage where I find a group of Poles roaming around — they have come from Shakhrisabz to see if they can loot anything.

There is no sign of any Russian authorities, nobody has come to take over the care of the sick remnants of our Orphanage. Who will feed the ill children? Who will care for them? Why had the sick children not been dispatched to a Russian hospital a few days in advance of our departure? I cannot go to the sick-bay and look the sick children in the eye — I simply cannot. The lorry arrives, we climb in and leave.

I never discover what happens to these children and try not to think about them to this day because the memories are too painful. My colleague the Jew found the children alone, with nobody there, when he returned that night to the deserted Orphanage to clean up the girl who was suffering from pellagra. This time I have not 'deserted' from the army as in Tatischevo but left with it, in uniform. Perhaps it was the wrong decision, perhaps I should have remained with the sick children?

We spend the night on the station at Shakhrisabz after which we journey to Krasnovodsk and there on the sandy beach we wait two days for our ship. The port at Krasnovodsk is big, the water in the Caspian Sea is warm though dirty. A sandstorm which blows up during the night prevents everybody from sleeping. The sand carried along by the strong wind penetrates everywhere and stings the face. Everybody coughs, there is sand in our eyes, noses and mouths and it becomes difficult to breathe. We try sitting with our backs to the wind but this helps little either until the Orphanage cleaner erects a sort of screen from blankets behind which we can shelter. The morning dawns to find us all very tired from lack of sleep.

On the day of departure, before we embark, an officer 'treasurer' makes a round amongst us, carrying a large sack into which he instructs us to throw all the roubles we may have, saying that once we are on board, the Russians will arrest anybody found carrying Russian money. The sack — which is quite a large one — is quickly filled up — no receipts are issued. The treasurer boards the ship with this sack and joins a group of higher ranks whom the Russians do not bother to search. Meanwhile the rest of us grey masses undergo a thorough search and naturally the Russian customs men find no roubles on anybody, whilst the treasurer calmly stands to one side. The sack containing our money safely reaches Pahlevi and — disappears.

The sick-bay is located below deck — it is hot and stuffy and becomes permeated with a stench because the majority of the children have diarrhoea. Some of the children are too weak to walk and have to be carried below deck. To the last moment we are anxious and nervous that the Russians will query their fitness to travel but since the children had previously been sorted out, the Russians are no longer interested in them. Looking after the children below deck there are several nurses and myself. Uneasily, I wonder what sort of journey we shall have — the bunks are in tiers and I cannot imagine how we shall manage to reach up in order to attend to all the children. Leaving the sick-bay, I find the deck in the open is very overcrowded, there is simply no room to pass because nobody wants to be below deck and people have all encamped here. We set sail — there is a heavy swell and the ship begins to roll — and I had always thought of the Caspian Sea as one huge pond. People on the deck start being sea-sick and when I return to the sick-bay, I find a similar situation there: the swaying nurses still trying to minister to the children. Back in this airless and stinking surroundings I am also overcome with sea-sickness and have to lie down near a porthole where I feel better immediately. I do not remain lying down for very long — the wind is strong and blows in droplets of moisture through the porthole — sea spray I think but when I examine the 'droplets' more closely, I see that they contain particles of corned-beef. I am forced to close all the portholes, causing the atmosphere to become stuffier and hotter, not to mention the already pervading presence of a combined aroma of sea-sickness and diarrhoea. The ship's rolling motion increases even more and now even the nurses have to lie down. I must go up on deck to bring somebody down to help with the children but some hope! Even in the open, in the fresh air, people are laid flat and only from time to time will somebody get up to make a dash for the ship's side. I can find nobody willing to help.

One ten-year-old girl dies. I knew her well and — later in Teheran — I am able to tell the mother who is searching for her daughter, of her death and burial at sea. In Teheran many mothers turn to me to ask about the fate of their children. Unfortunately, the only children I know well are those from the original Orphanage in Semipalatynsk and I cannot remember the names of the other hundred or so who came to us from Guzar and the environs of Shakhrisabz. Also to complicate matters, our list of children's names gets lost during the crossing of the Caspian Sea and the Supervisor has to try to reproduce the list from memory. Then I lose touch with the staff and children after we disembark at Pahlevi. The children are placed in

Polish institutions and I am once again embraced into the army, into a tent on the beach.

We live like nomads on the beach at Pahlevi for about two weeks and I have many opportunities to observe people. Immediately upon our arrival here, trade begins to flourish with the Persians who bring food and fruit to barter. Amongst the Poles ham is much sought after because none of us have seen any since the outbreak of war. It also now becomes apparent that Russian roubles do have reasonable worth here but since all our roubles had gone into the 'treasurer's' sack it is the sheets, blankets and men's underwear which change hands in exchange for food in the business transactions — those very same 'riches' which we had been given to transport on behalf of the army. Values change — my christening present to the baby boy, the bracelet from Semipalatynsk, is given away in exchange for ham. His mother, the Orphanage Supervisor shamefacedly admits to having 'consumed' the bracelet in the form of ham.

Women who are starved if not literally, then at least starved of meat and fruit are easy prey for unscrupulous men. An invitation to an elegant dinner is often a temptation impossible to resist.

The early stages of freedom are neither easy nor attractive.

From the time of our arrival in Pahlevi, I am never again to go hungry — this is the start of a life which is 'secure' though by no means comfortable or happy.

The acquired 'burden' always remains.